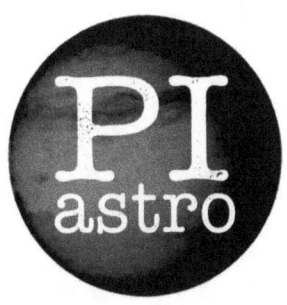

Www.psychic-insights-astrology.com

Copyright © 2017 by G. Desiree Fultz
All rights reserved. This book or any portion thereof
may not be reproduced or used in any manner whatsoever
without the express written permission of the artist.

Printed in the United States of America

ISBN-13: 978-1977848369

ISBN-10: 1977848362

Follow the artist on social media by searching:

G. Desiree Fultz

World of Elementals
Coloring Book

Vol 1.

Art by G. Desiree Fultz

Travel-Size! Take your book with you. Got 15 minutes? Exercise your creative energies; Do some art while you're in a waiting room, a passenger in a vehicle, at the park, or at home enjoying time in your meditative and artistic state of mind.

I know you'll love splashing your flavor of colors, textures, embellishments, and collaborative efforts onto these pages as much as I enjoyed creating the original art for you.

Post your renditions to social media and tag me so I can find yours! I can't wait to see how your voice shapes the images on the pages.

Www.psychic-insights-astrology.com

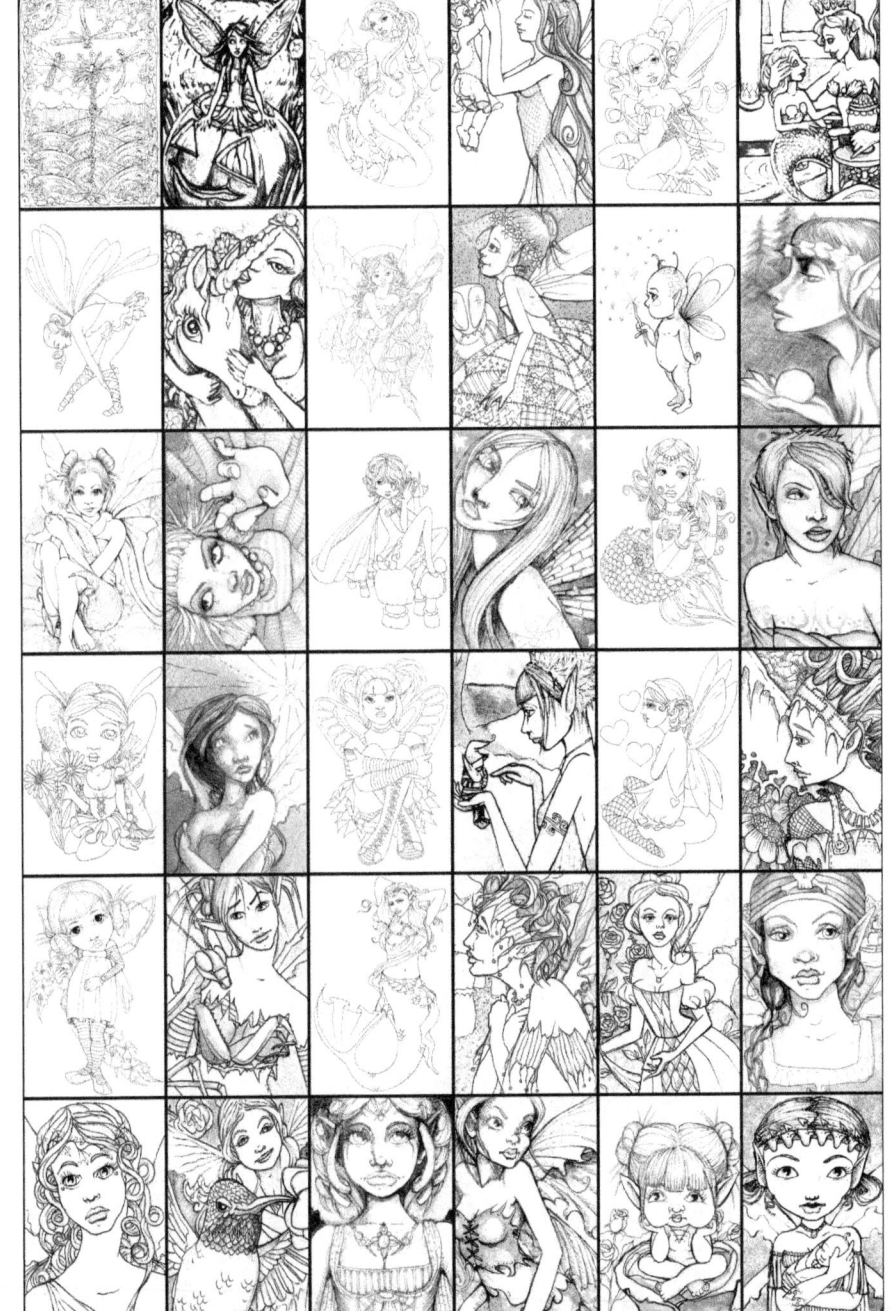

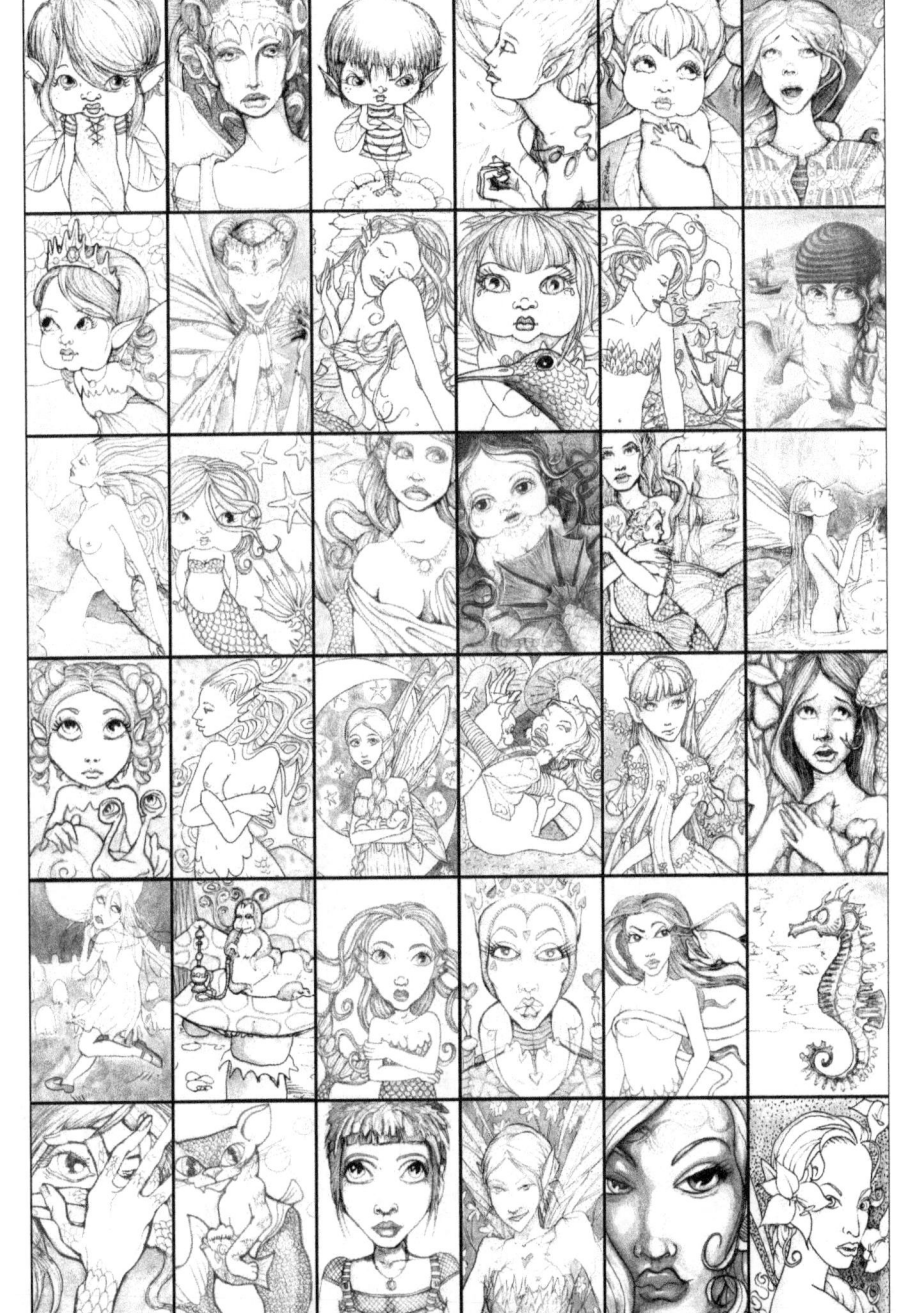

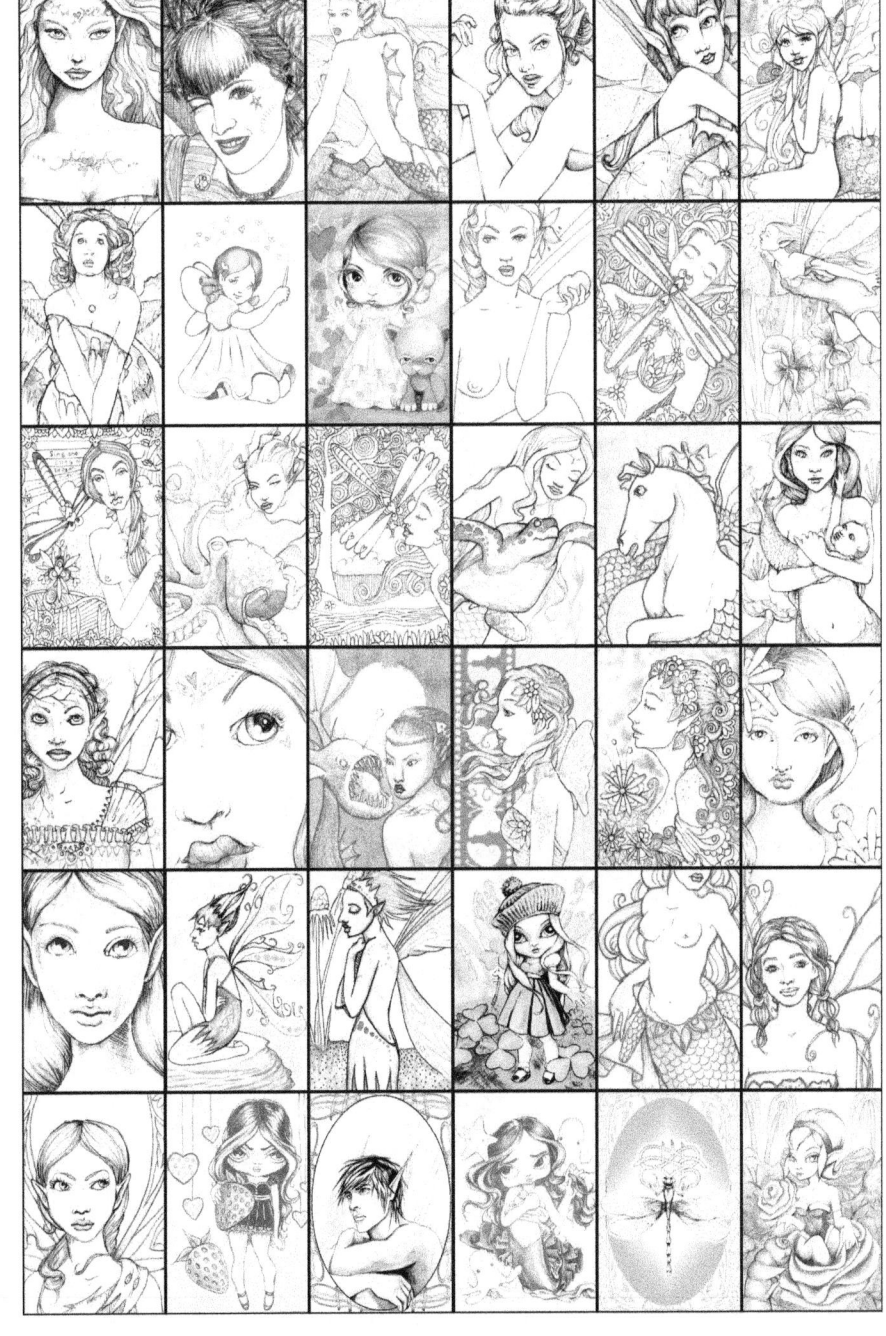

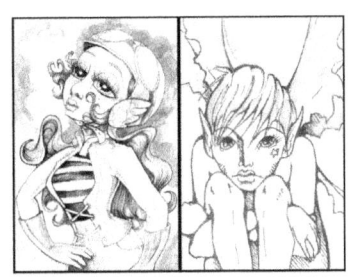

The images in this book were all created between 2005 and 2015 except for a few from 2017 that were included for the sake of variety. The selected images were chosen by theme from 10 years of artwork by G. Desiree Fultz. The color has been removed from finished work and rendered as line art so you can add your own colorful artistic flare.
Enjoy!

Images appear in the same order in this book as they do in the contents key.

Find me on Facebook as: G. Desiree Fultz
and on Instagram as: Vivian Hax
Visit my eBay store for original art and more:
https://www.ebay.com/usr/psychic-insights

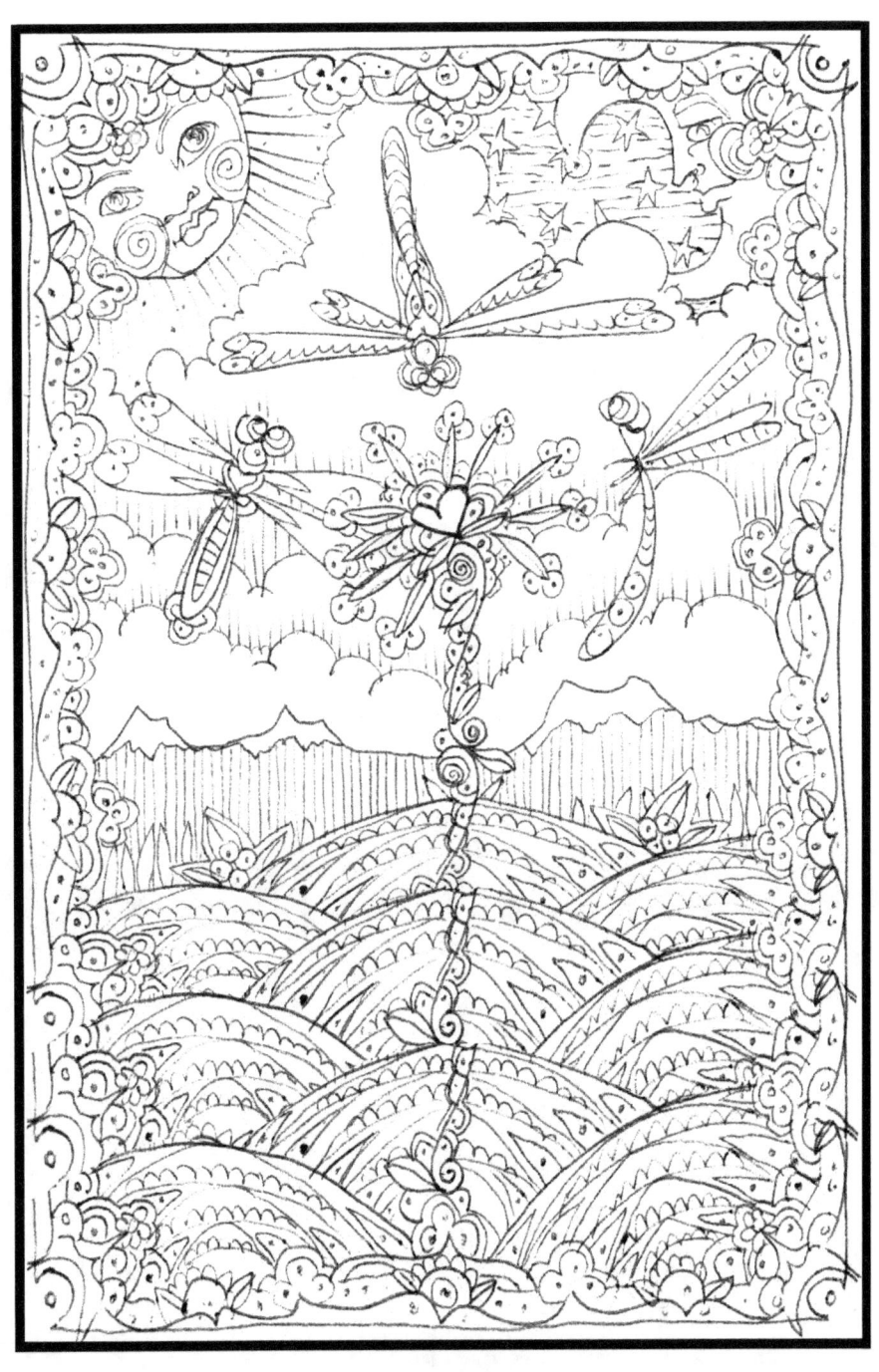

Dragonfly Hills

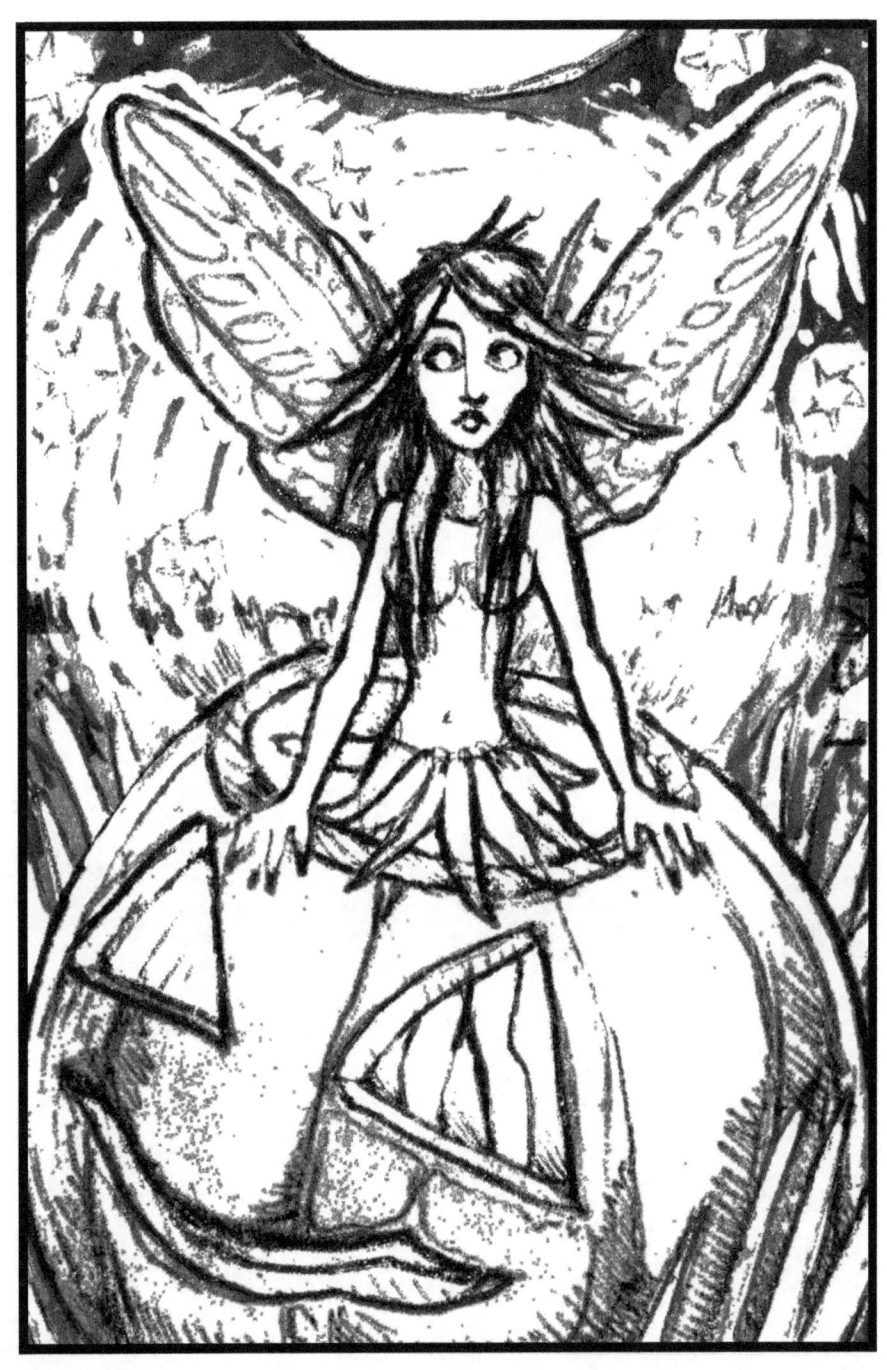

Farie Lantern

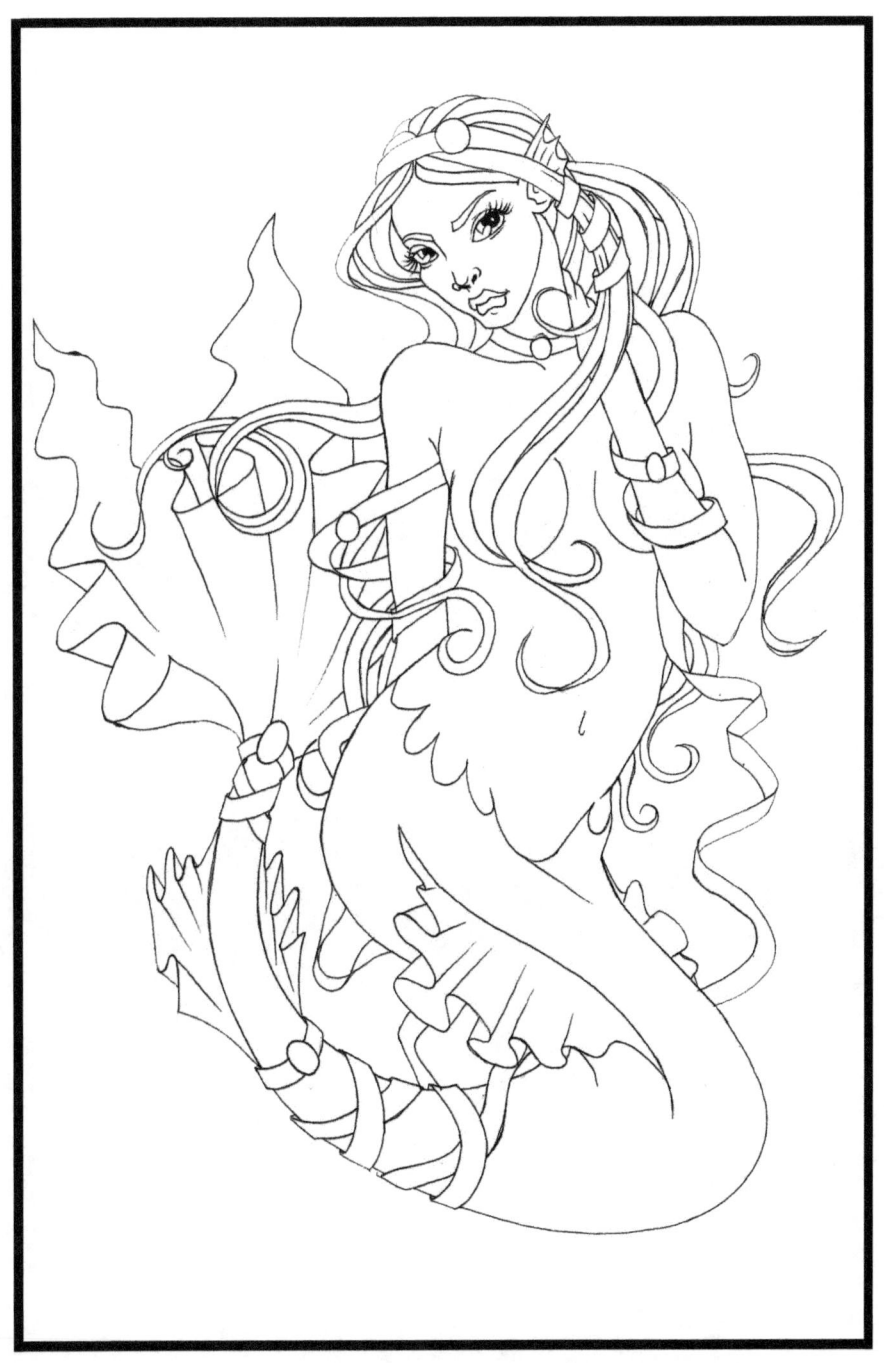

Ribbons & Fins

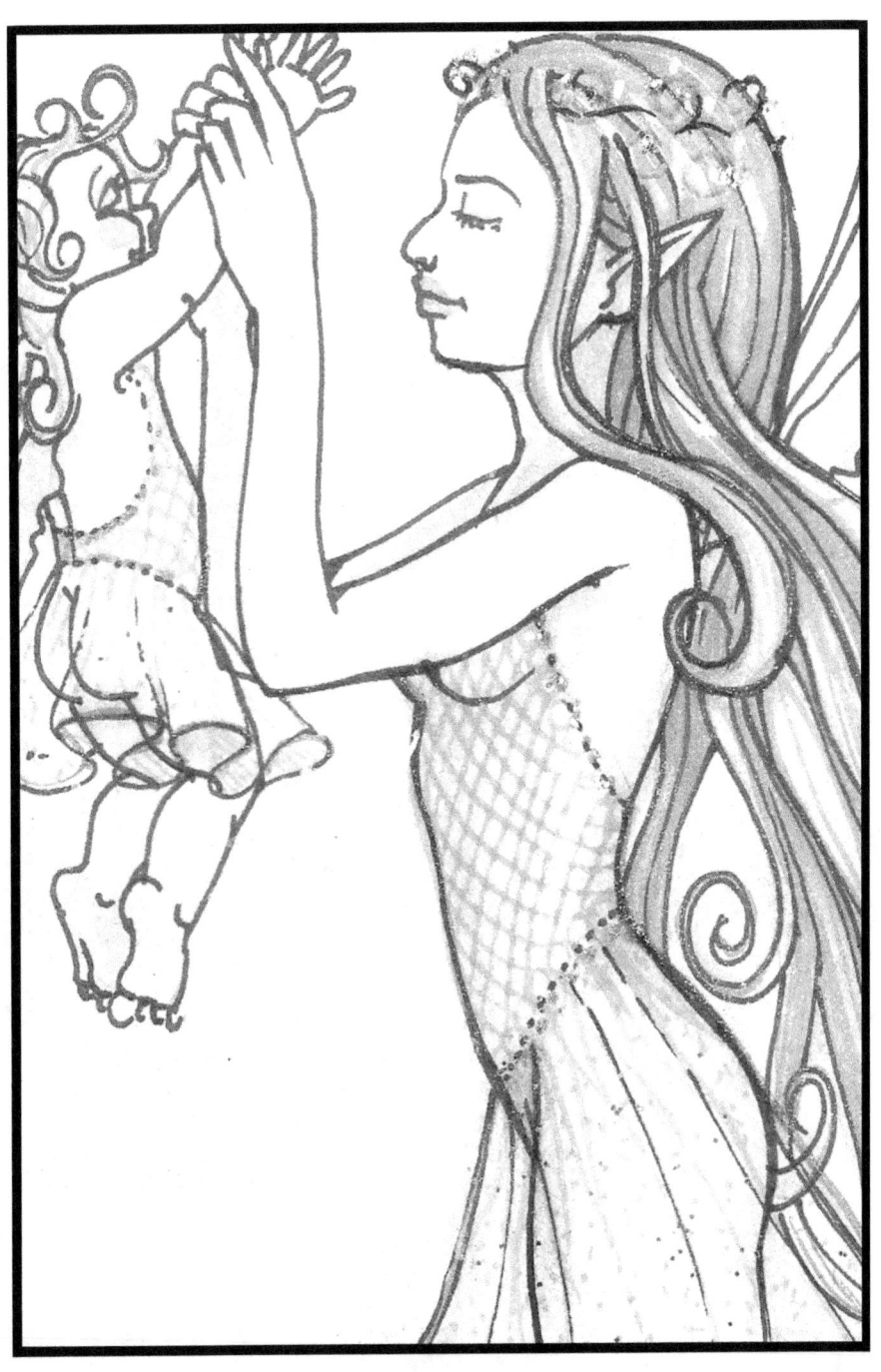

Playtime

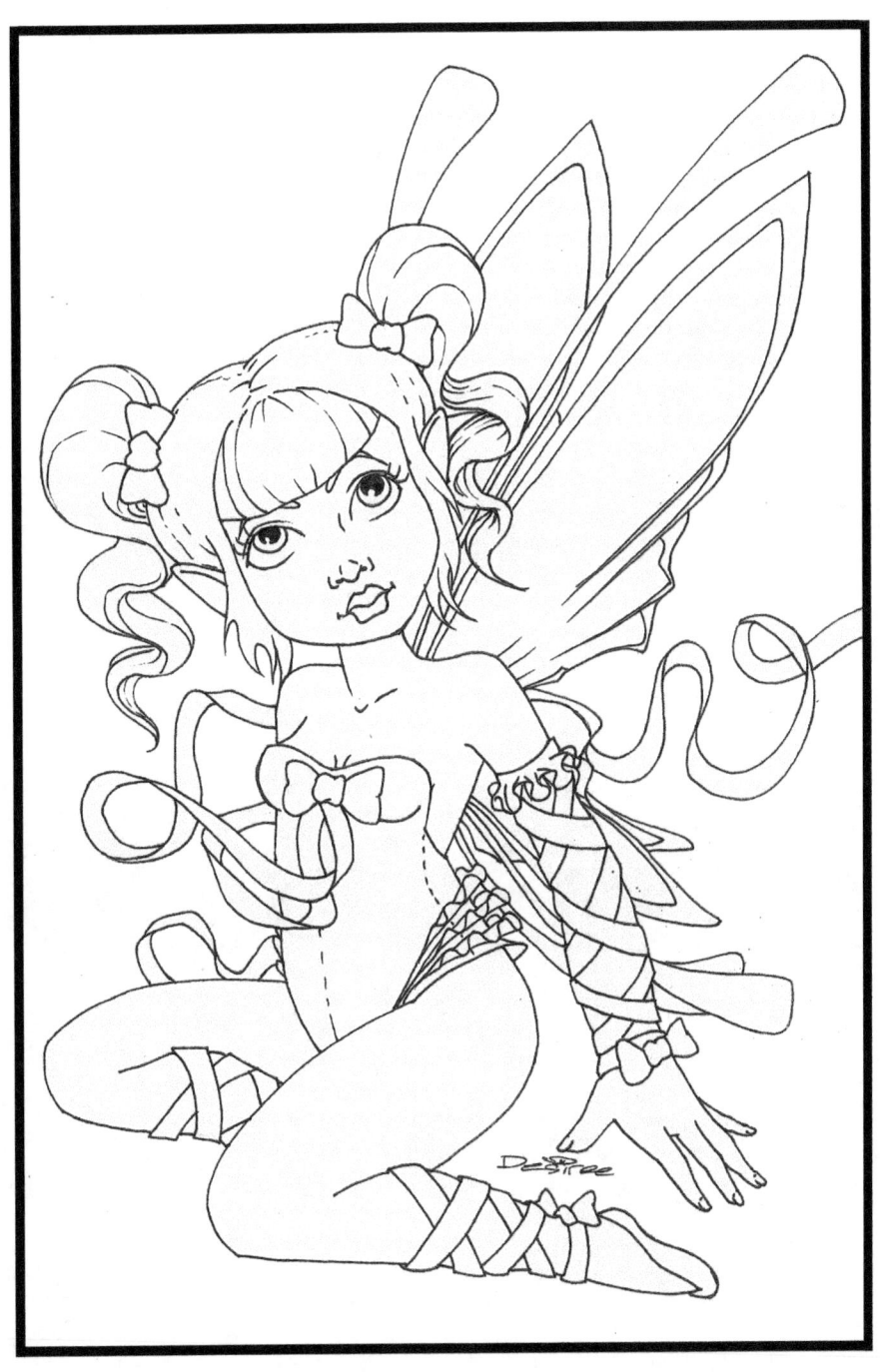

Ribbon Dancer

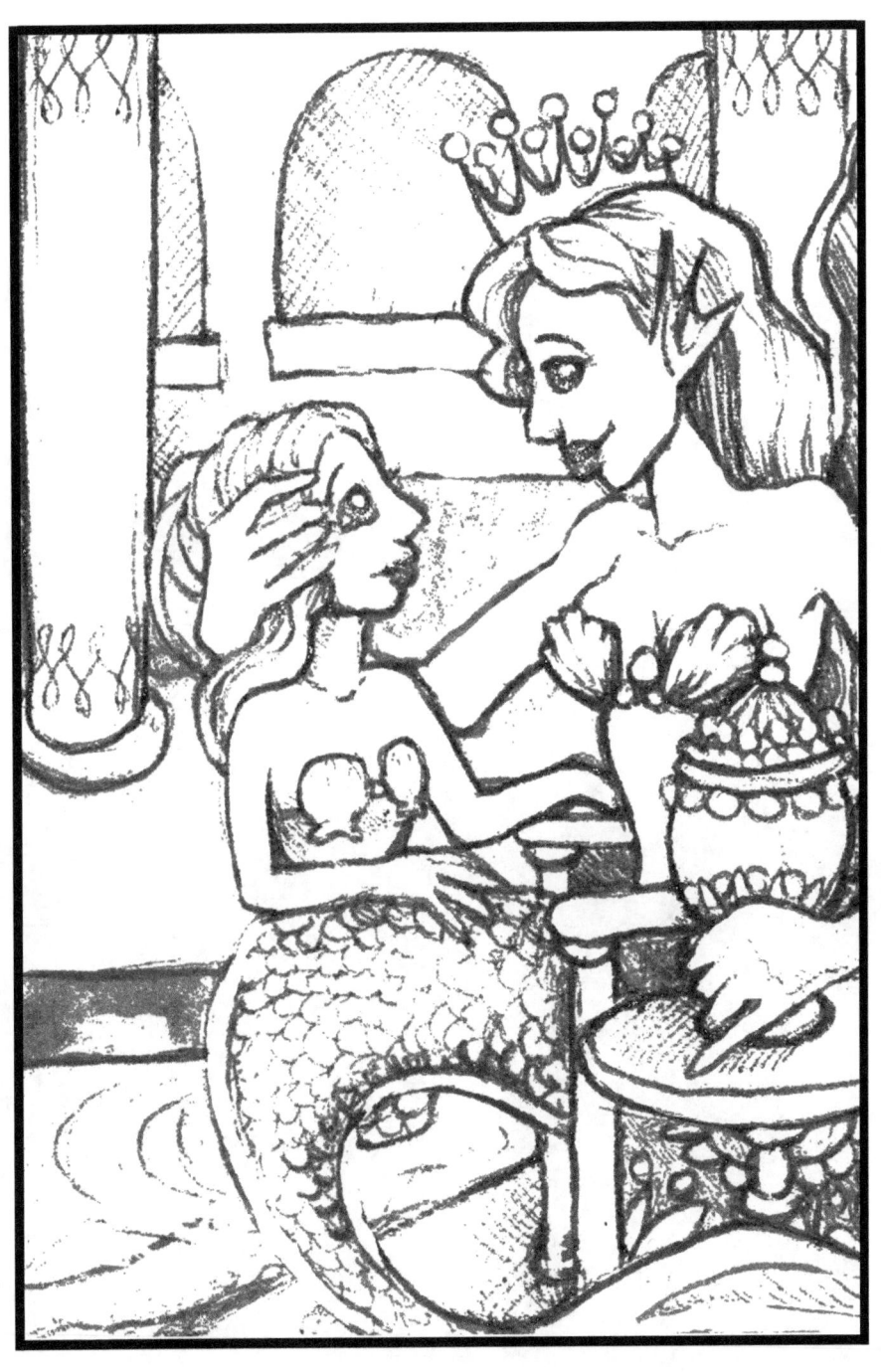

Queen of Cups

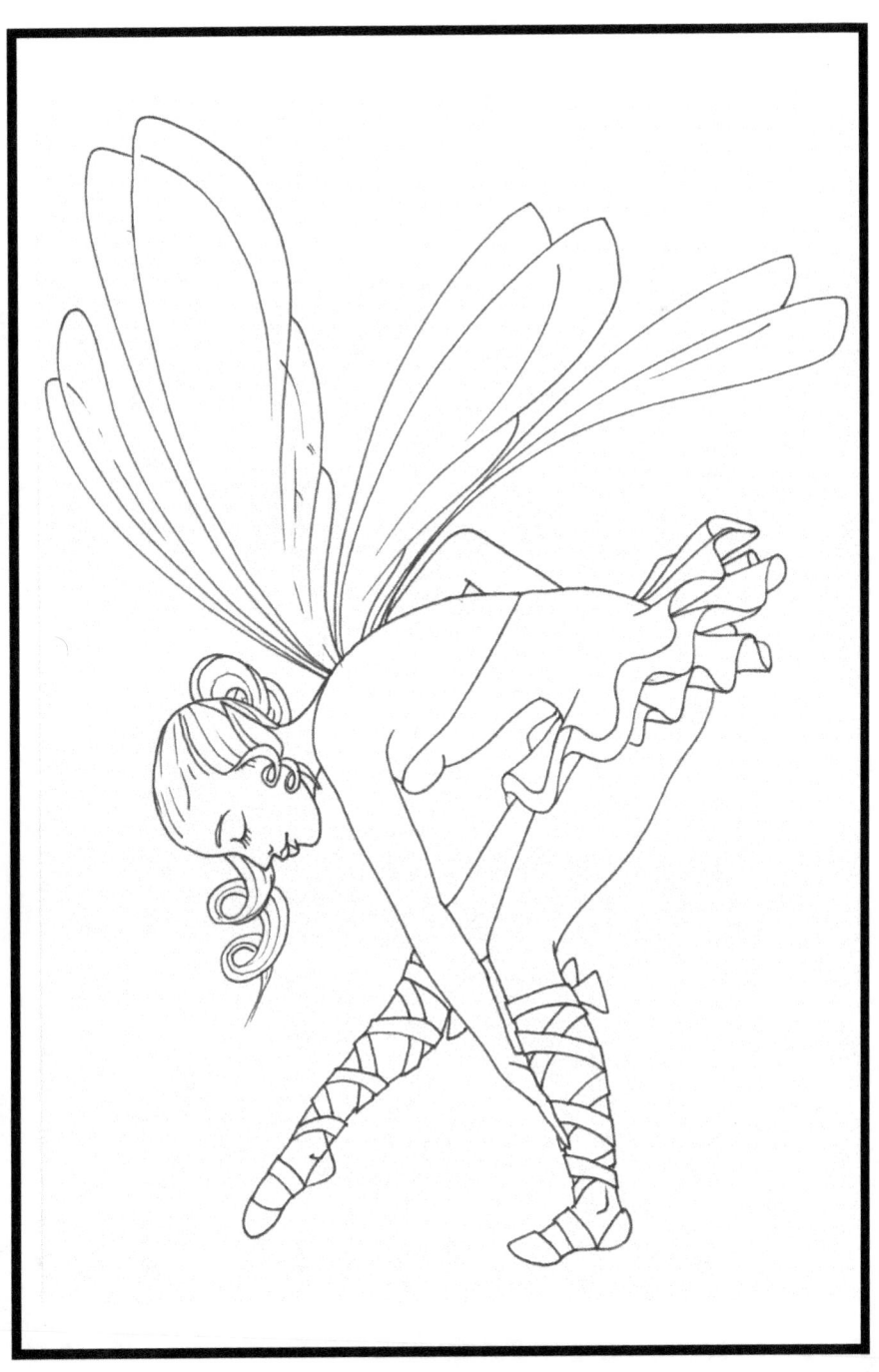

Ballet Faerie

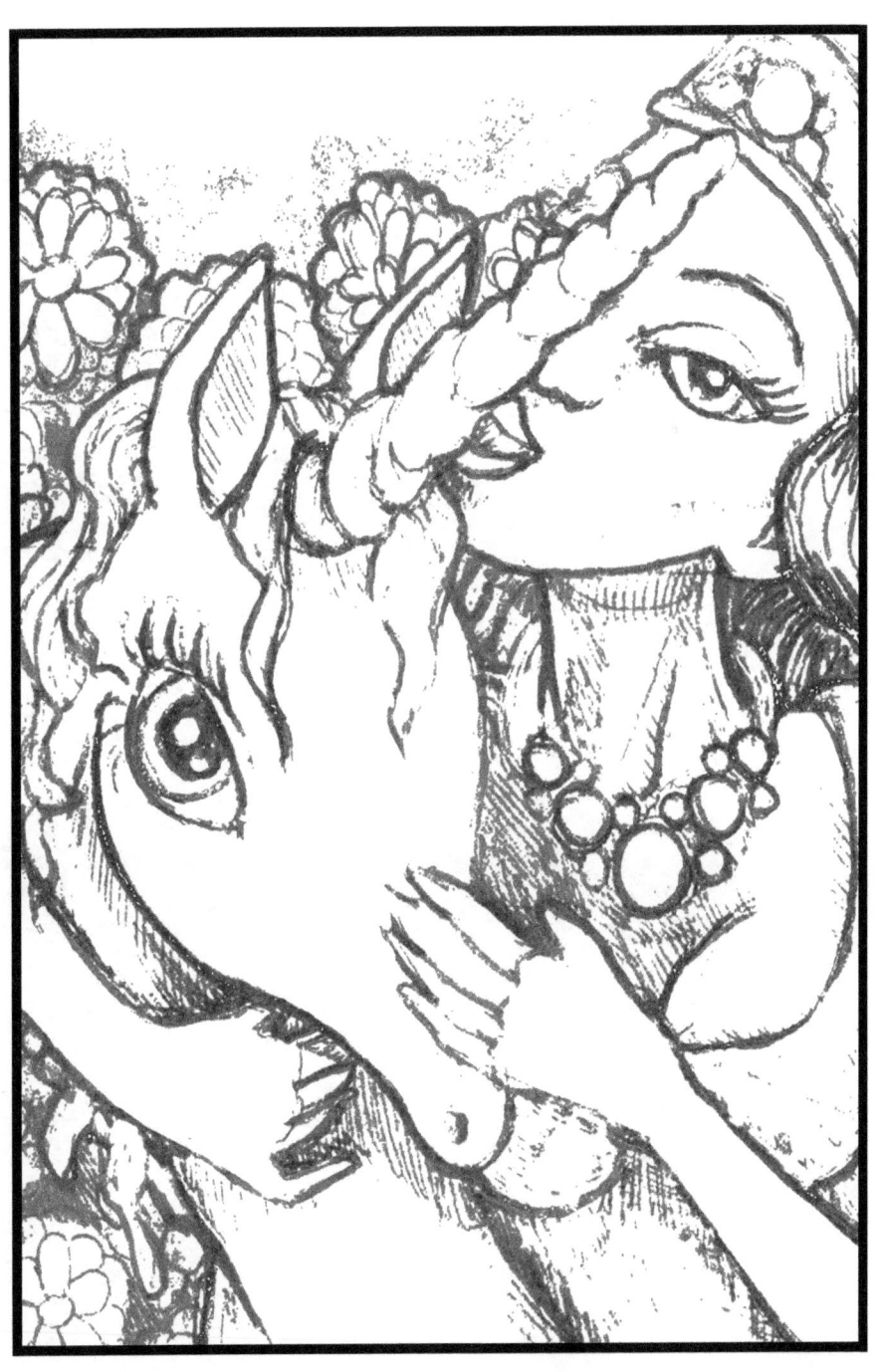

Unicorn Whisperer

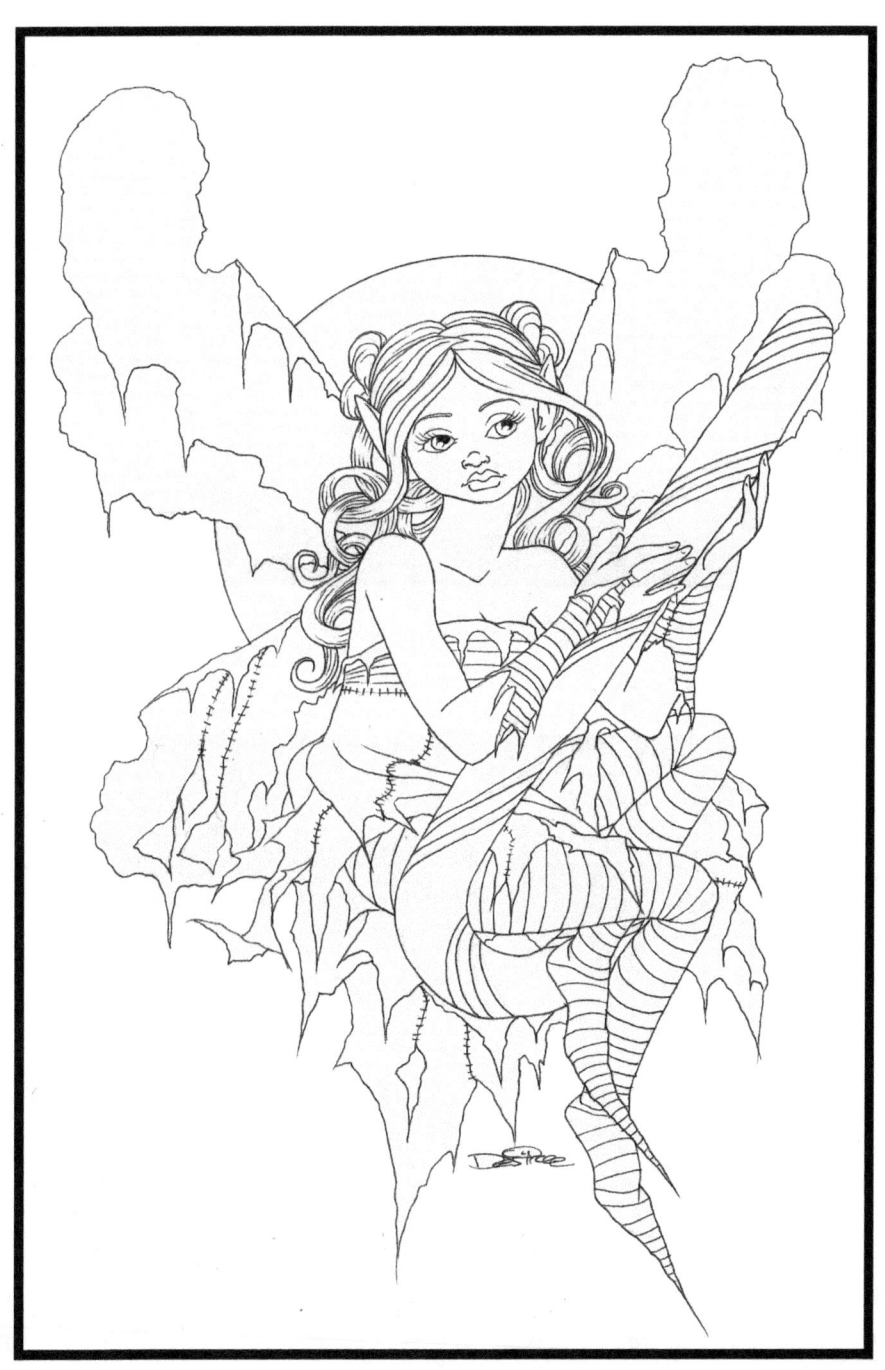

Candy Cane Faerie

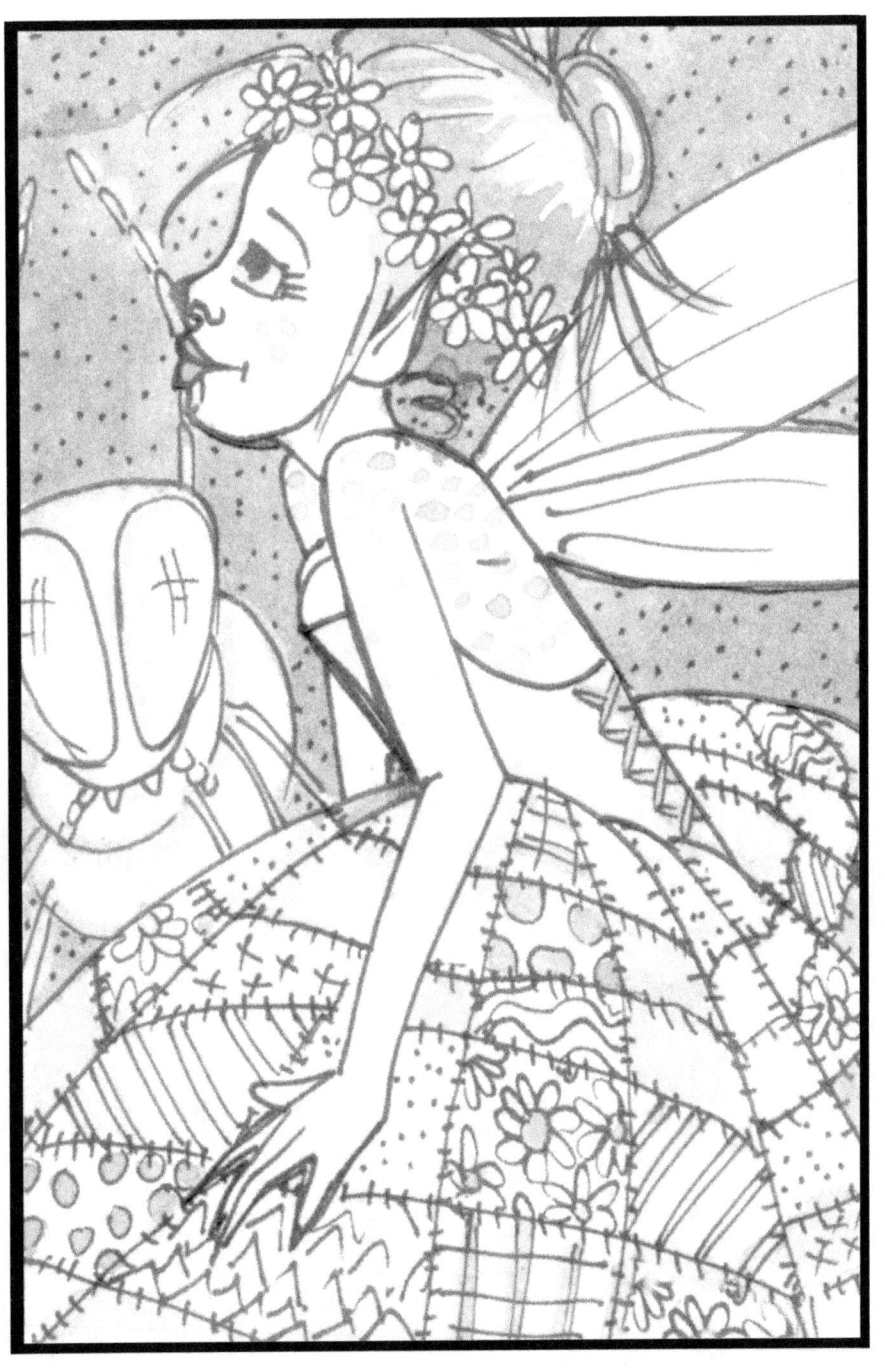

Patchwork

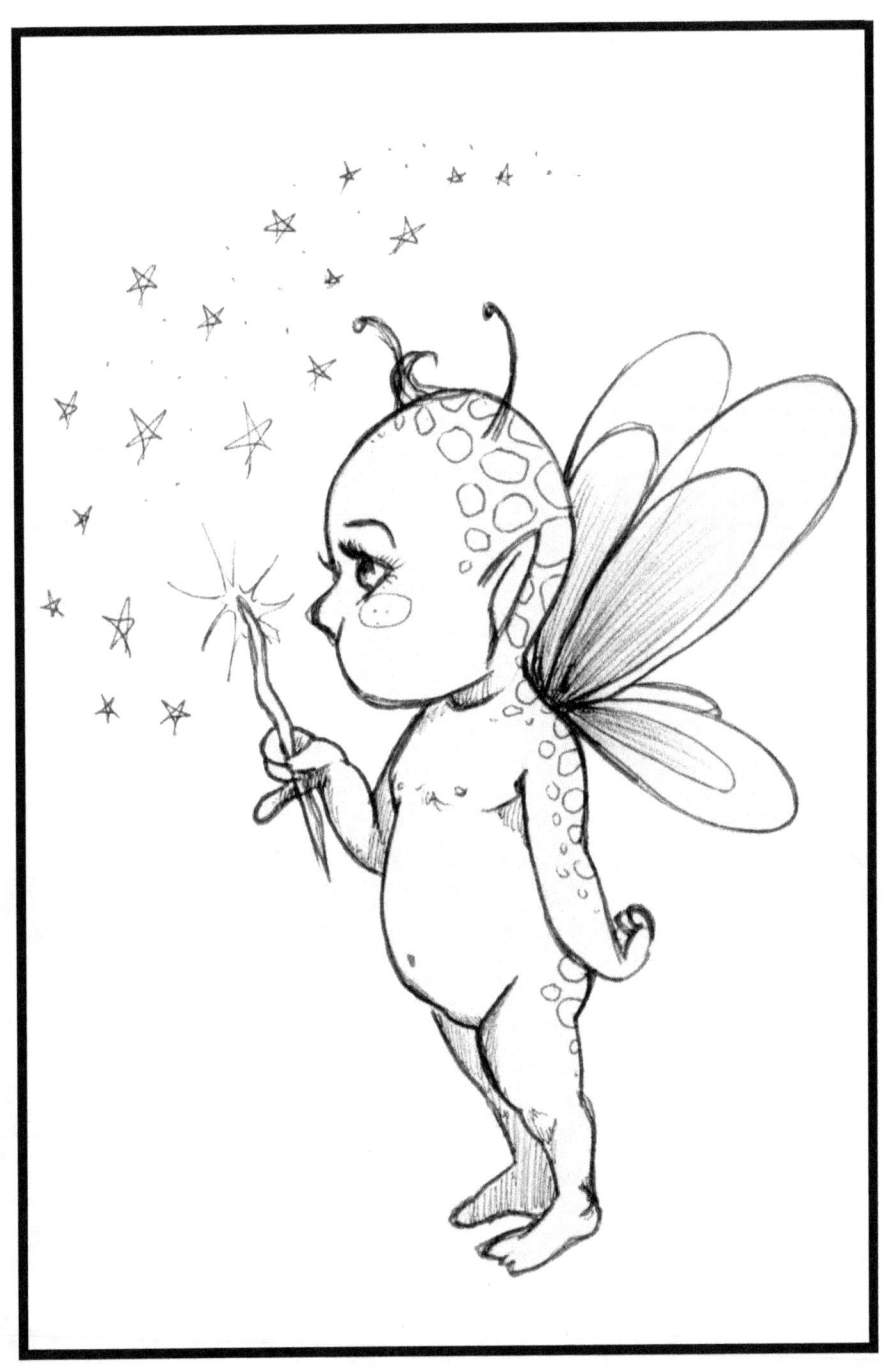

Pixie Dust

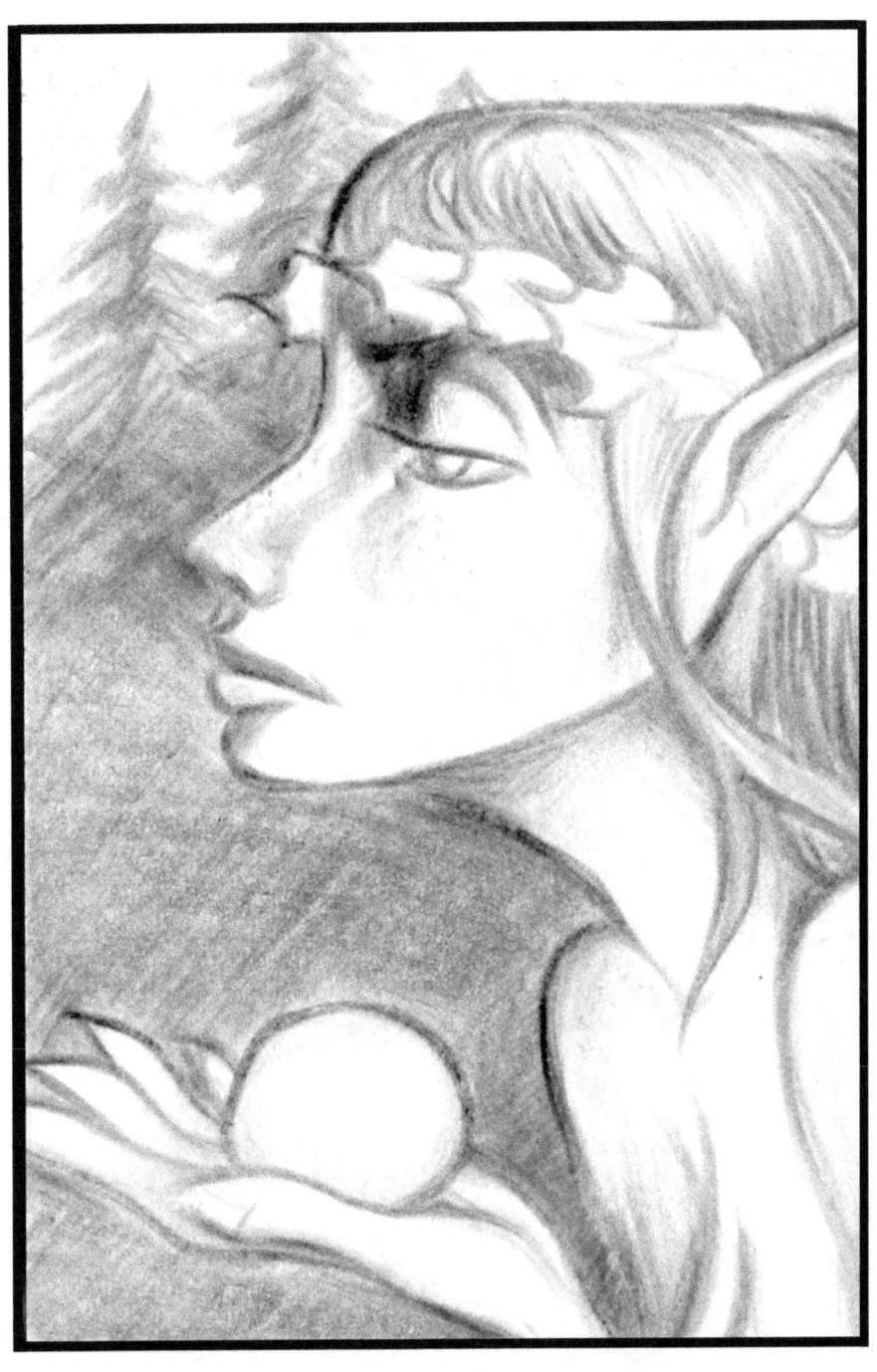

Faerie Princess & the Pea

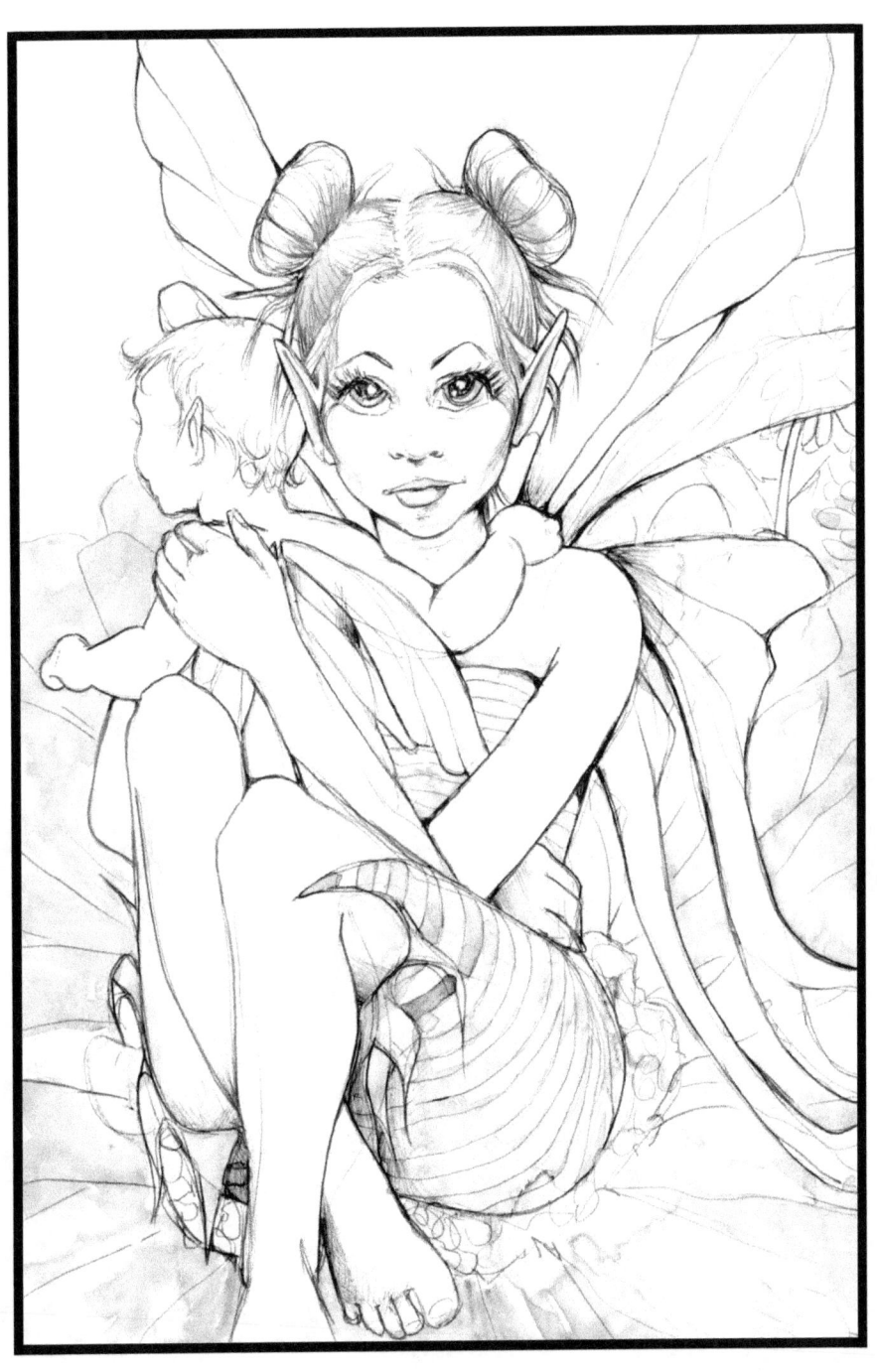

Mother Fae

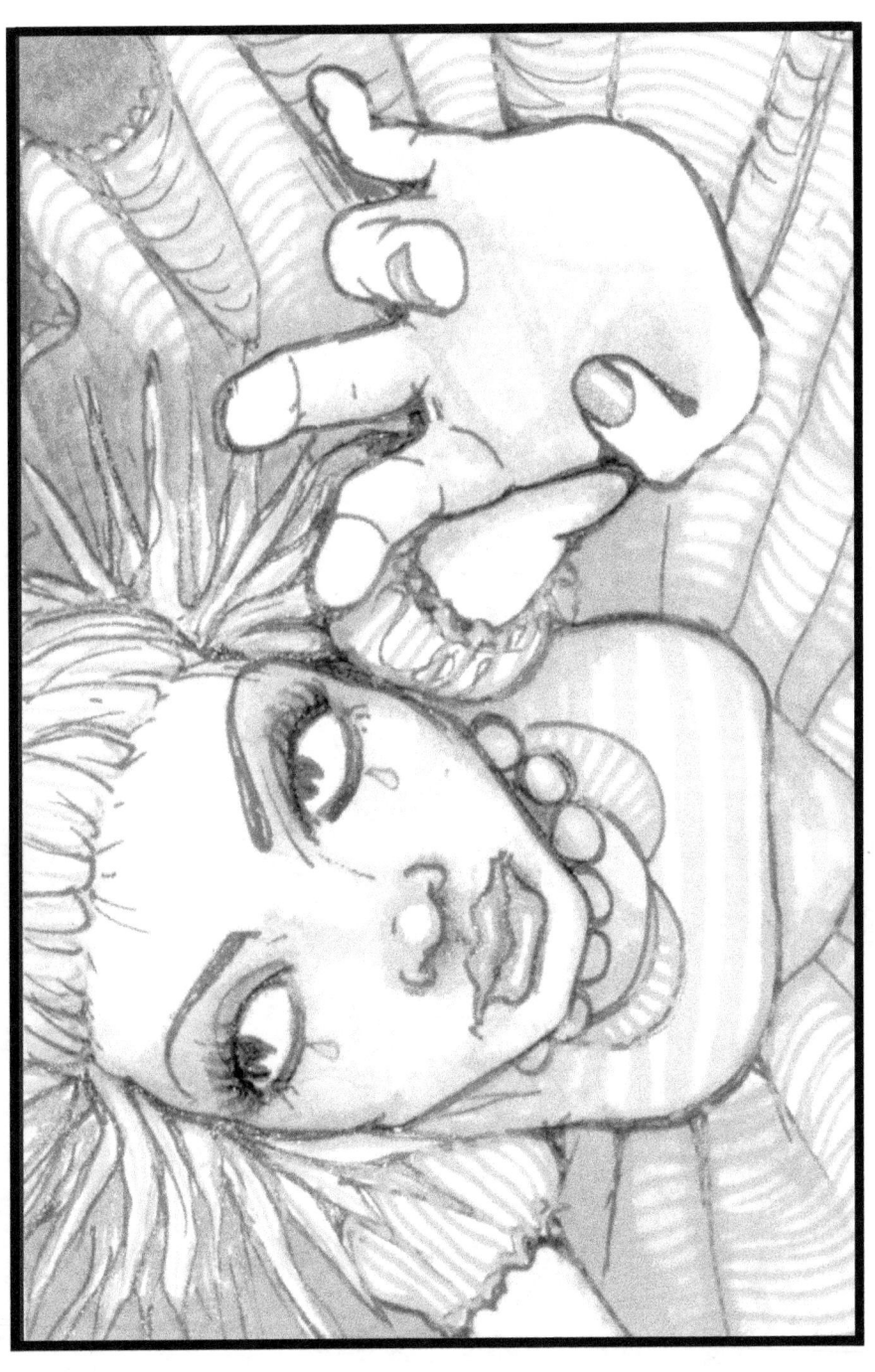

Seflie Faerie

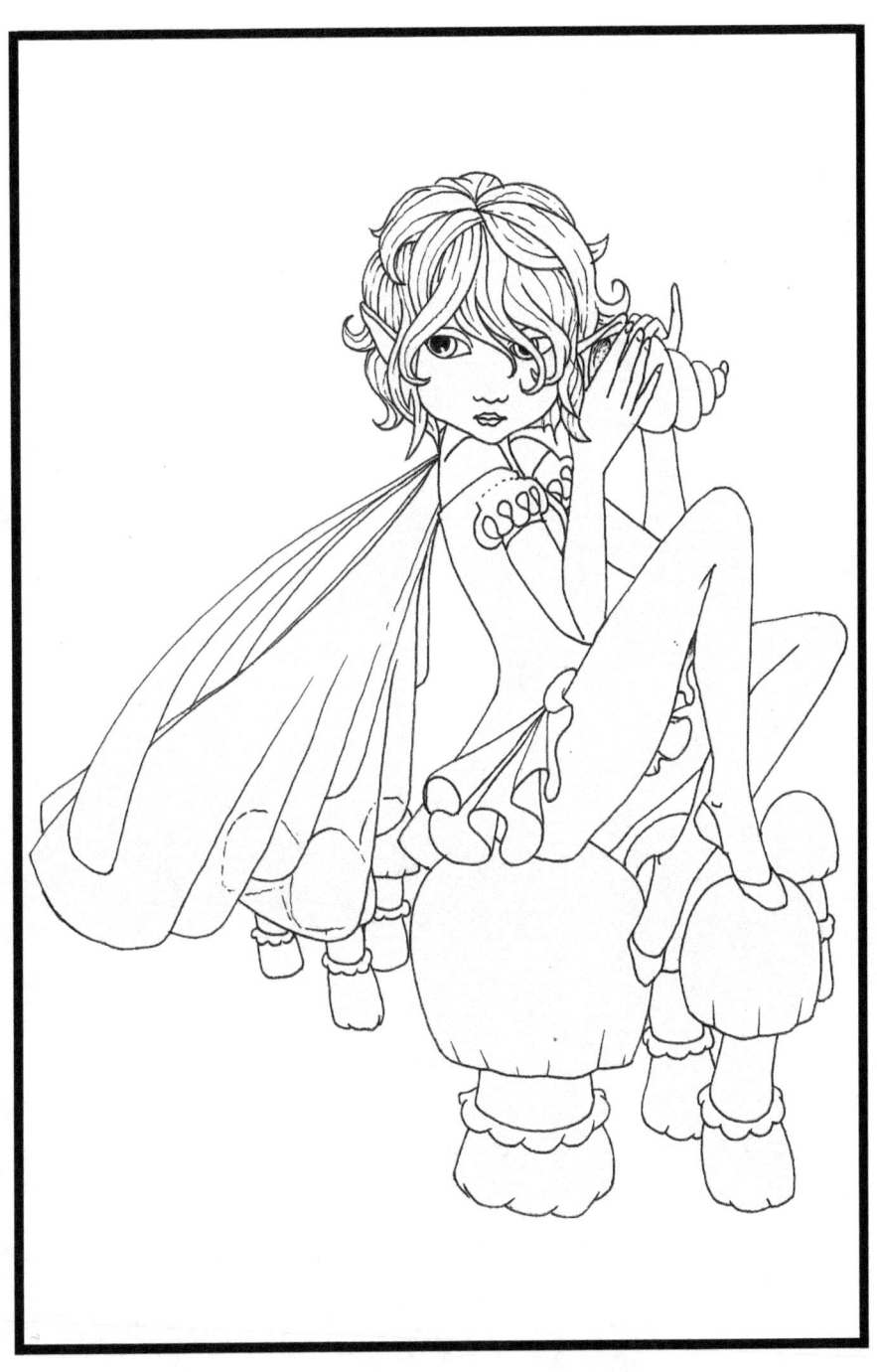

Secrets of a Shell

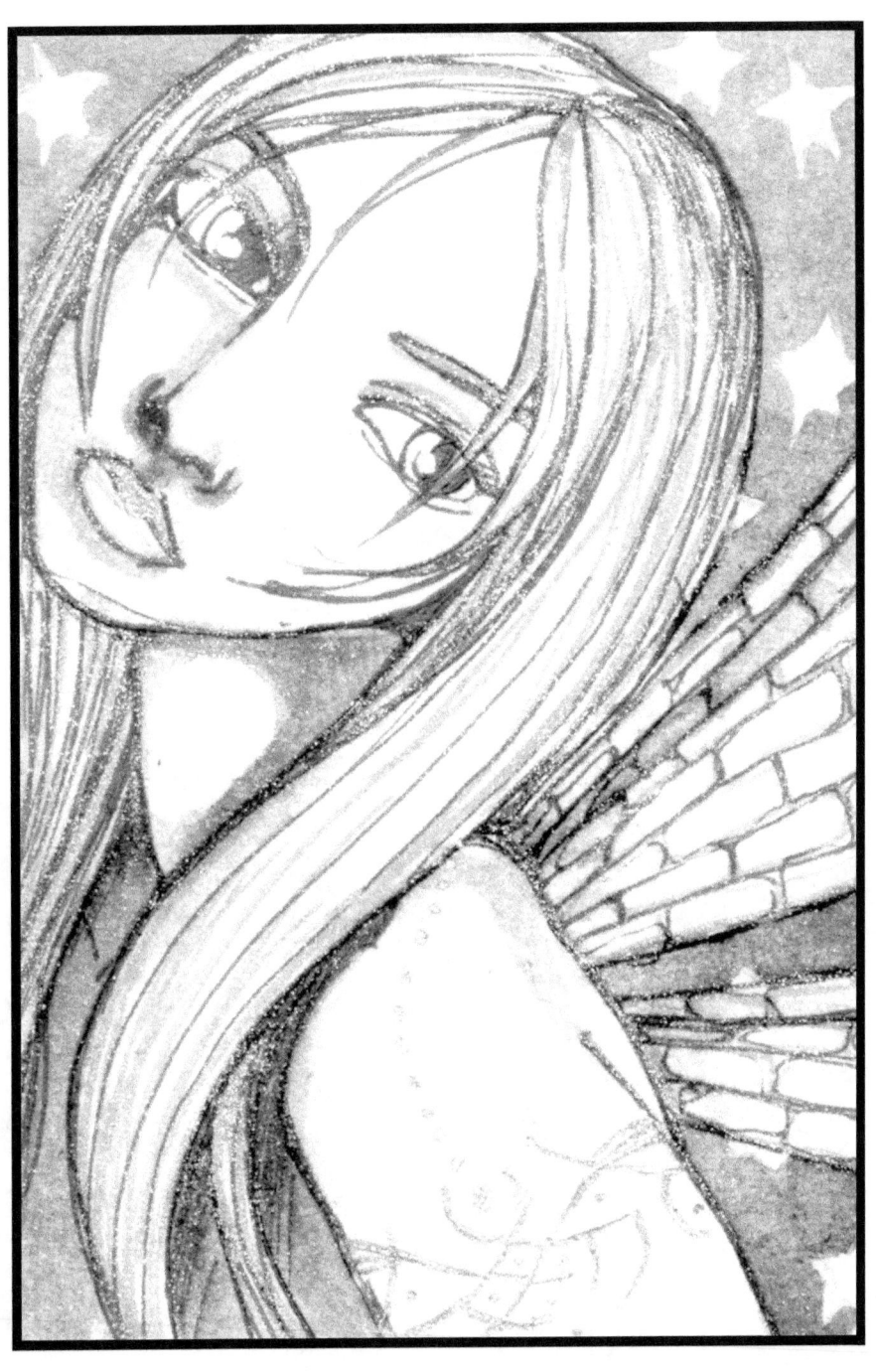

Dragonfly Damsel

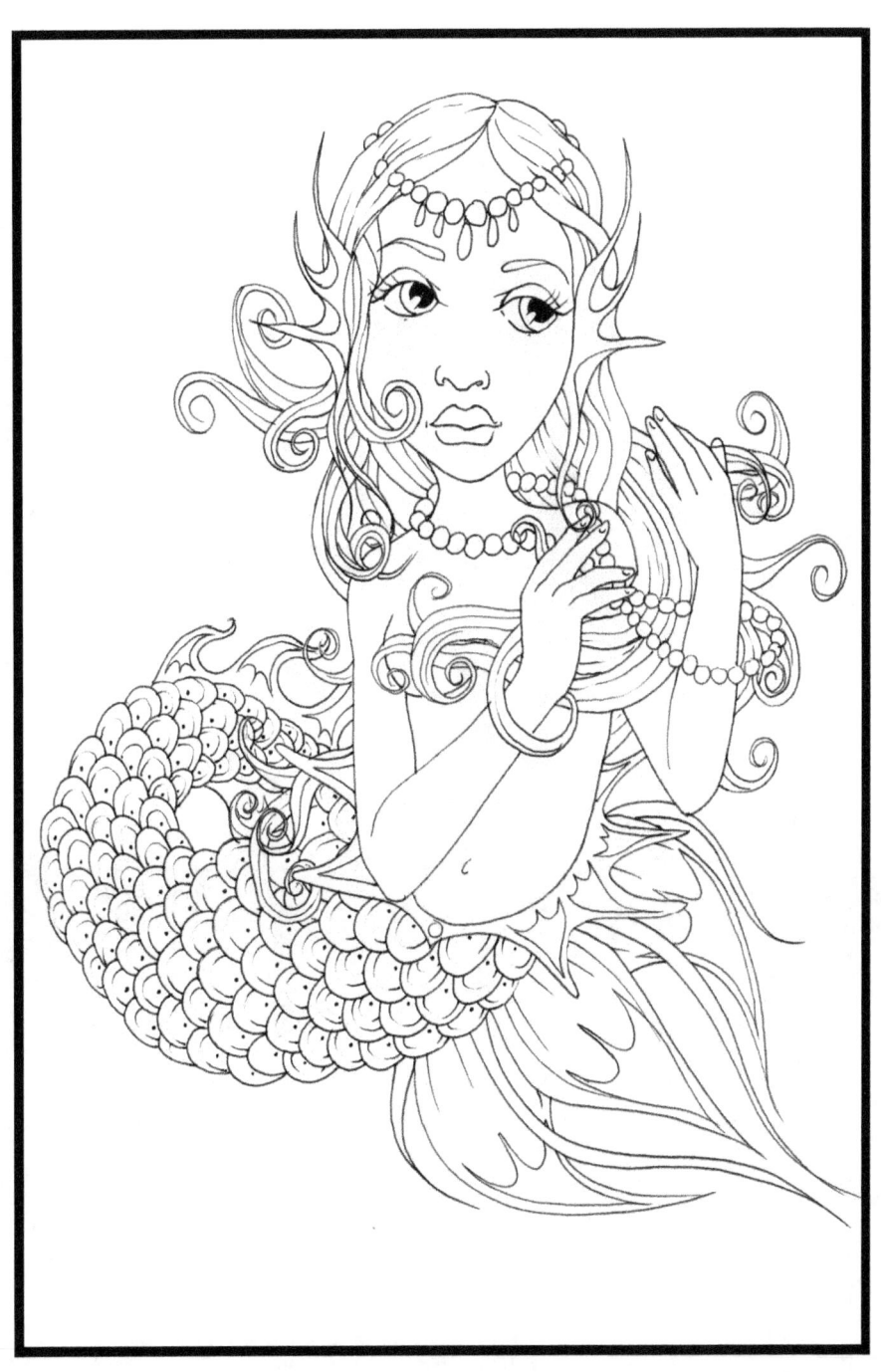

Pearl Necklace

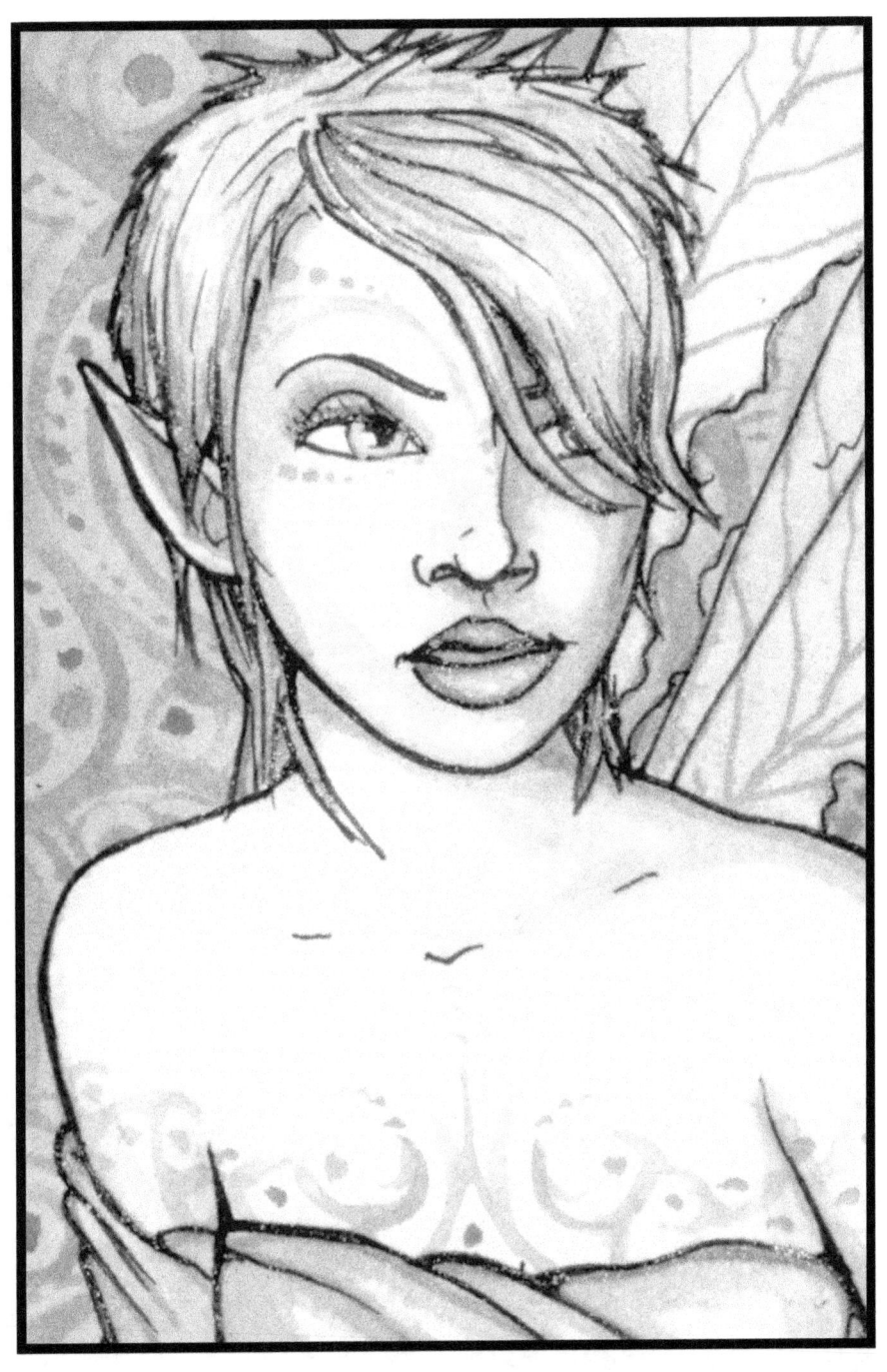

Tribal Fae

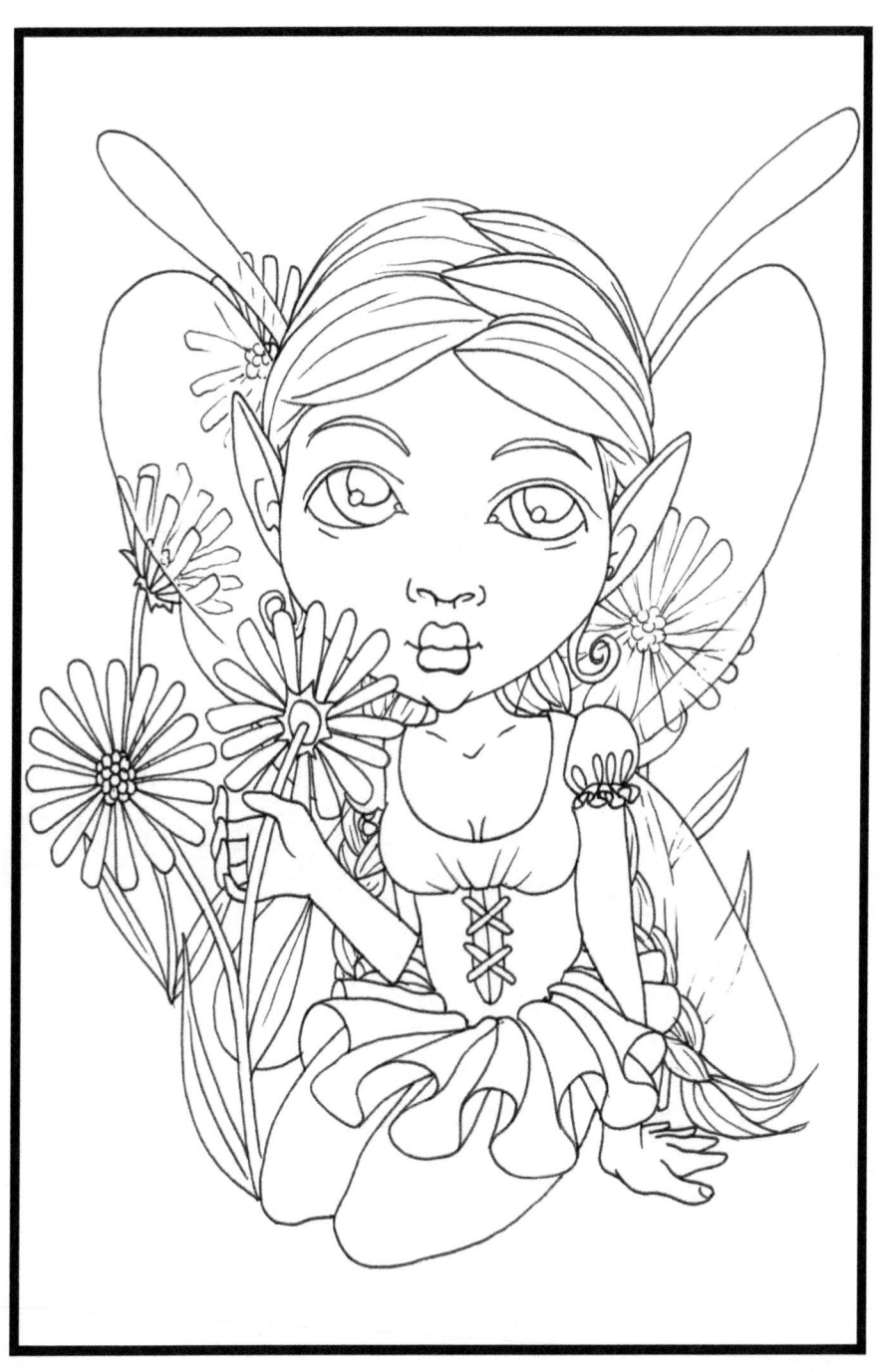

Daisies Are Awesome

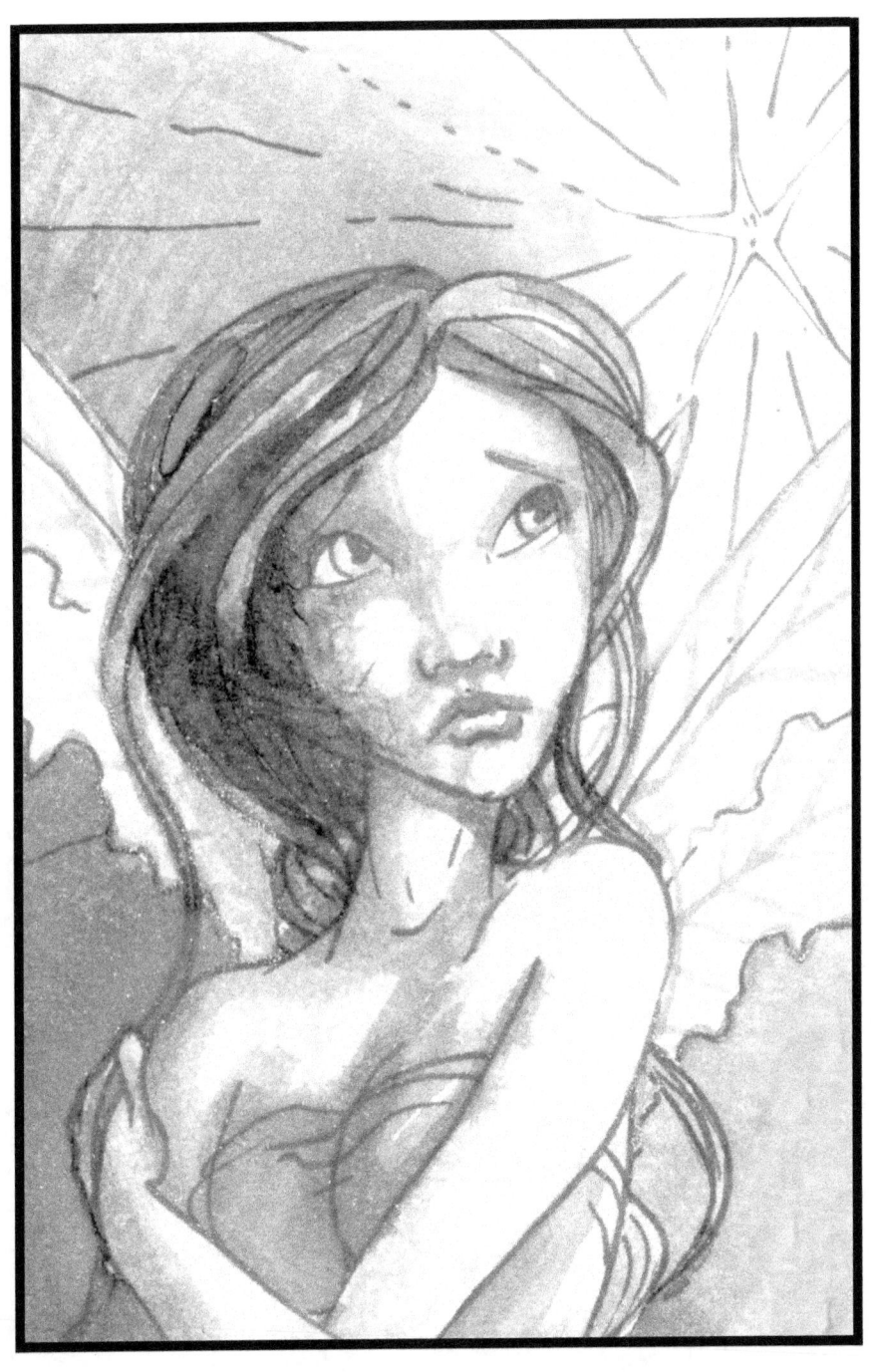

Wish on a Star

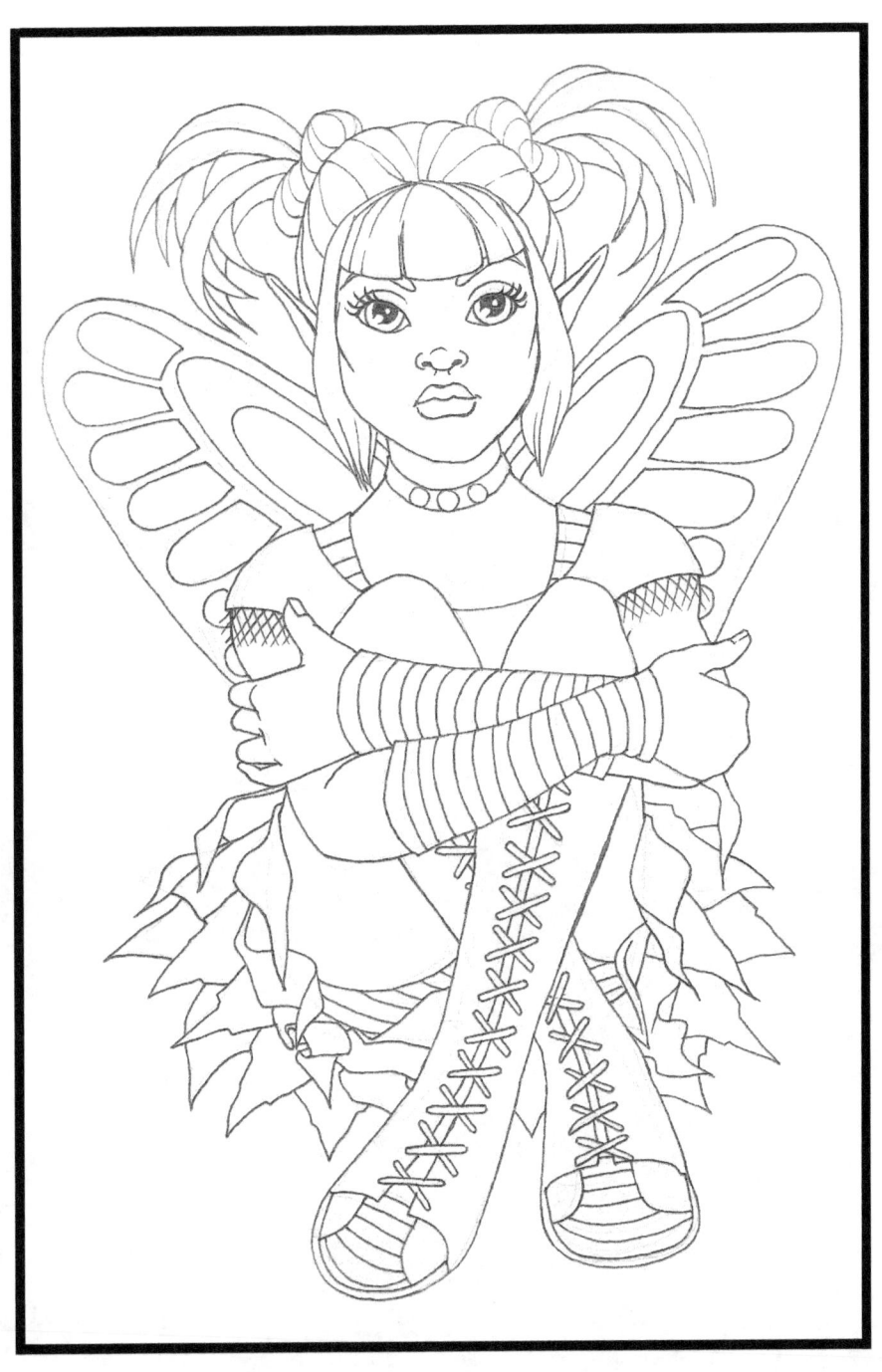

Bubble Gum Punk Faerie

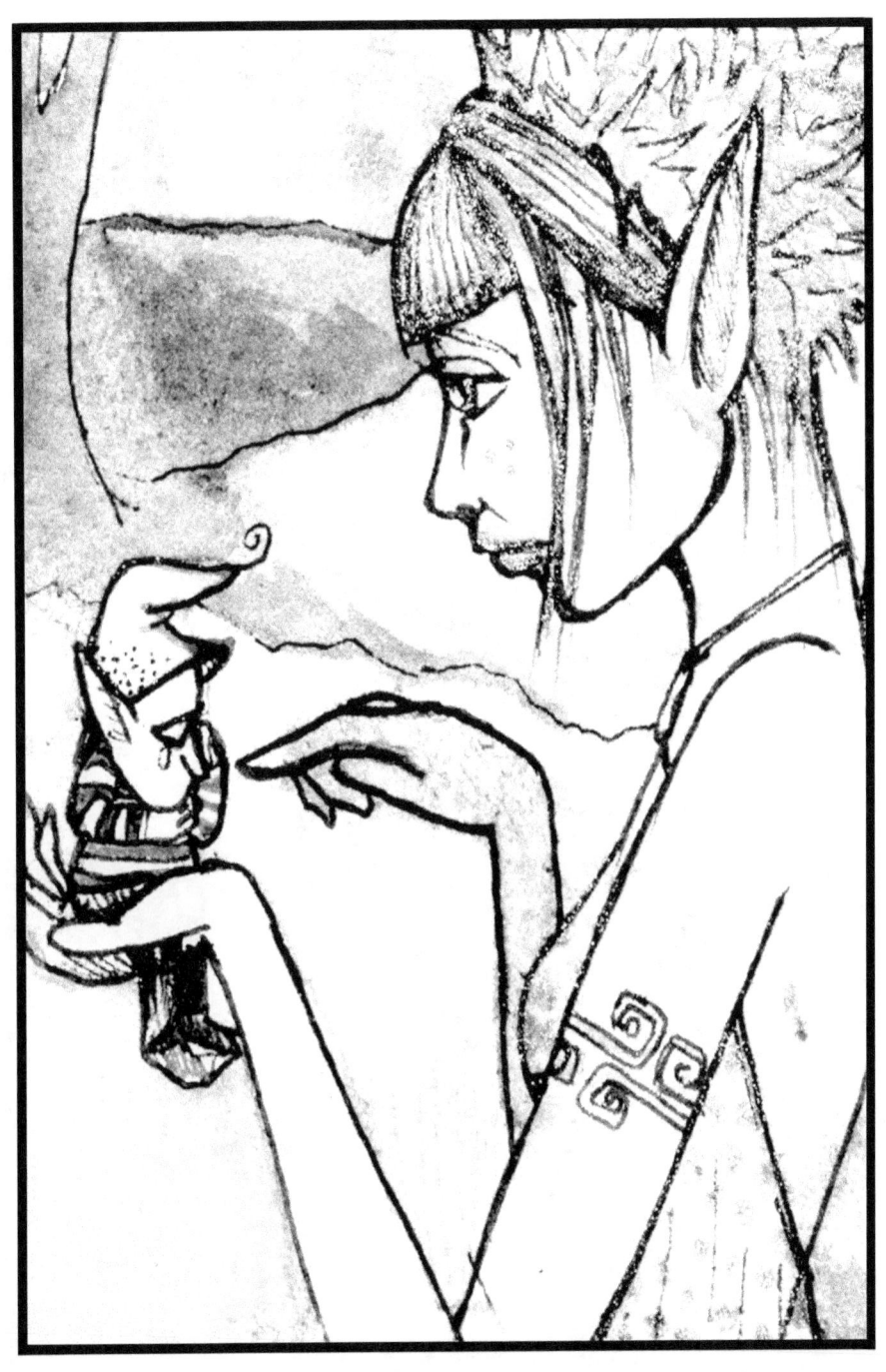

Consoling a Friend

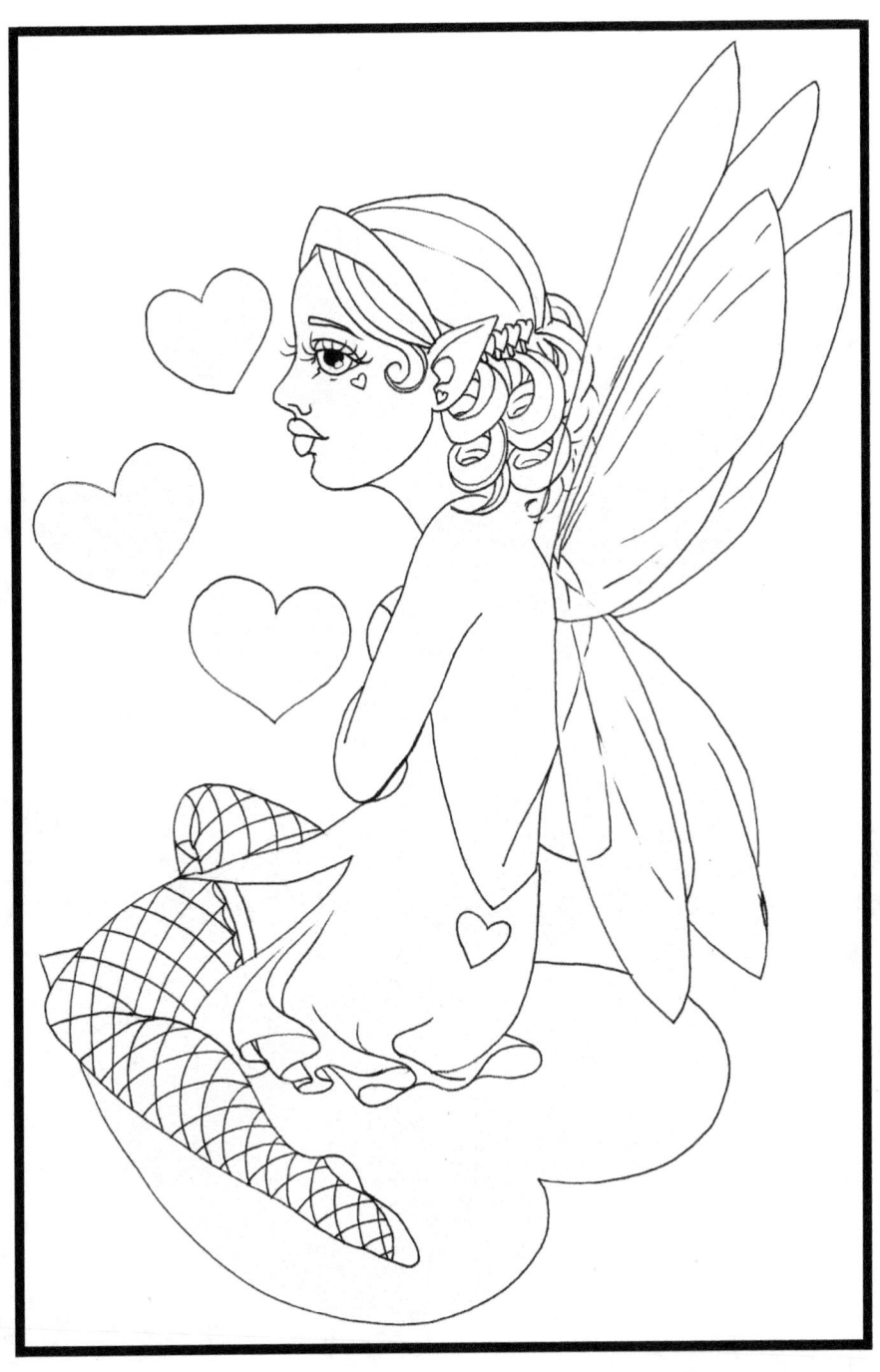

Heart's Desire

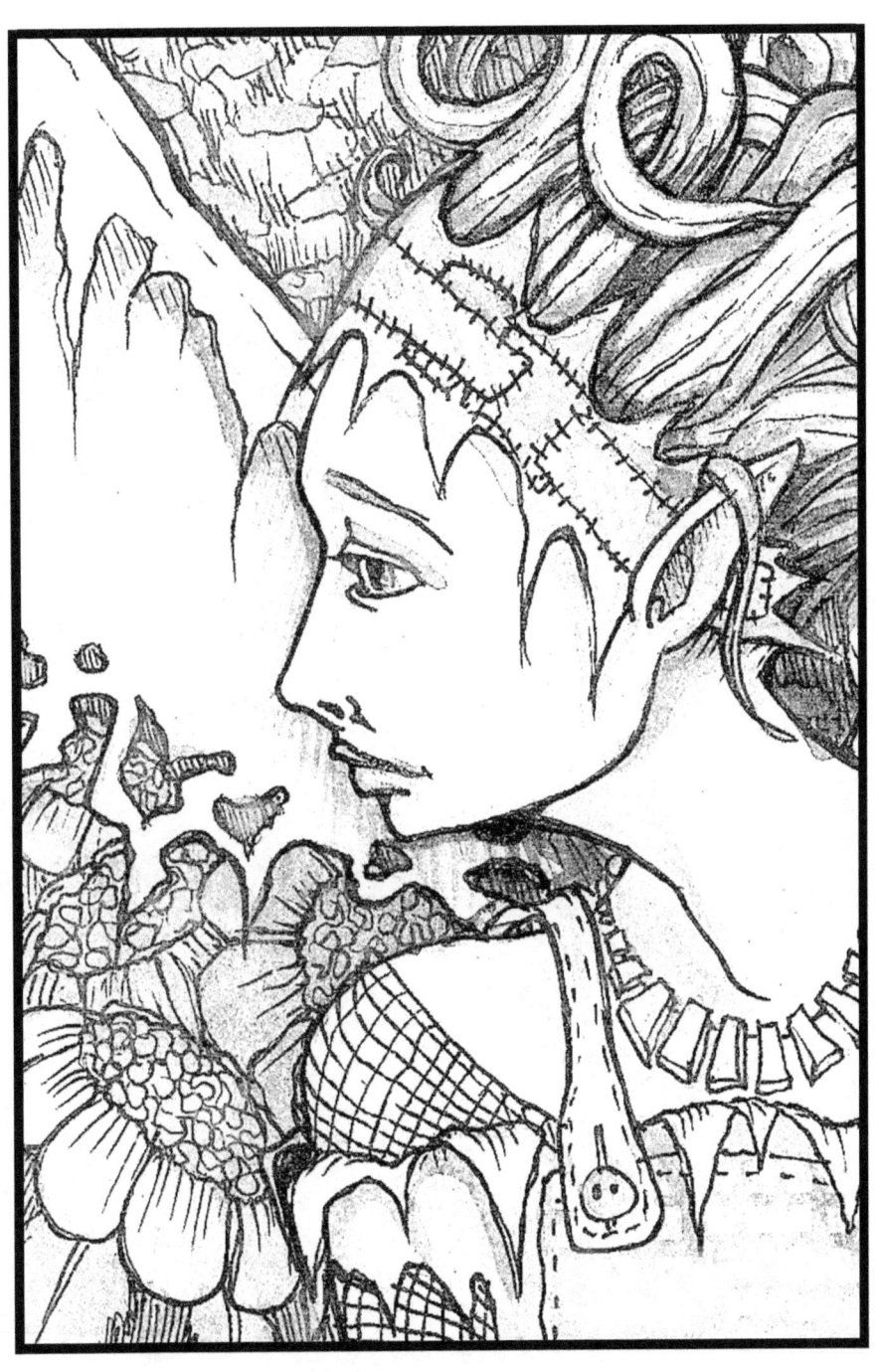

Upcycled Clothing

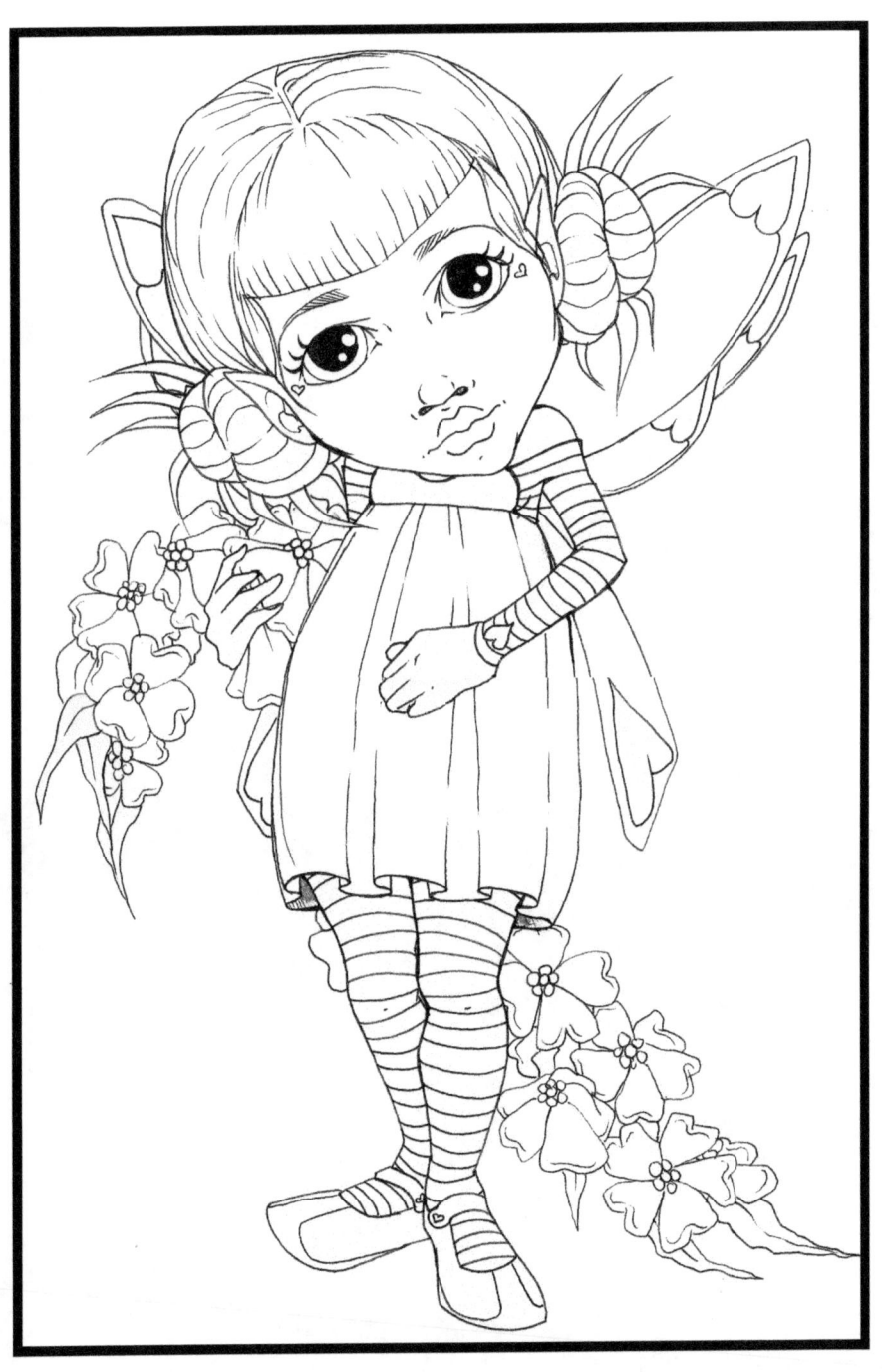

Gathering the Bouquet

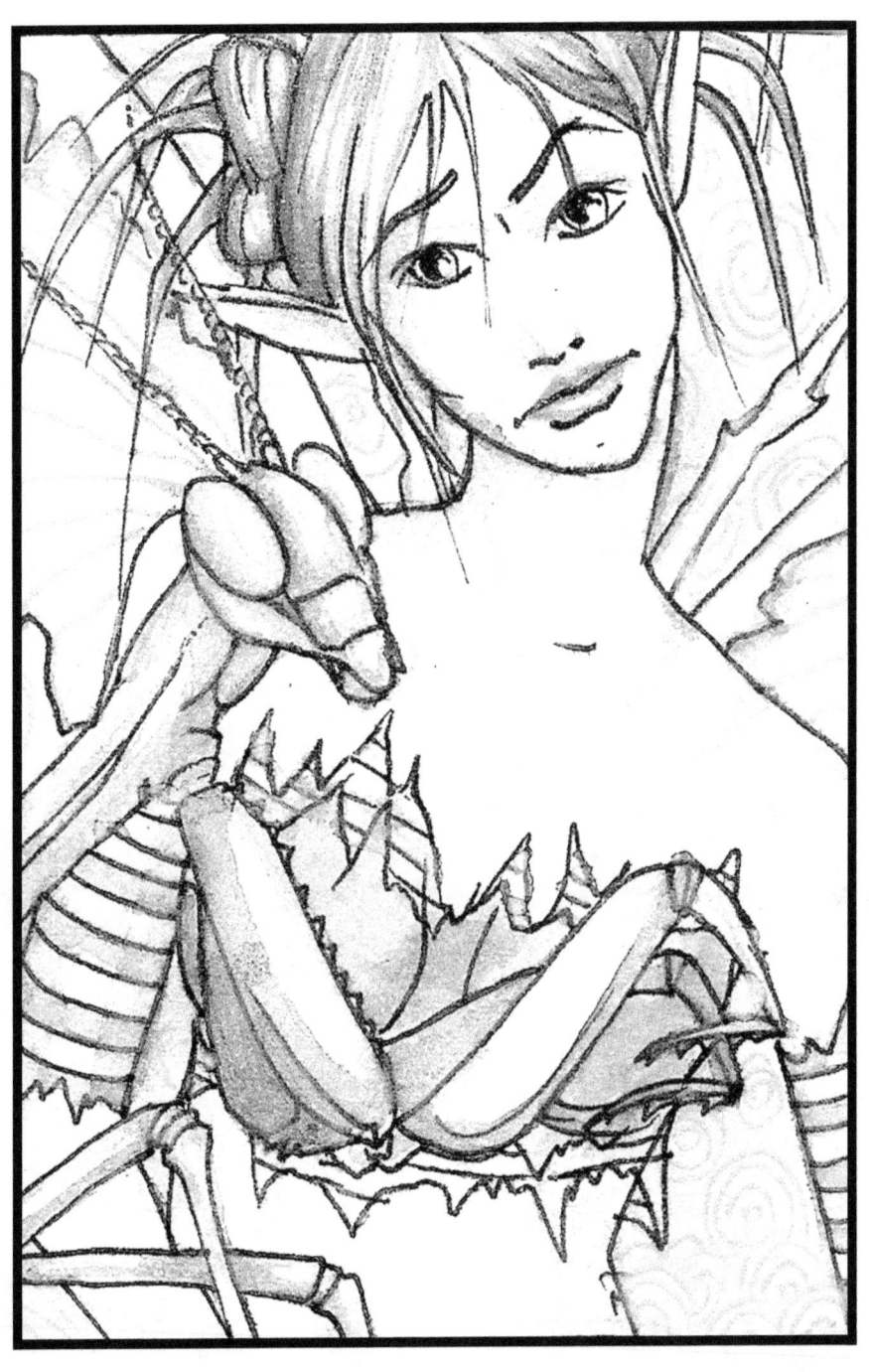

Mad at Manty

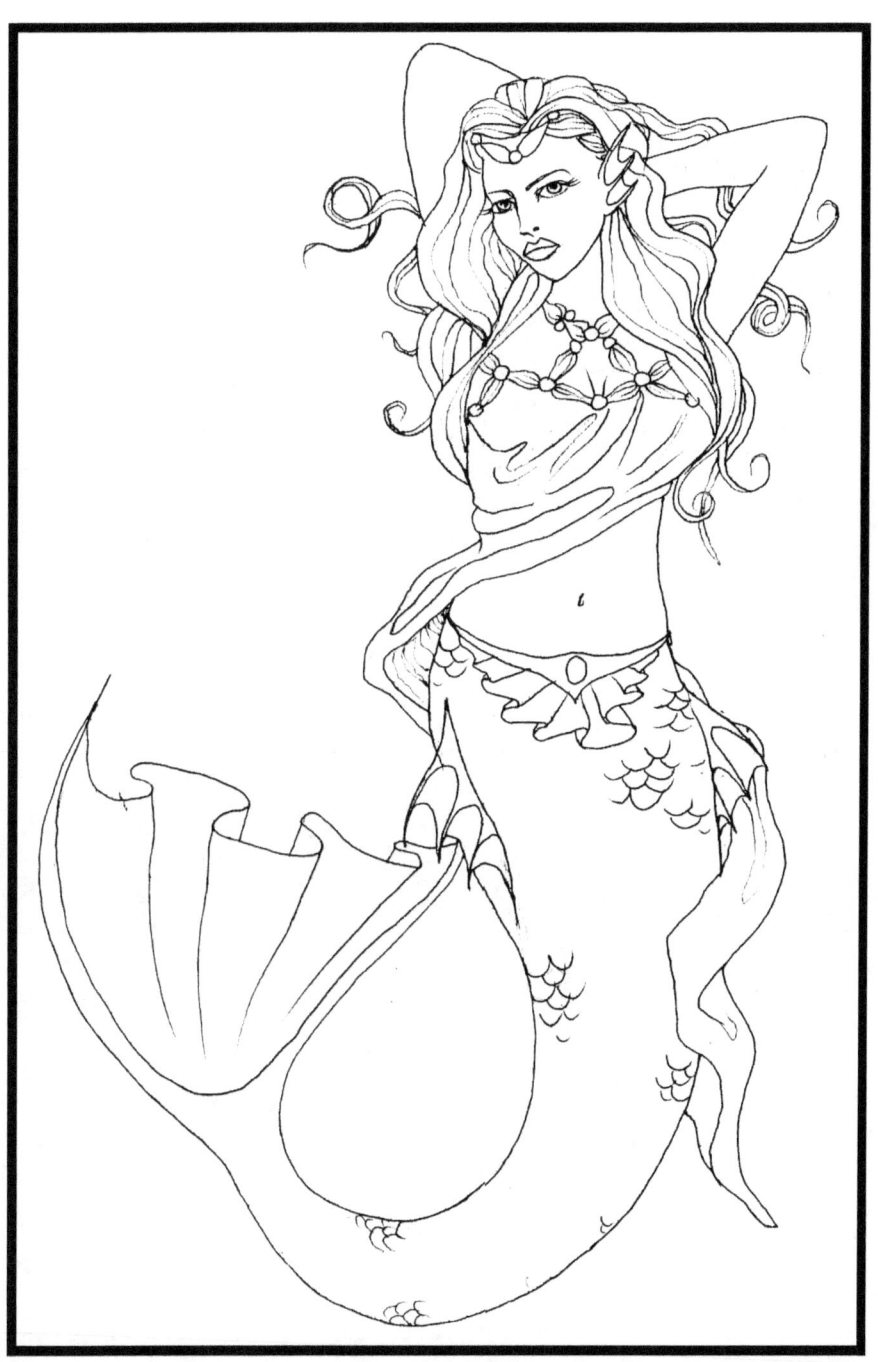

Floating, Thinking

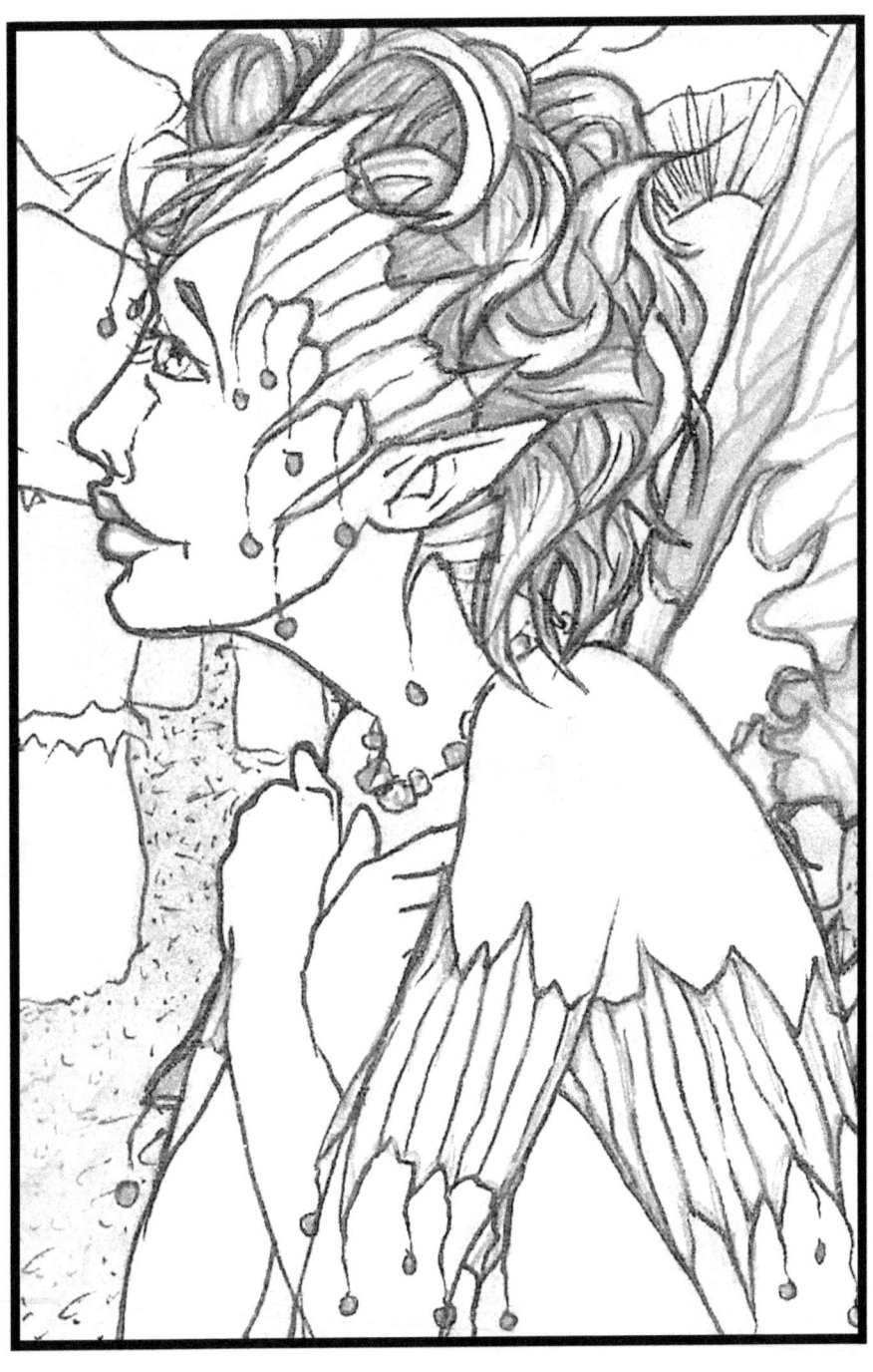

Missing Him

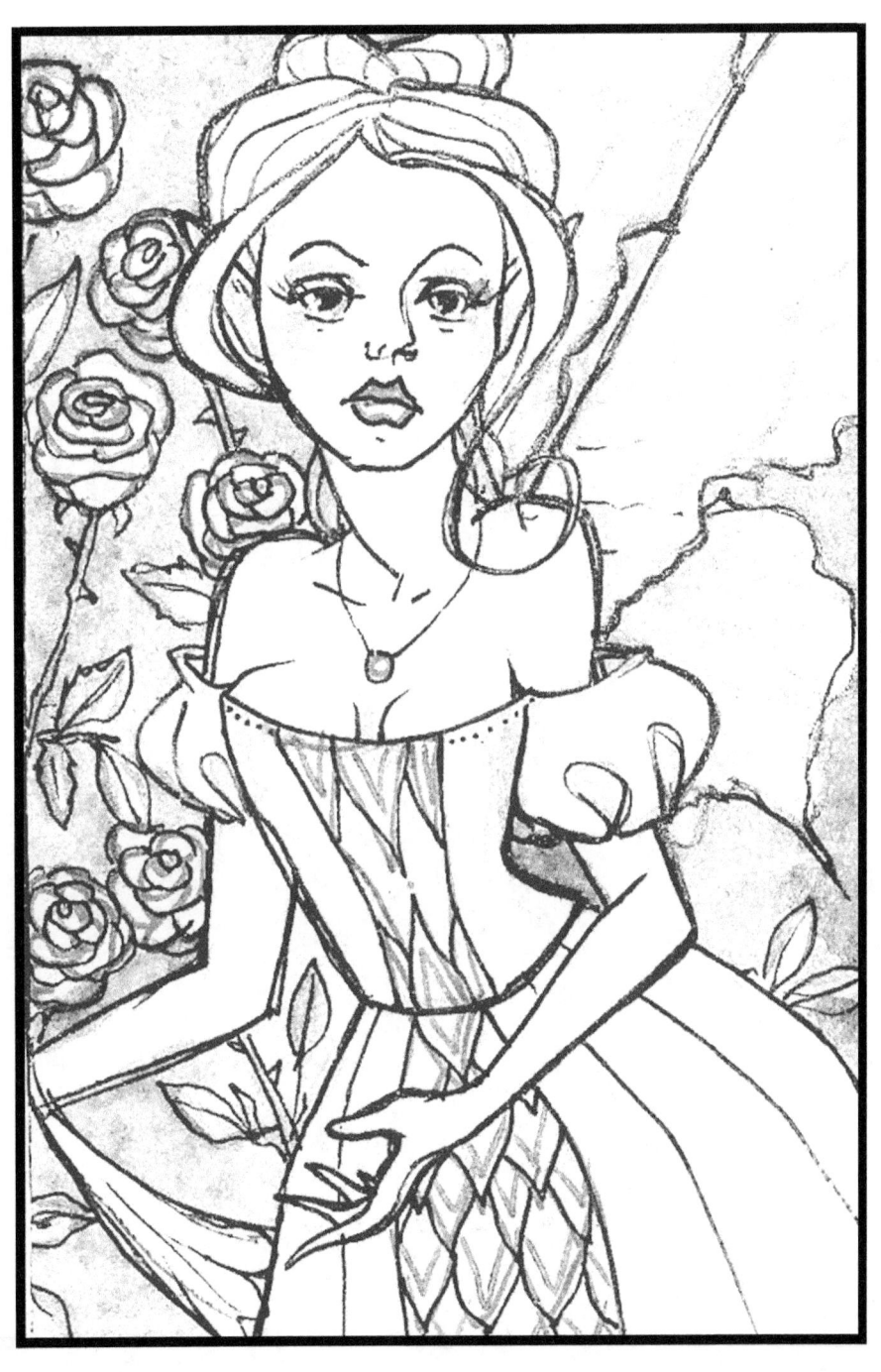

Roses are Red

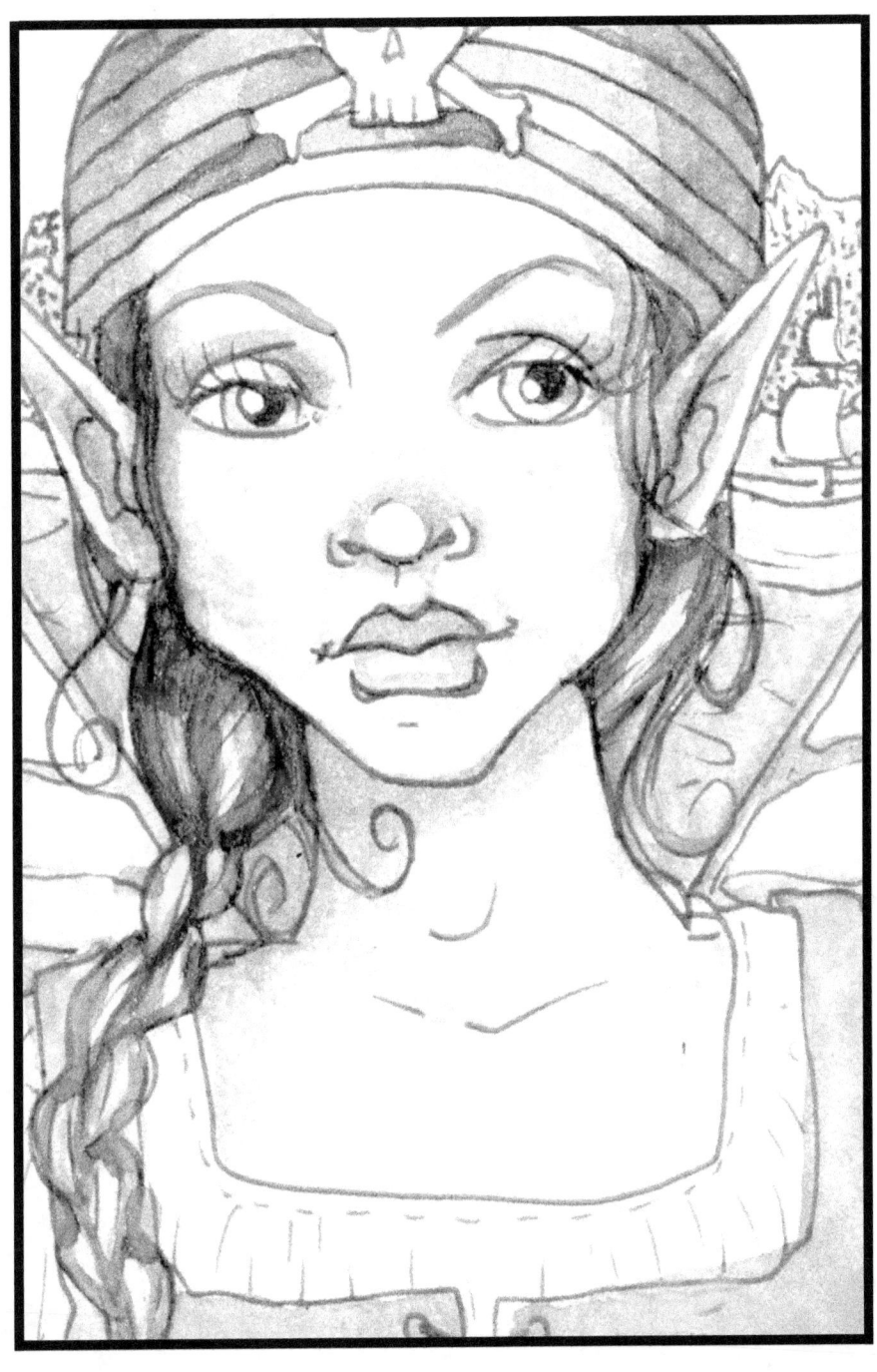

Pirate Fae

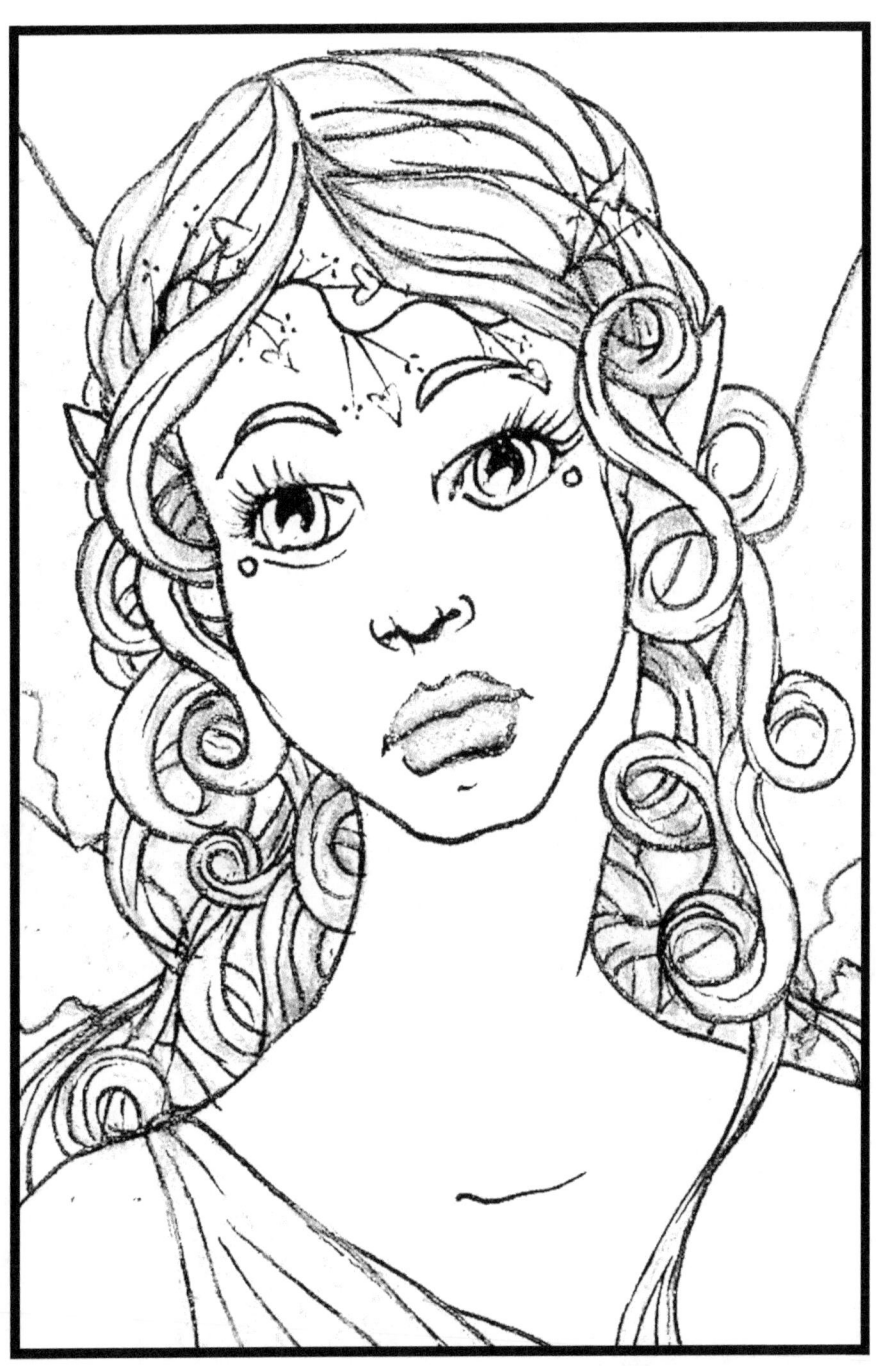

Curls

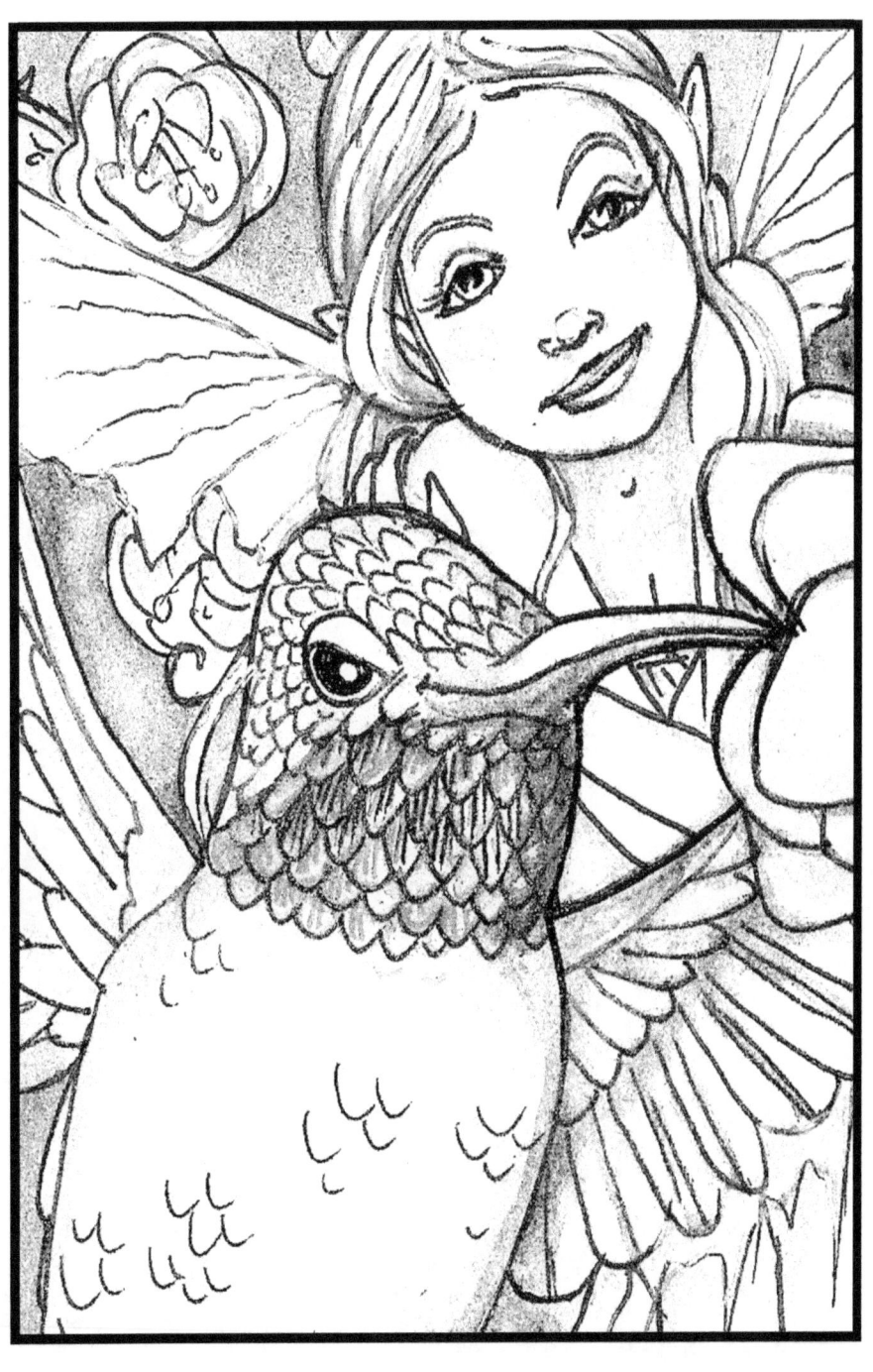

Flight of the Humming Bird

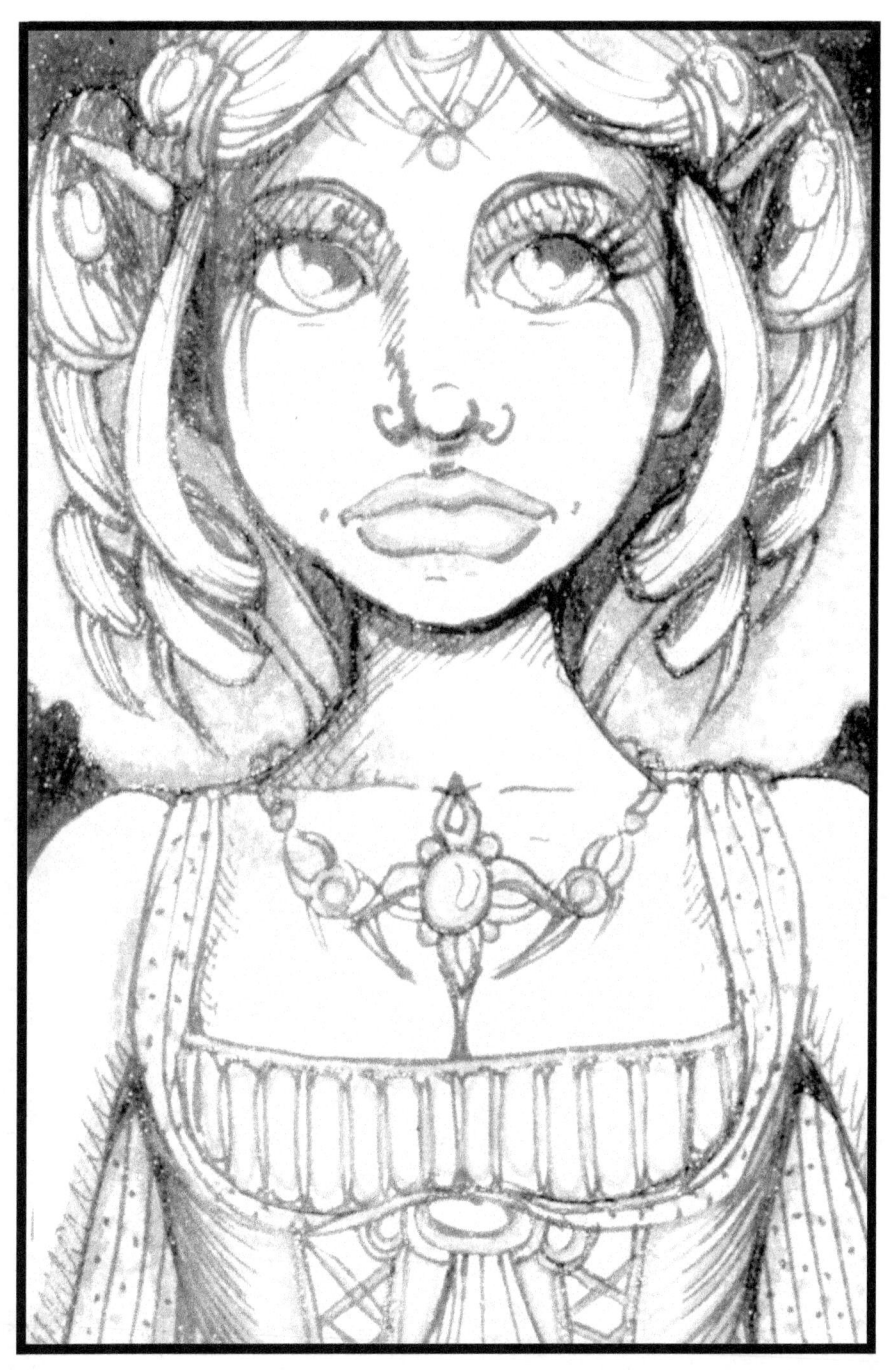

Dressed to Kill

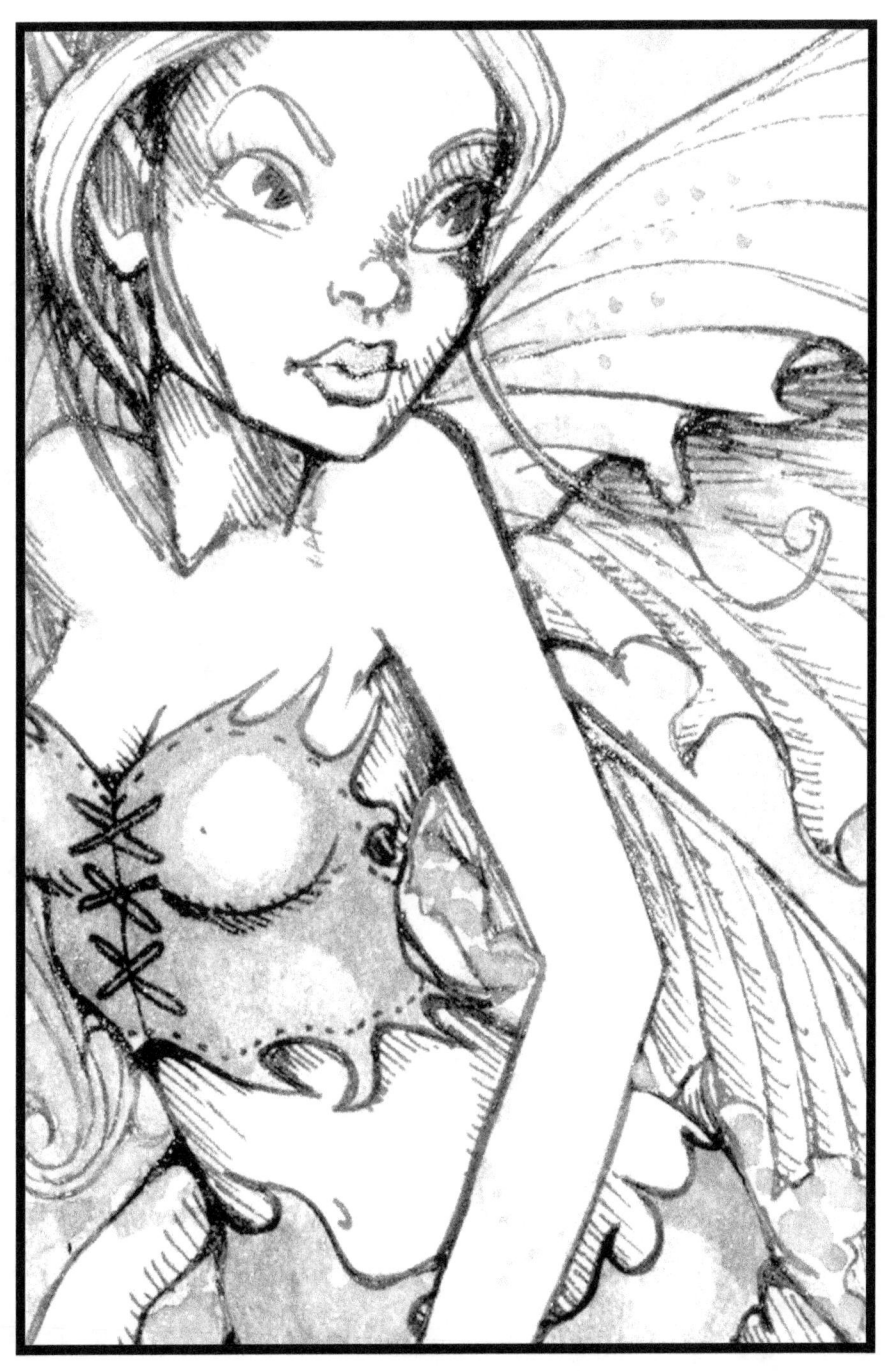

Autumn Faerie

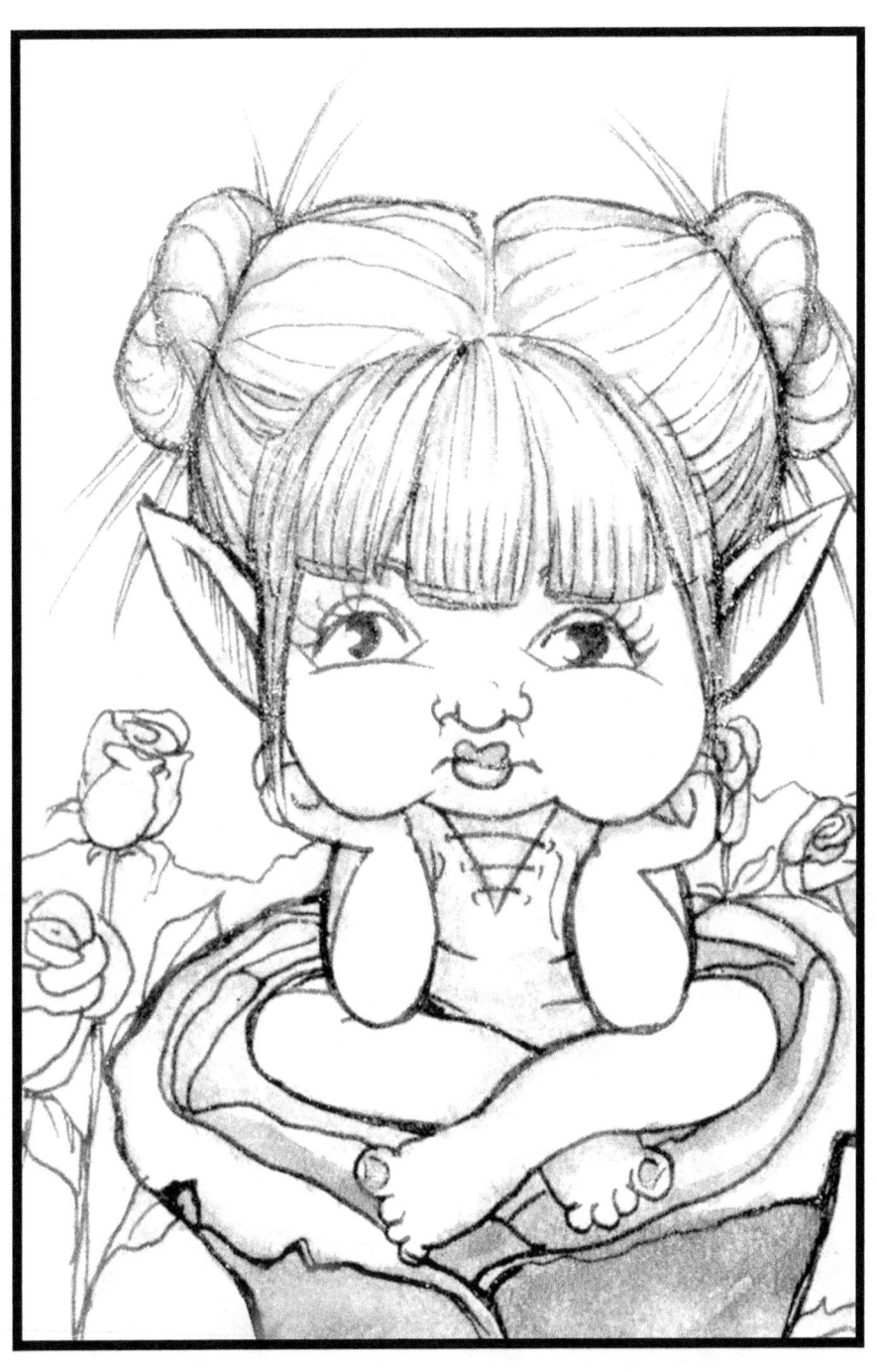

Roses are Red, and I Feel so Blue

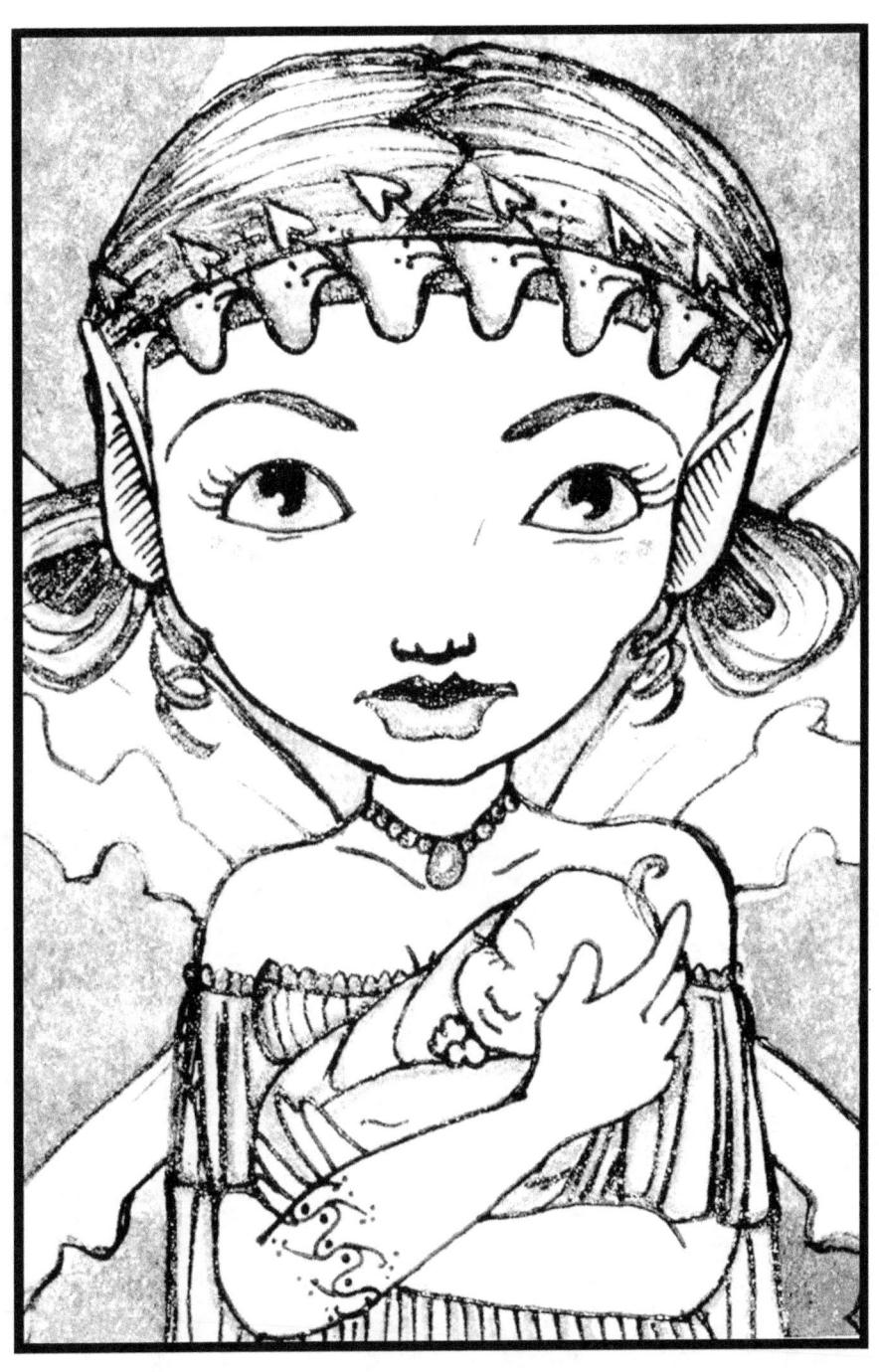

Newborn Love

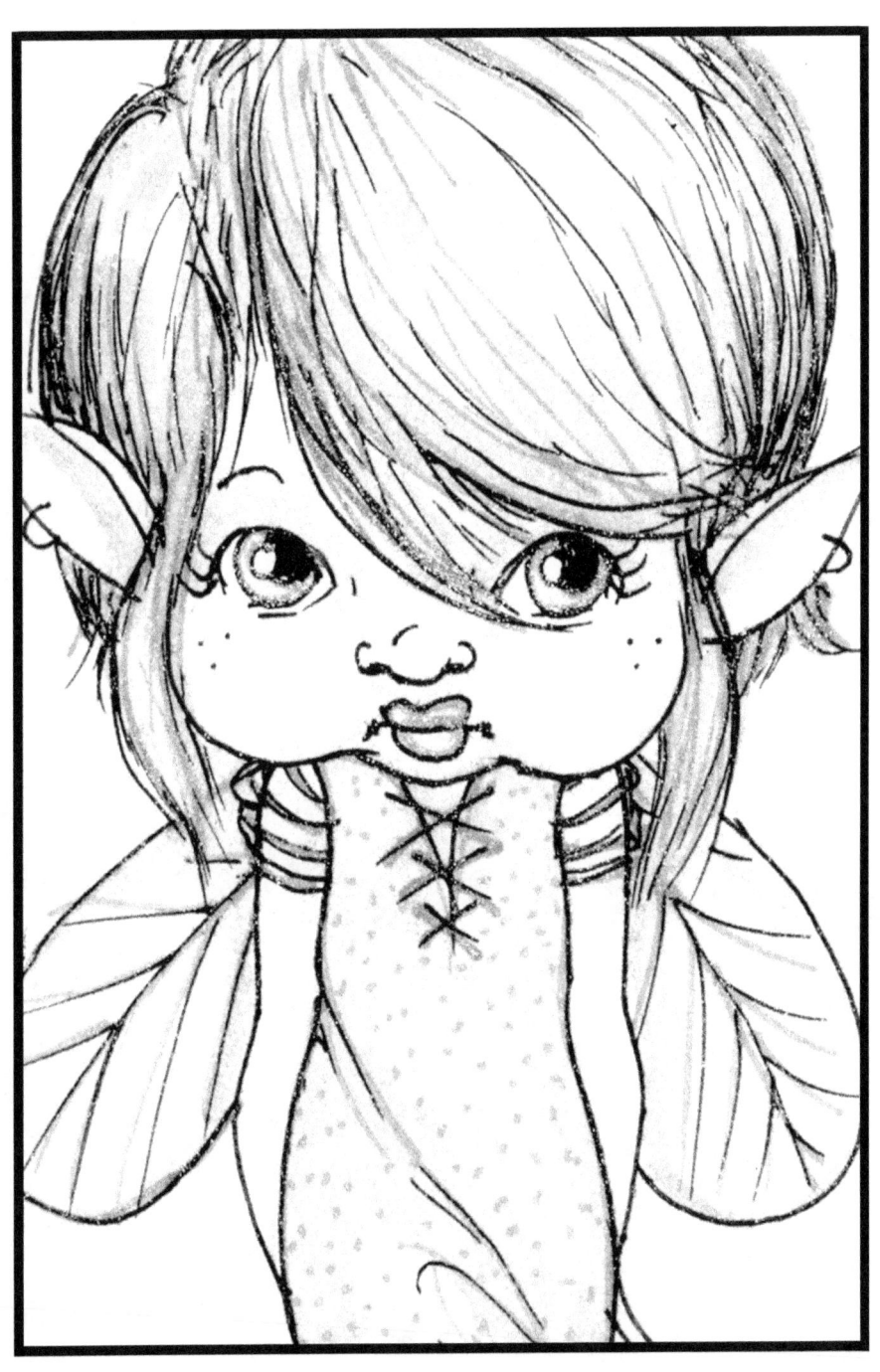

Modest One

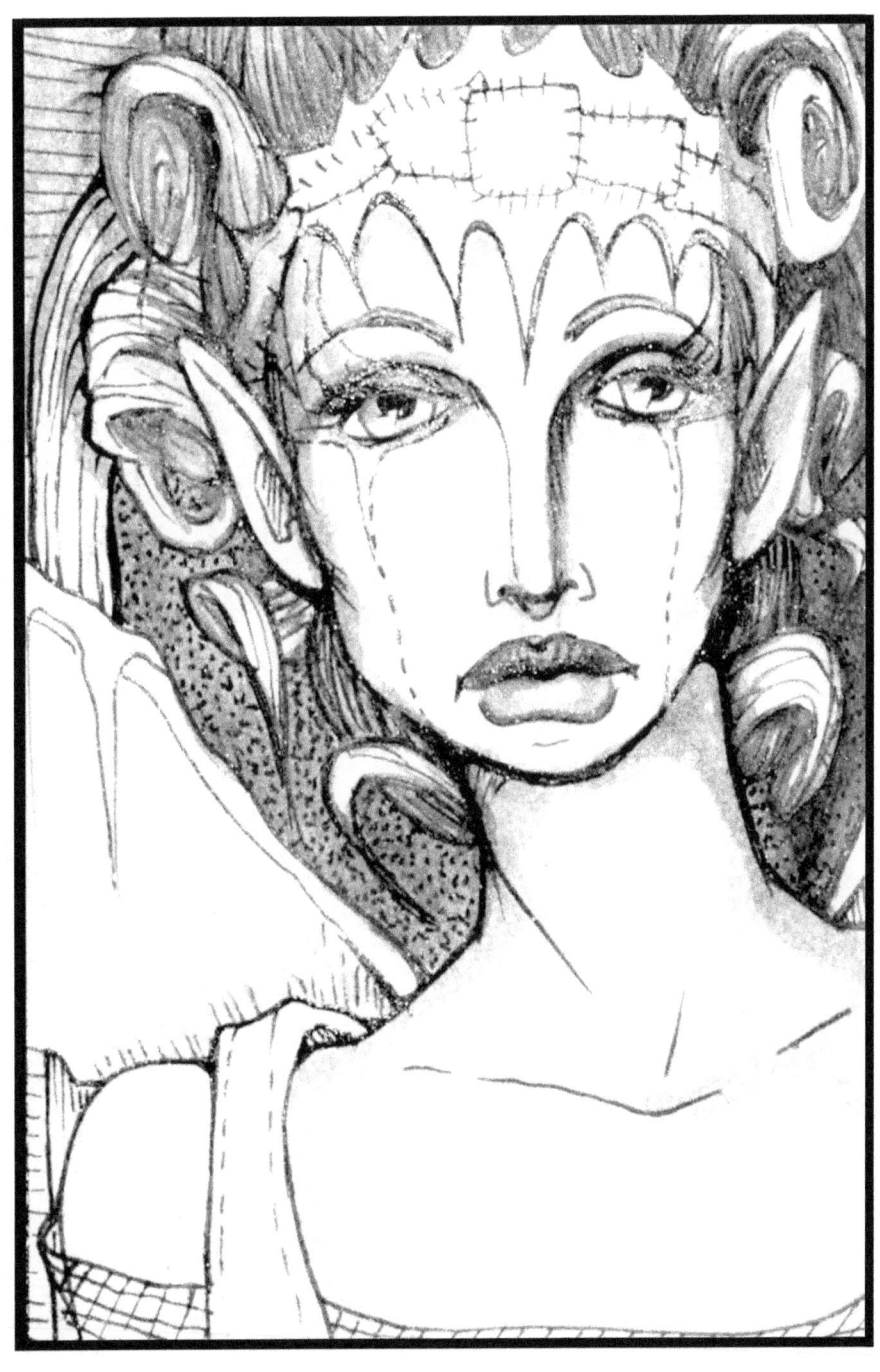

Tears

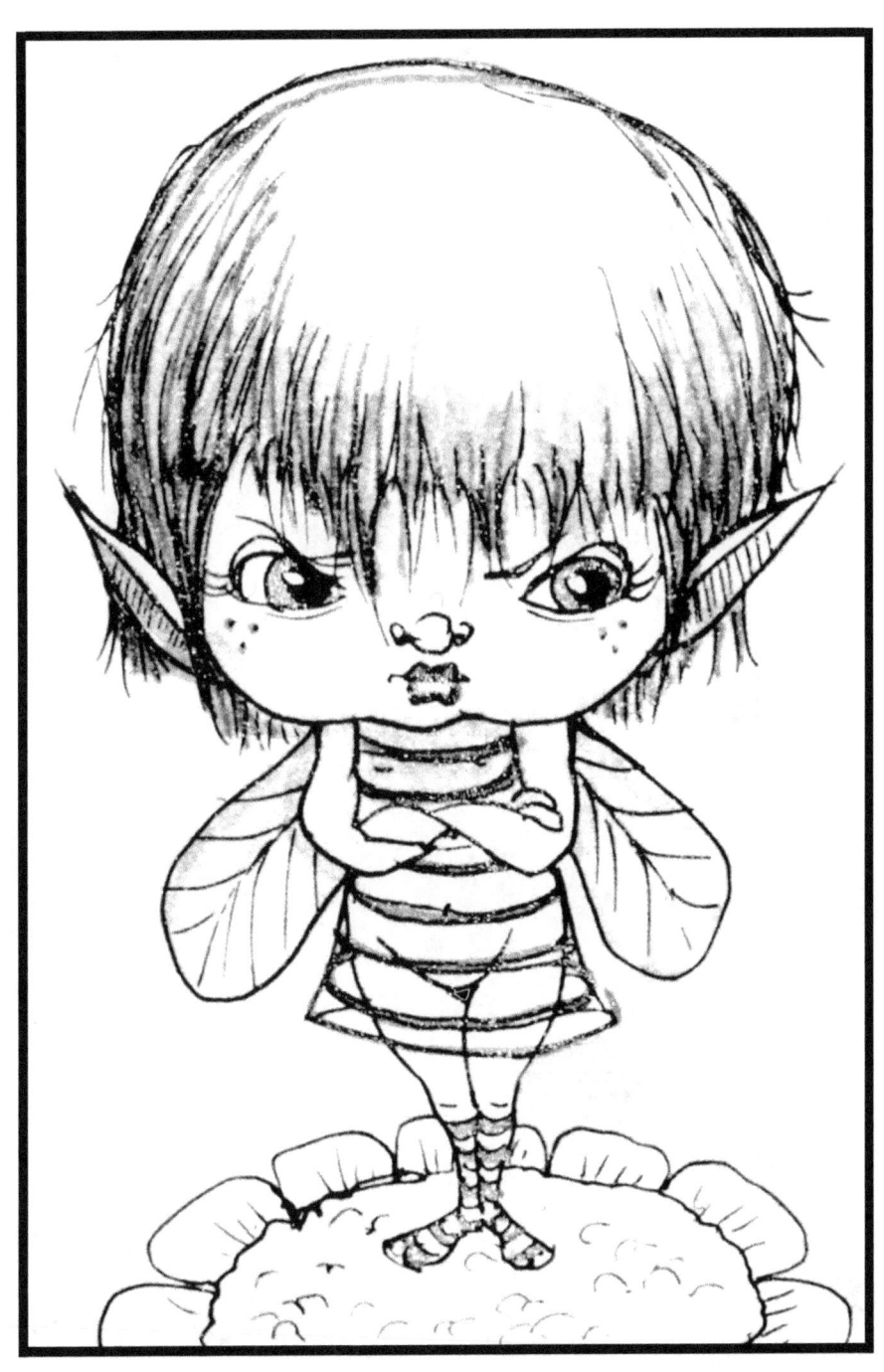

Sassy Attitude

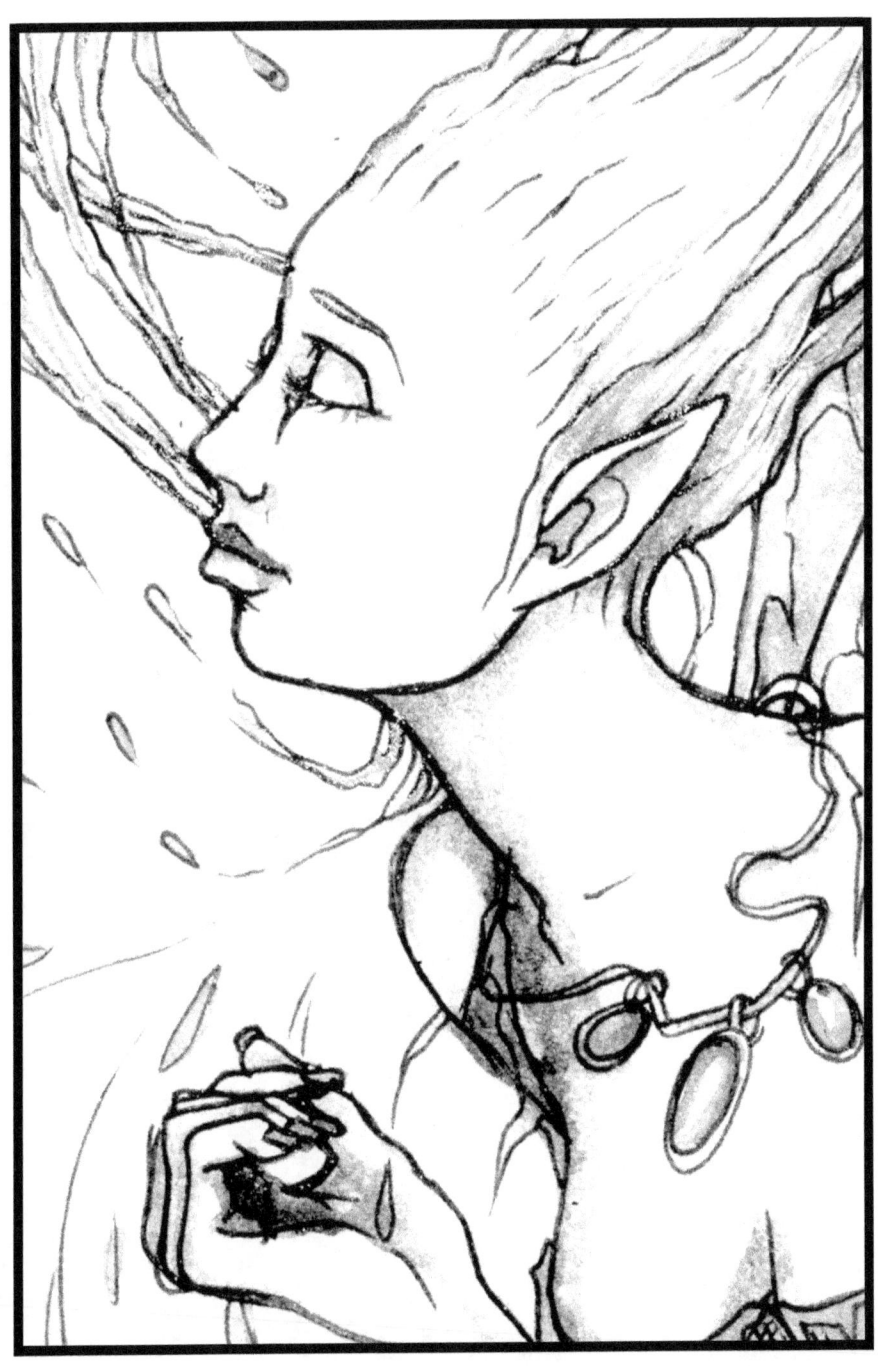

Splash

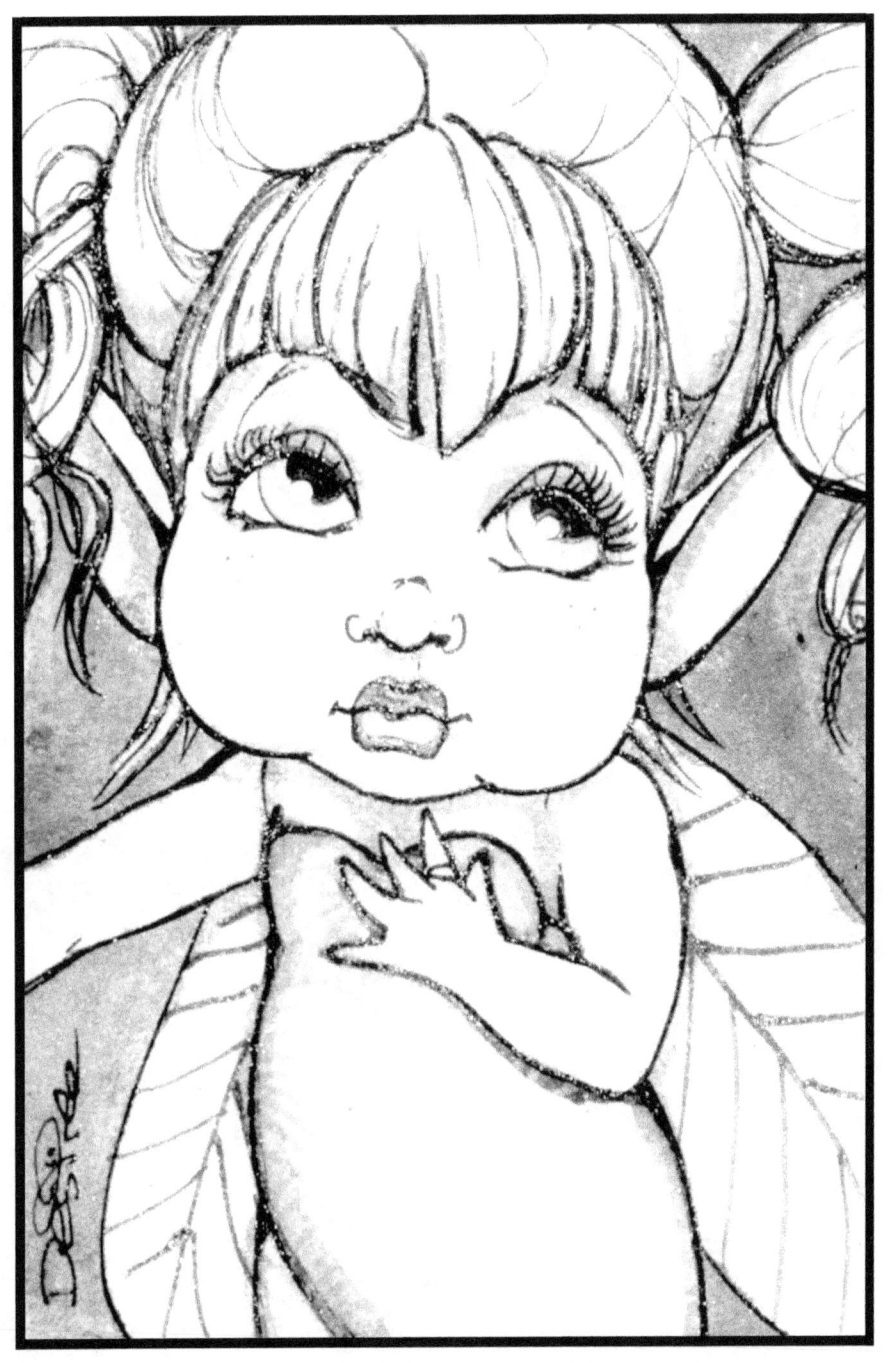

Heartfelt

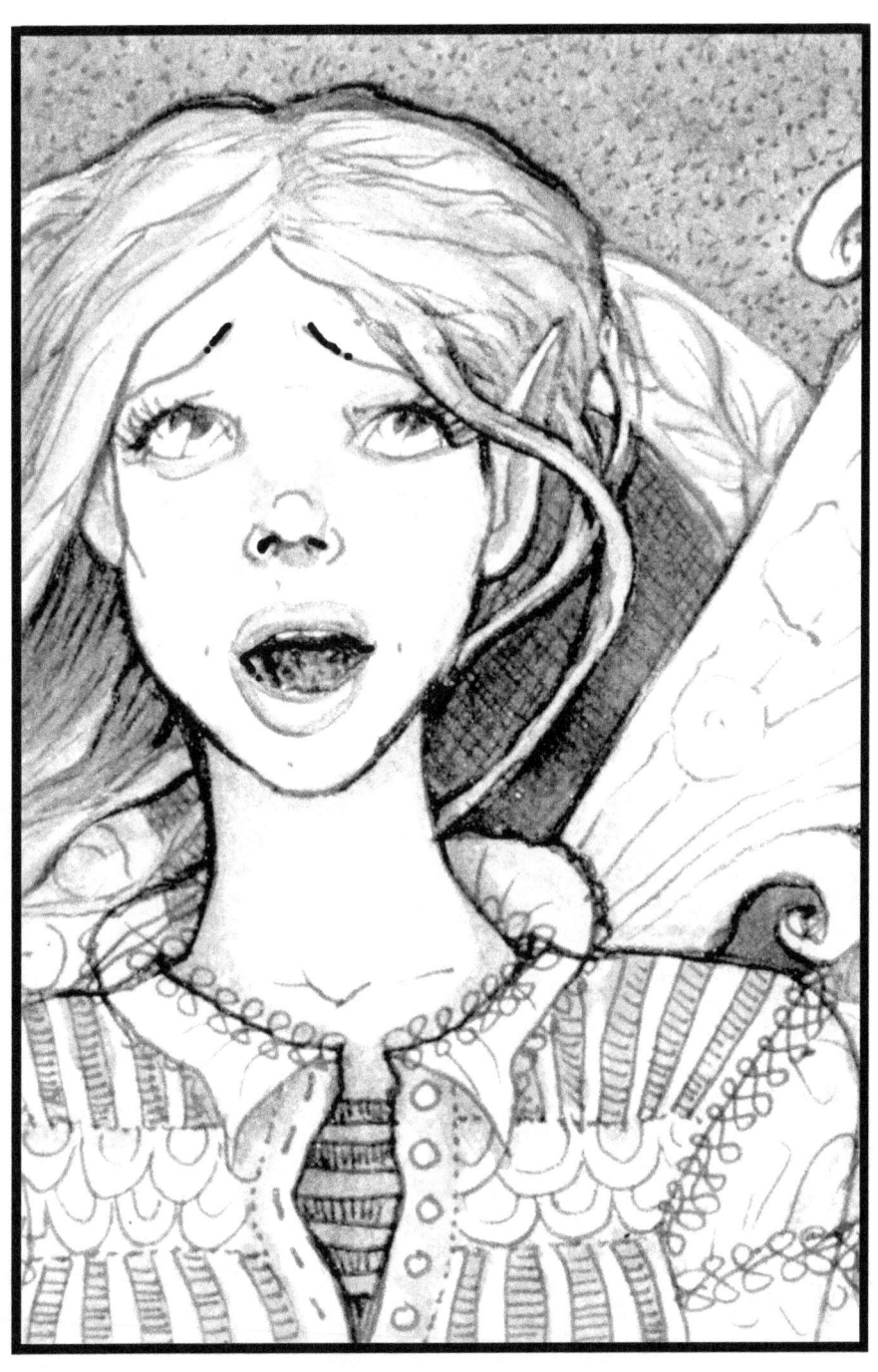

Singing Fae

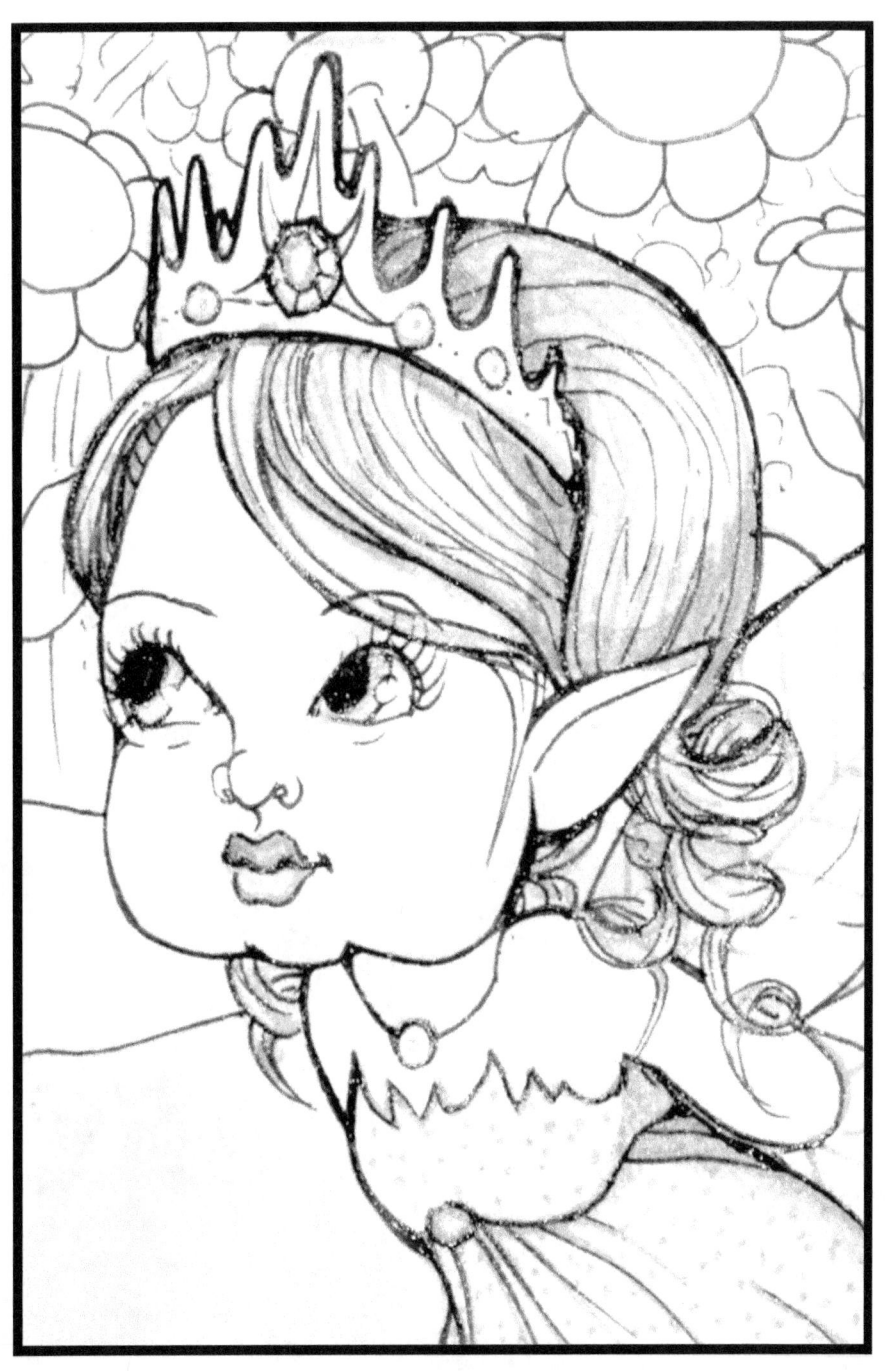

Stroll in the Flowers

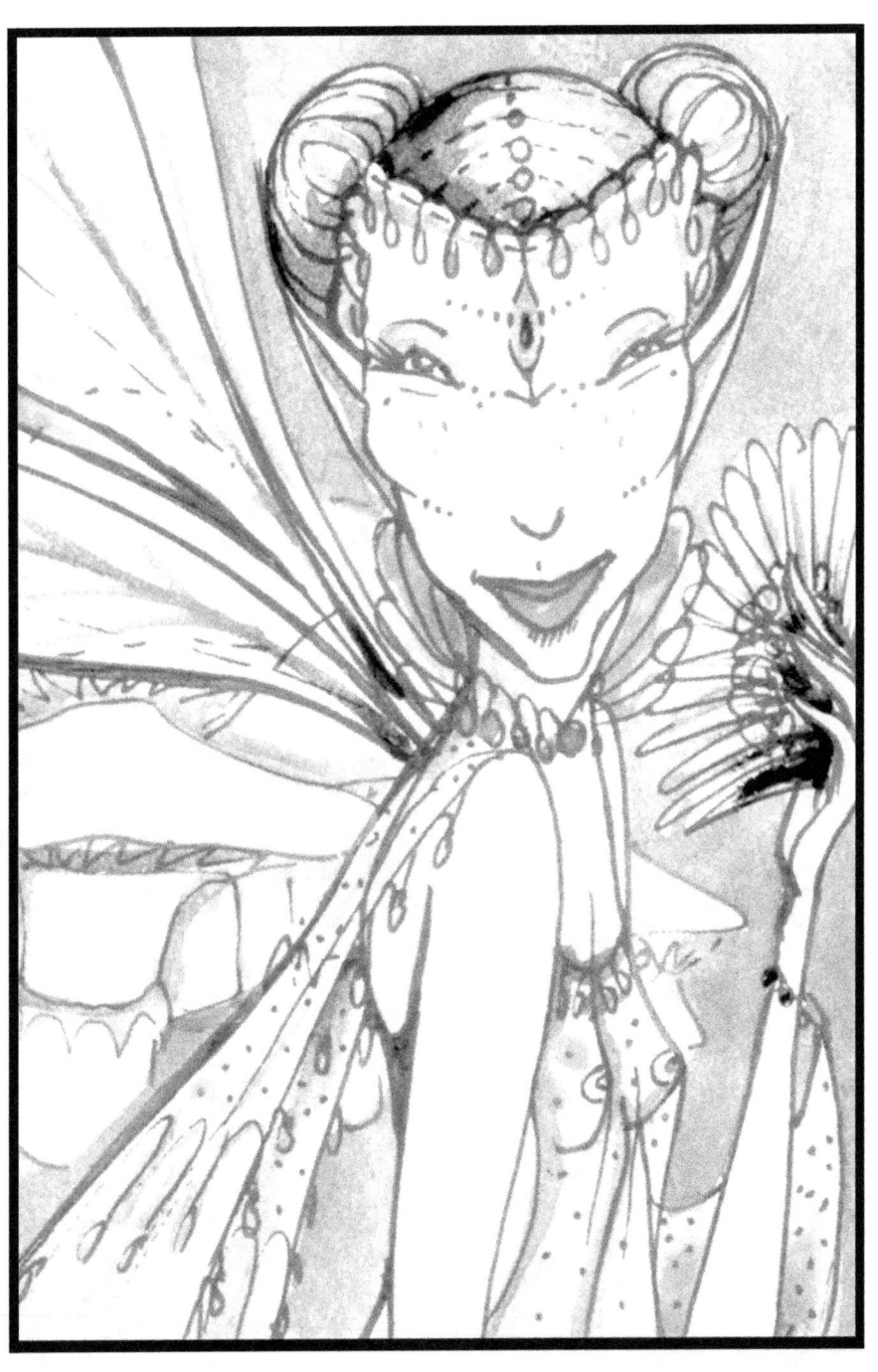

Nymph Queen

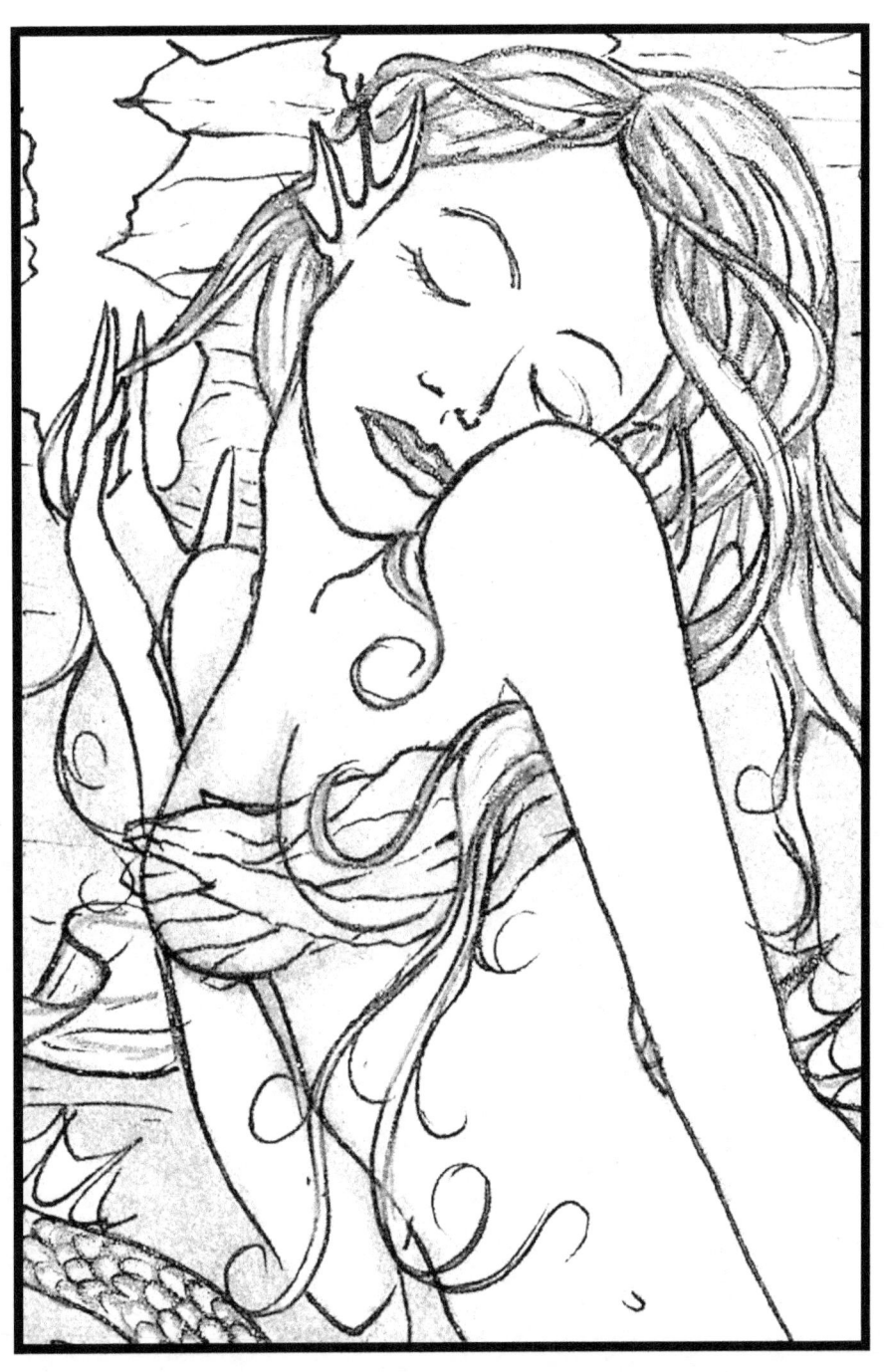

Grooming Underwater

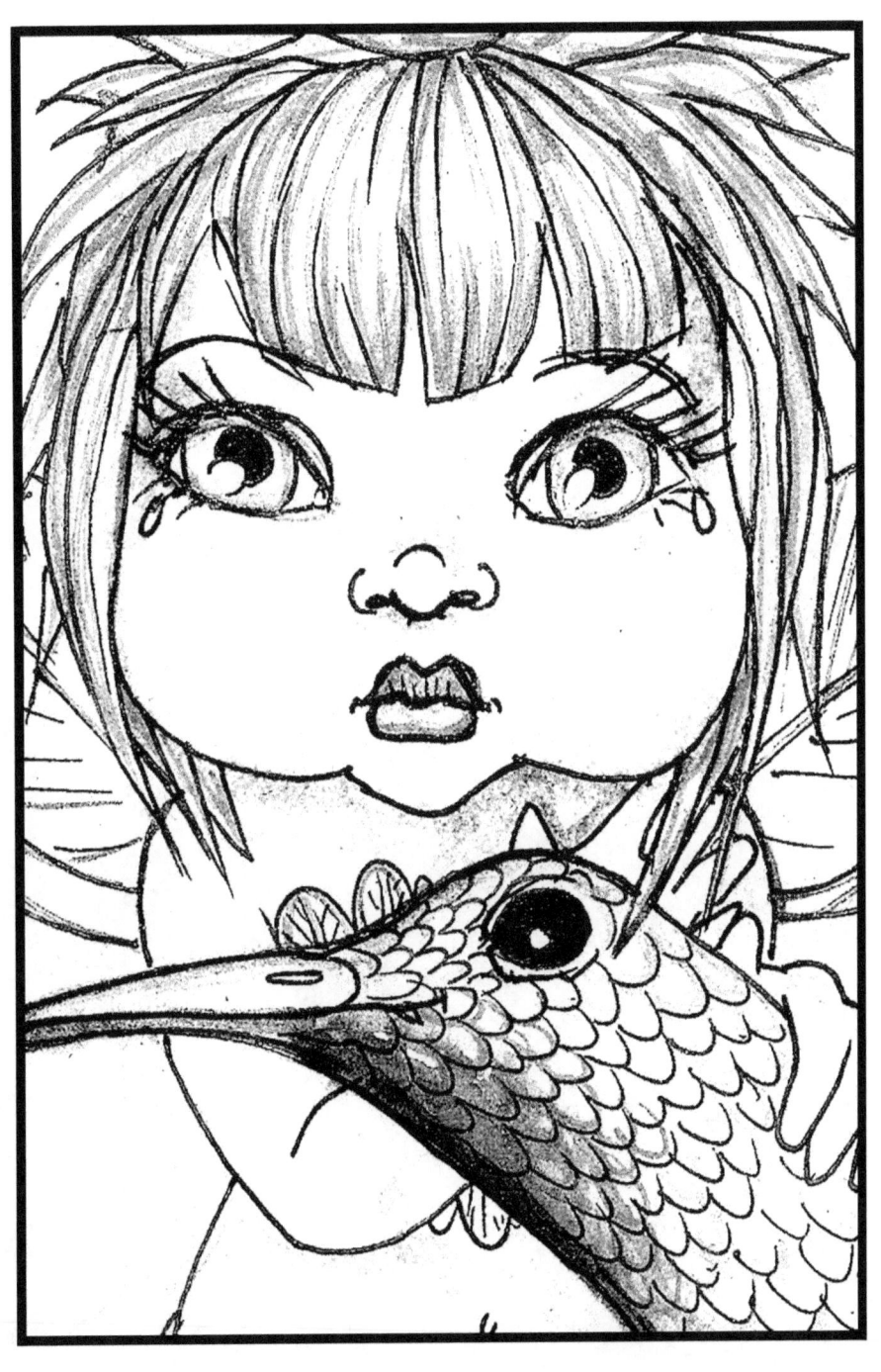

Humming Bird Companion

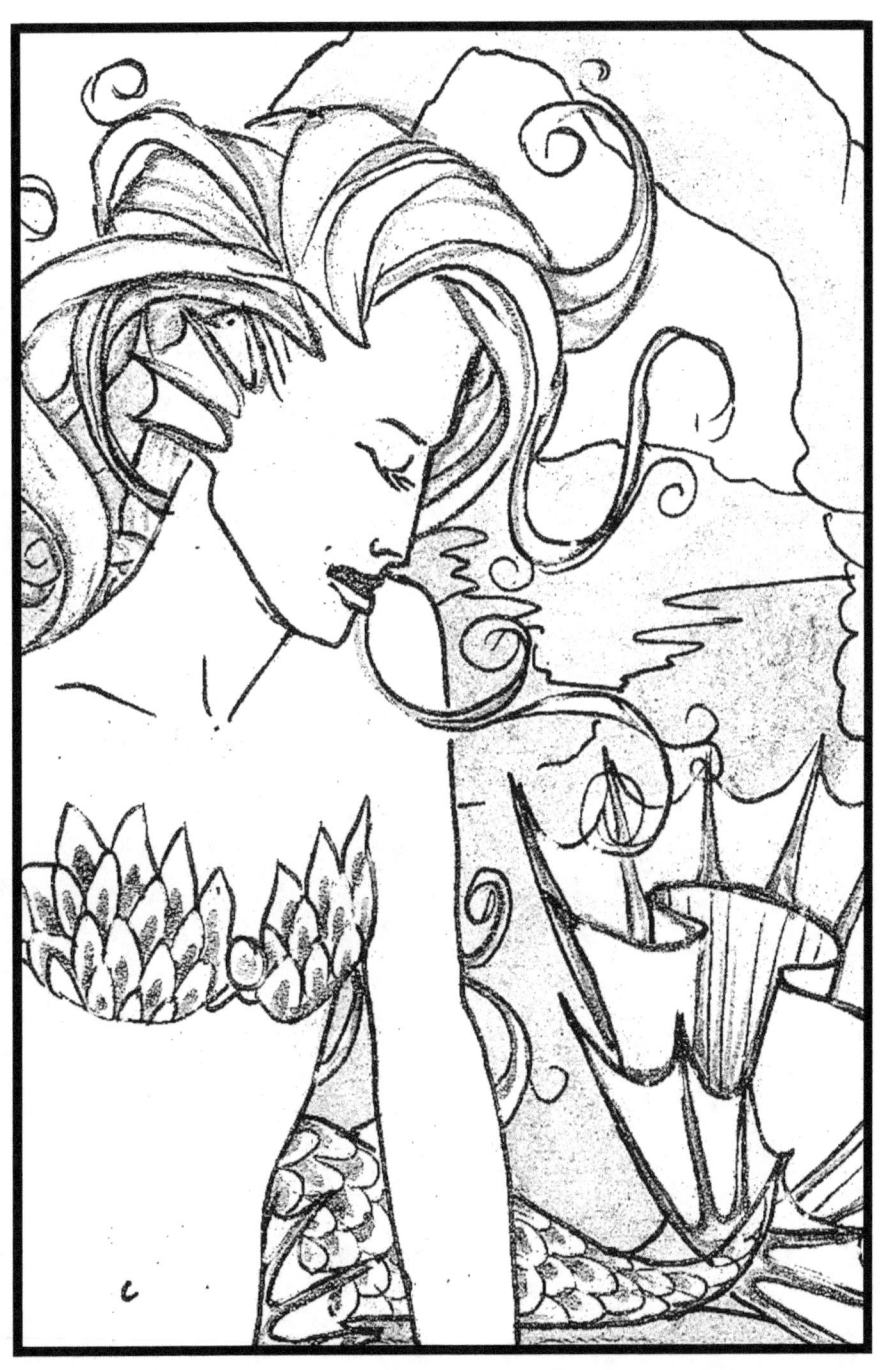

At Rest

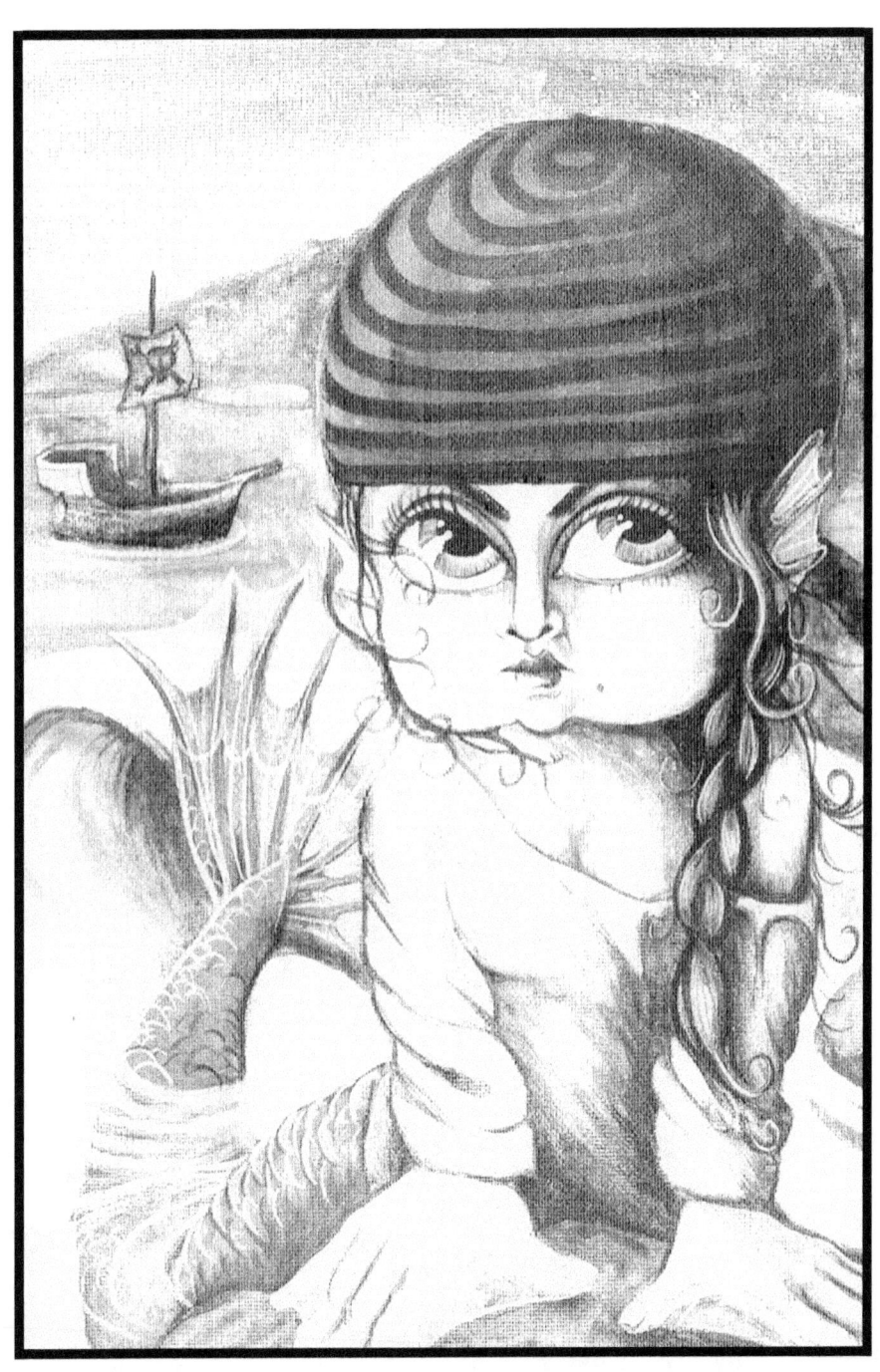

Siren of the Night

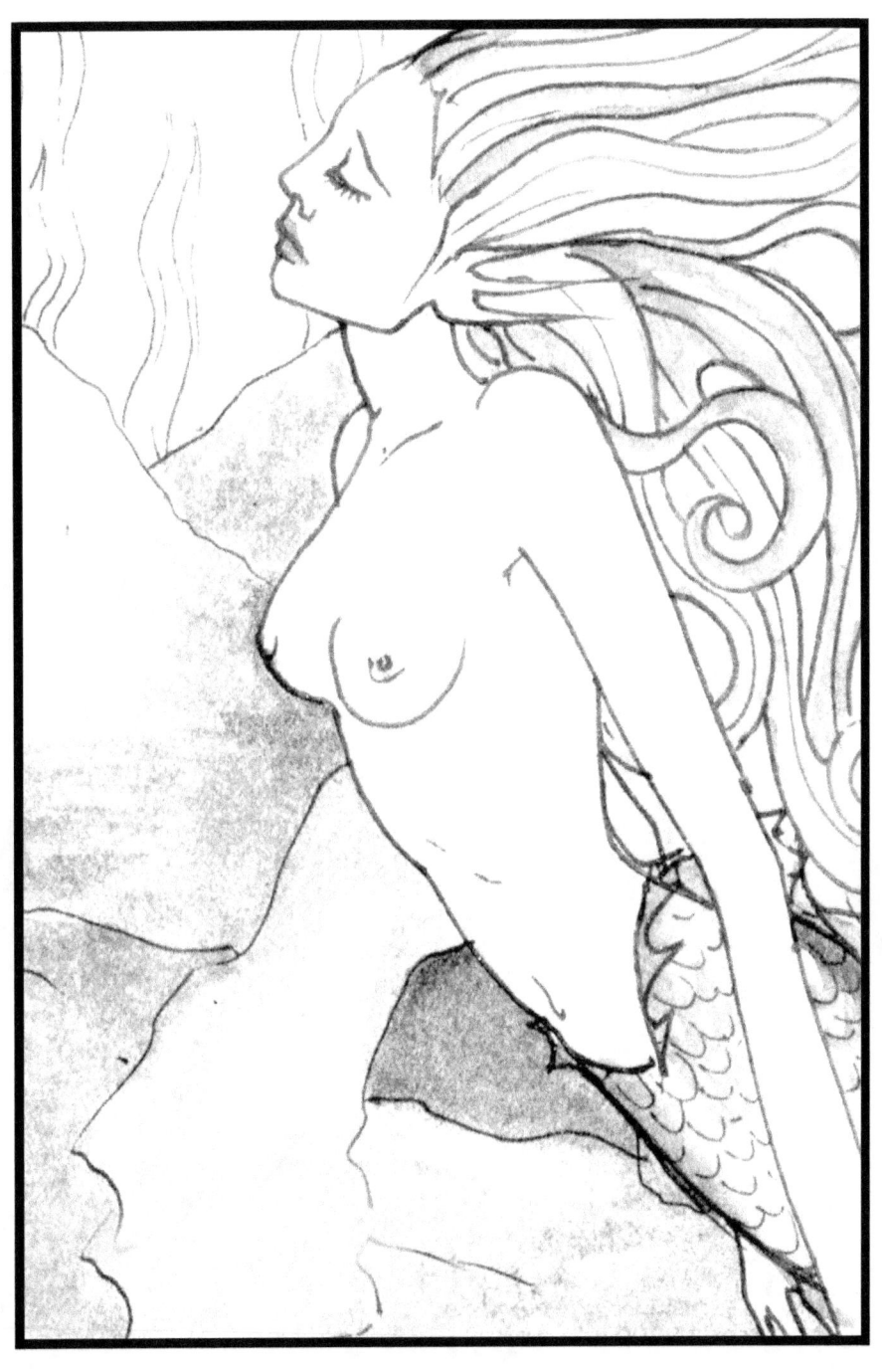

Sea Breeze

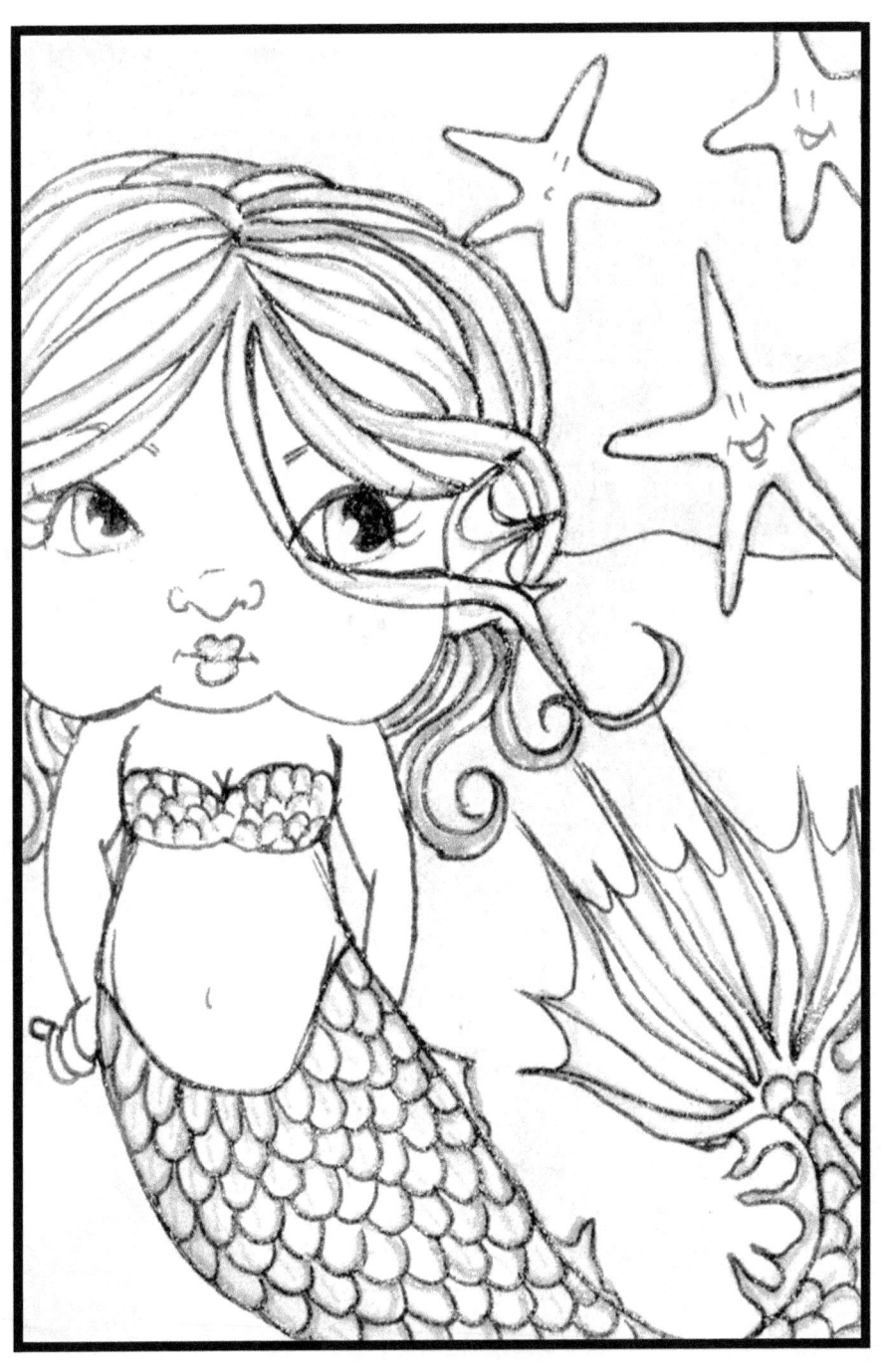

Starfish Friends

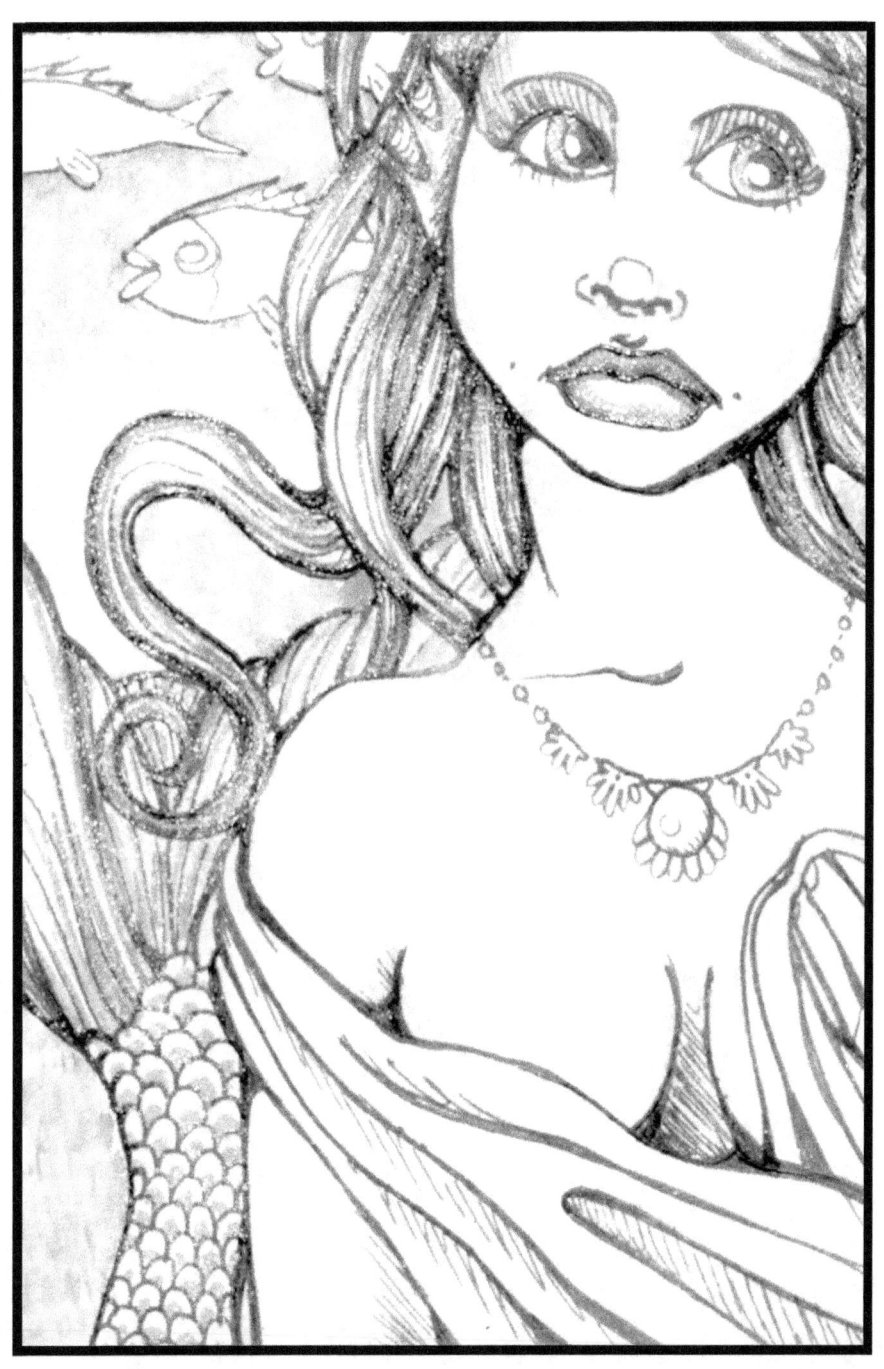

The Arrangement

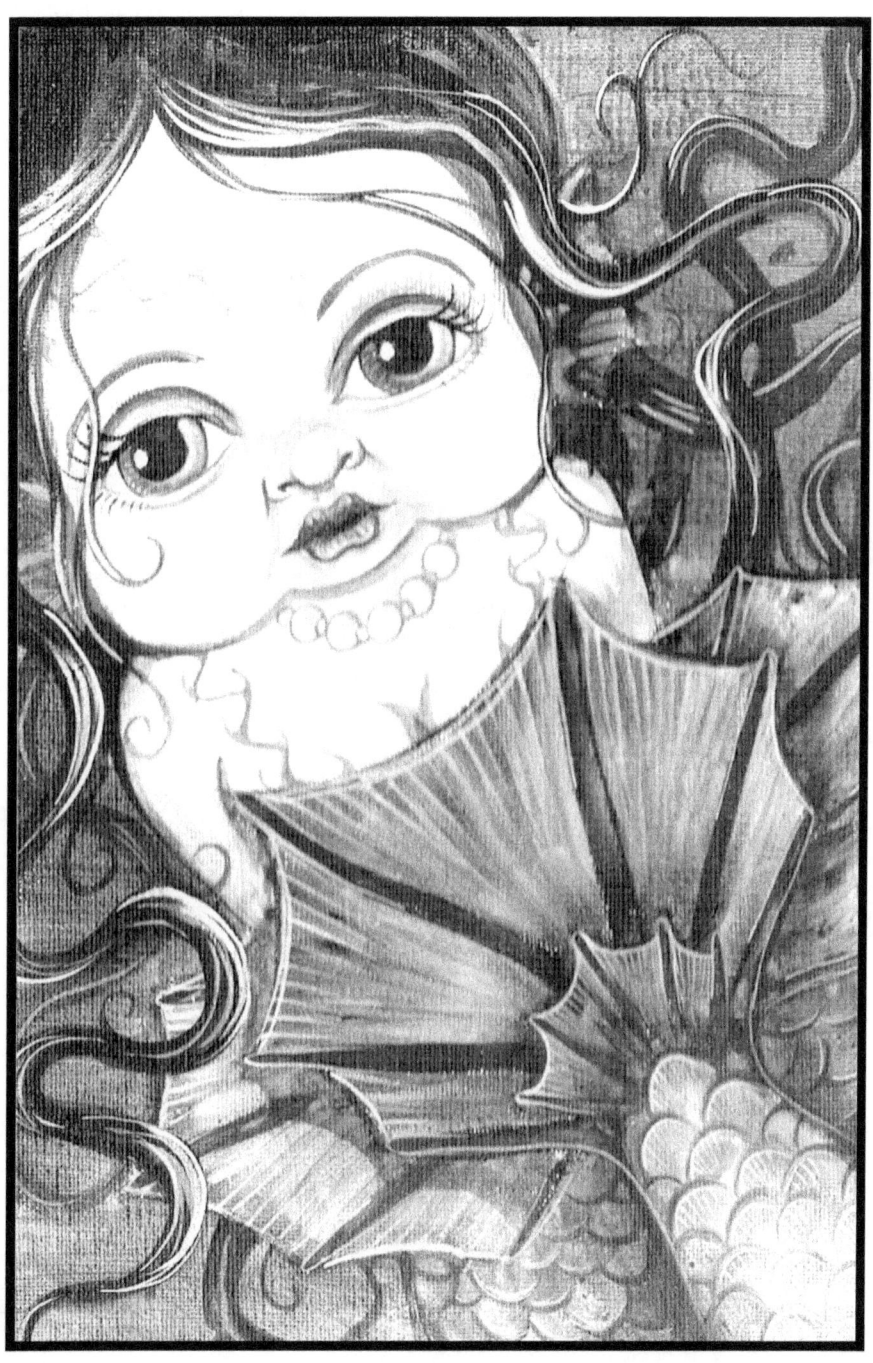

Fins

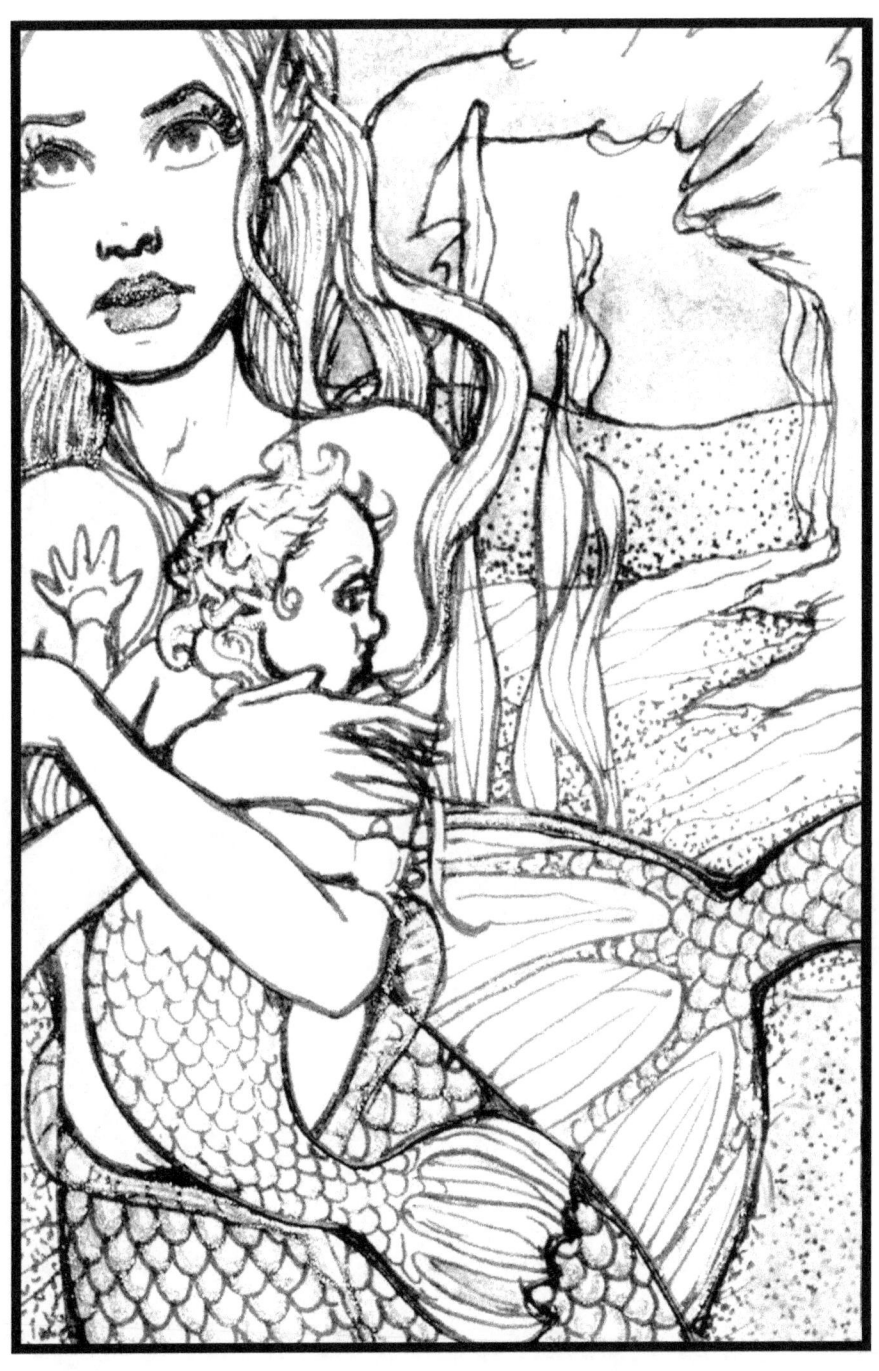

Cuddles

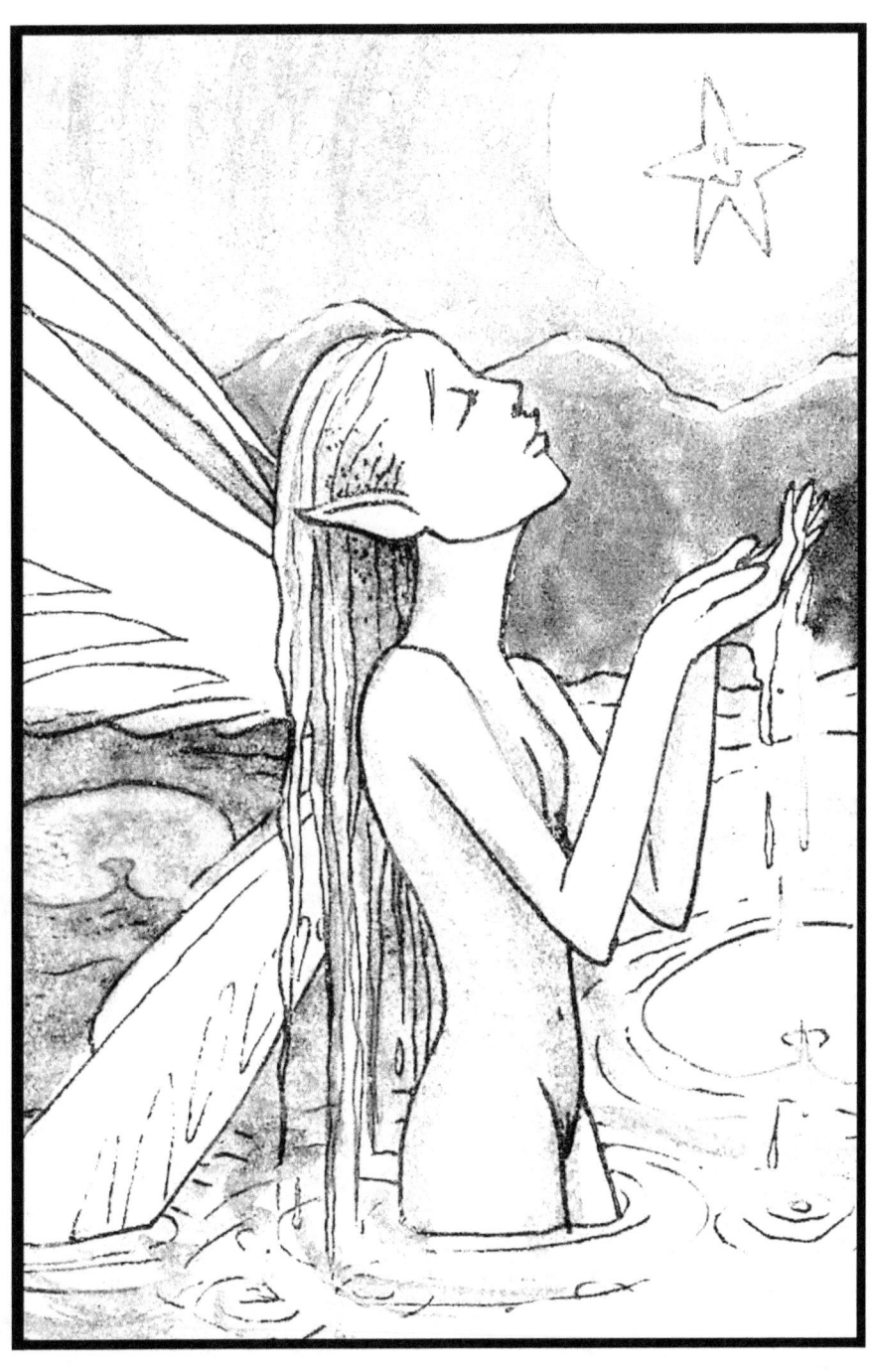

Starlight Bathing

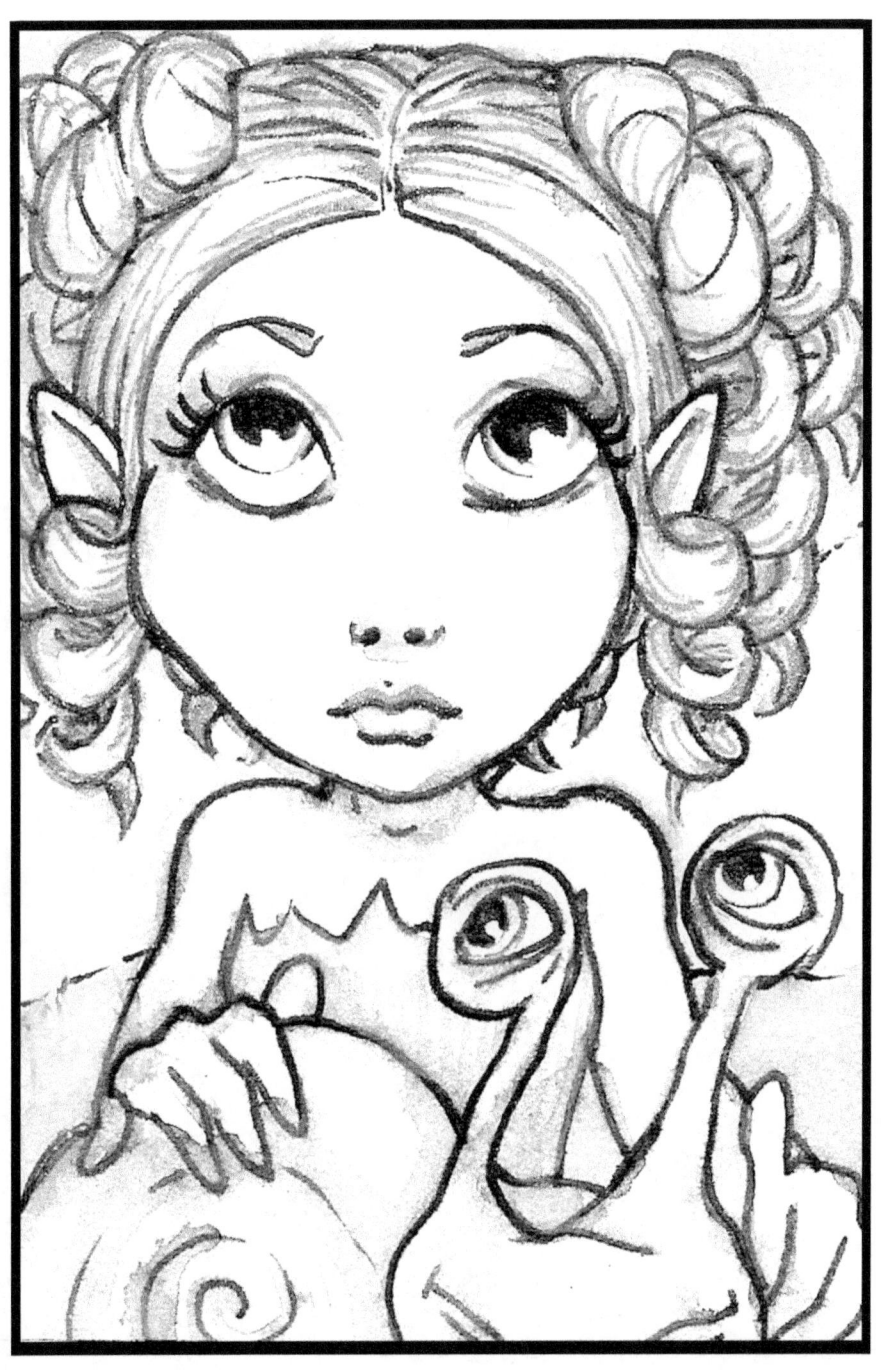

Snail Pal

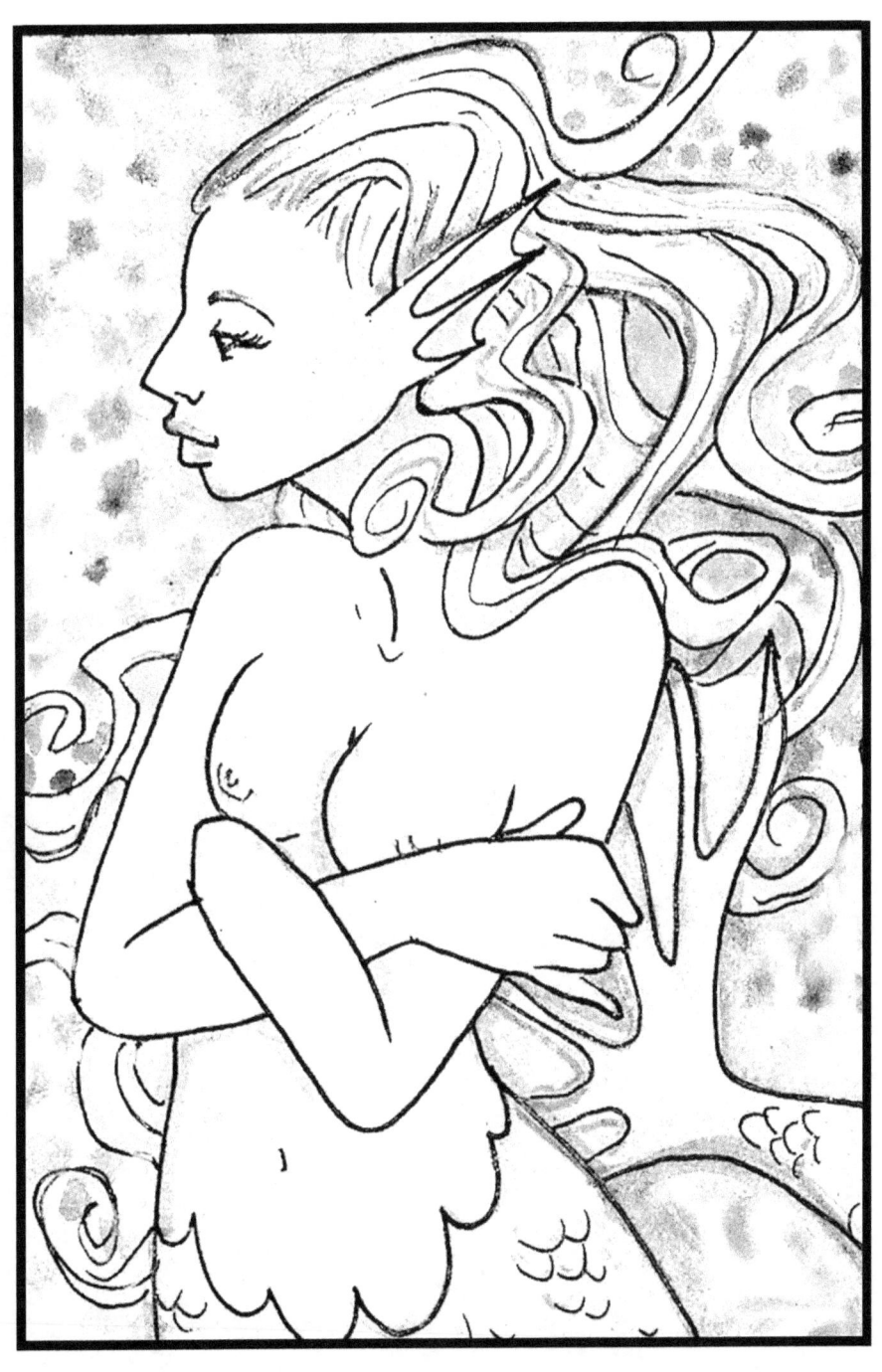

Enjoying the Water

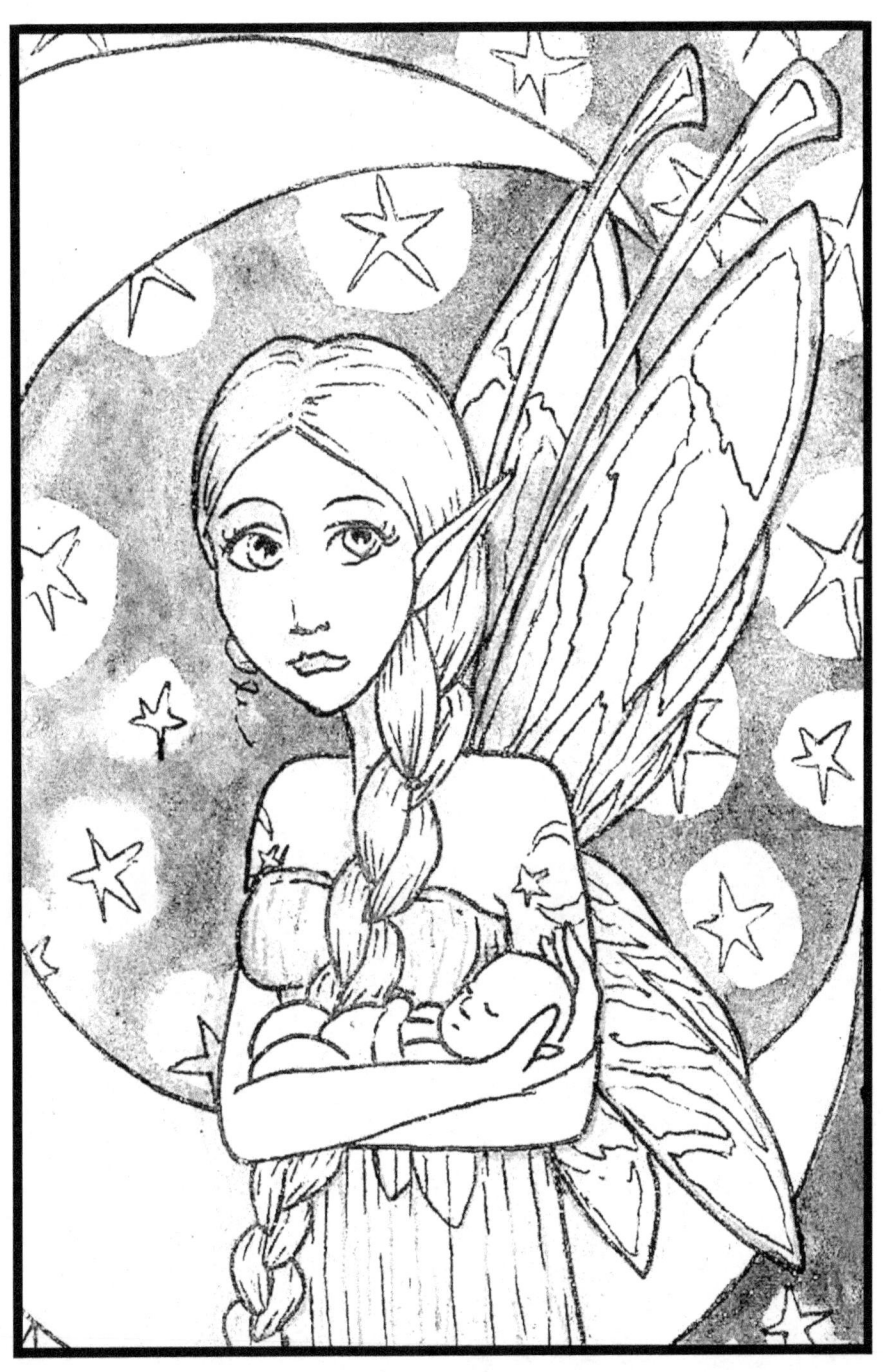

Up With Baby

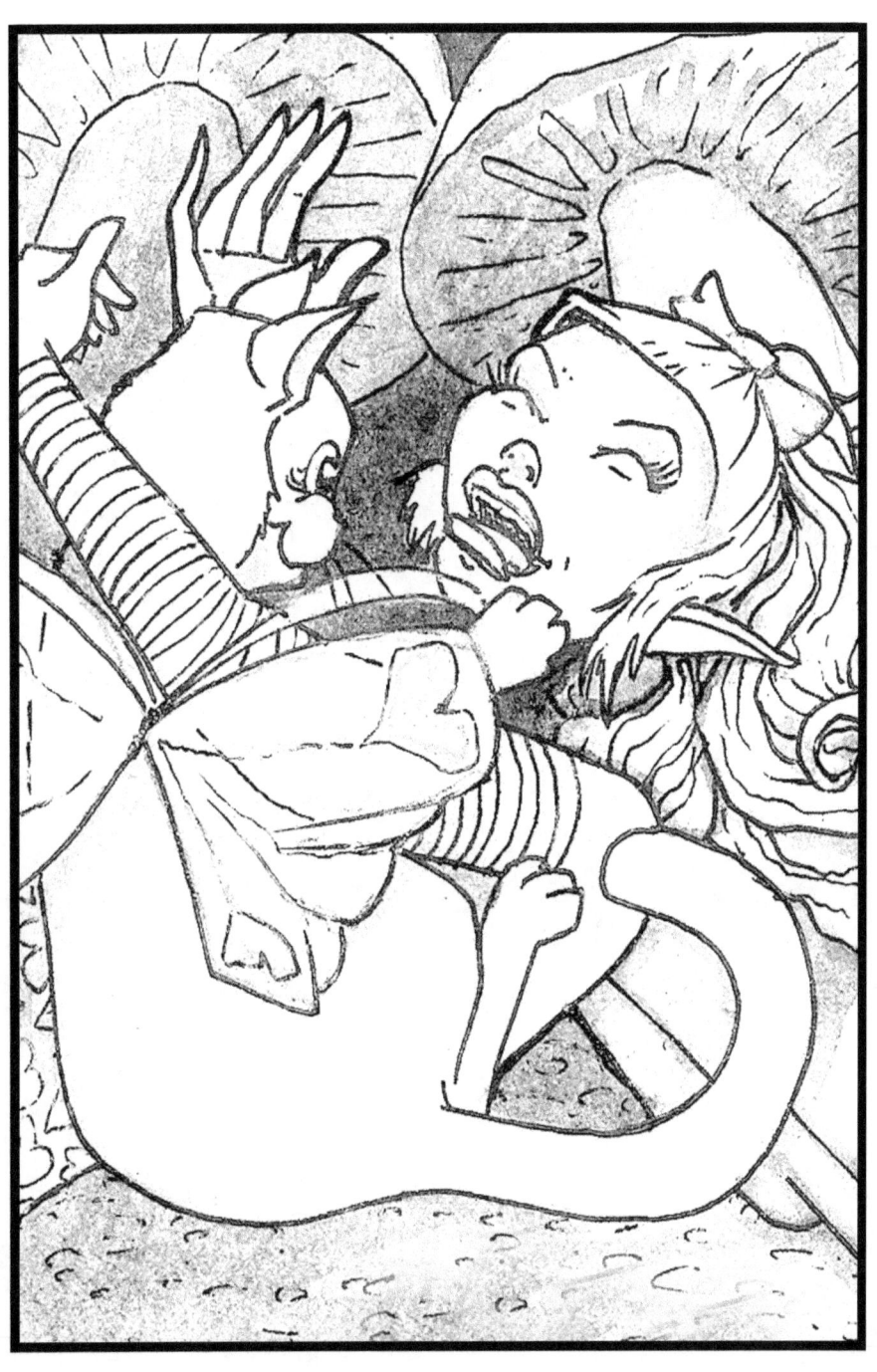

Kitty Companion

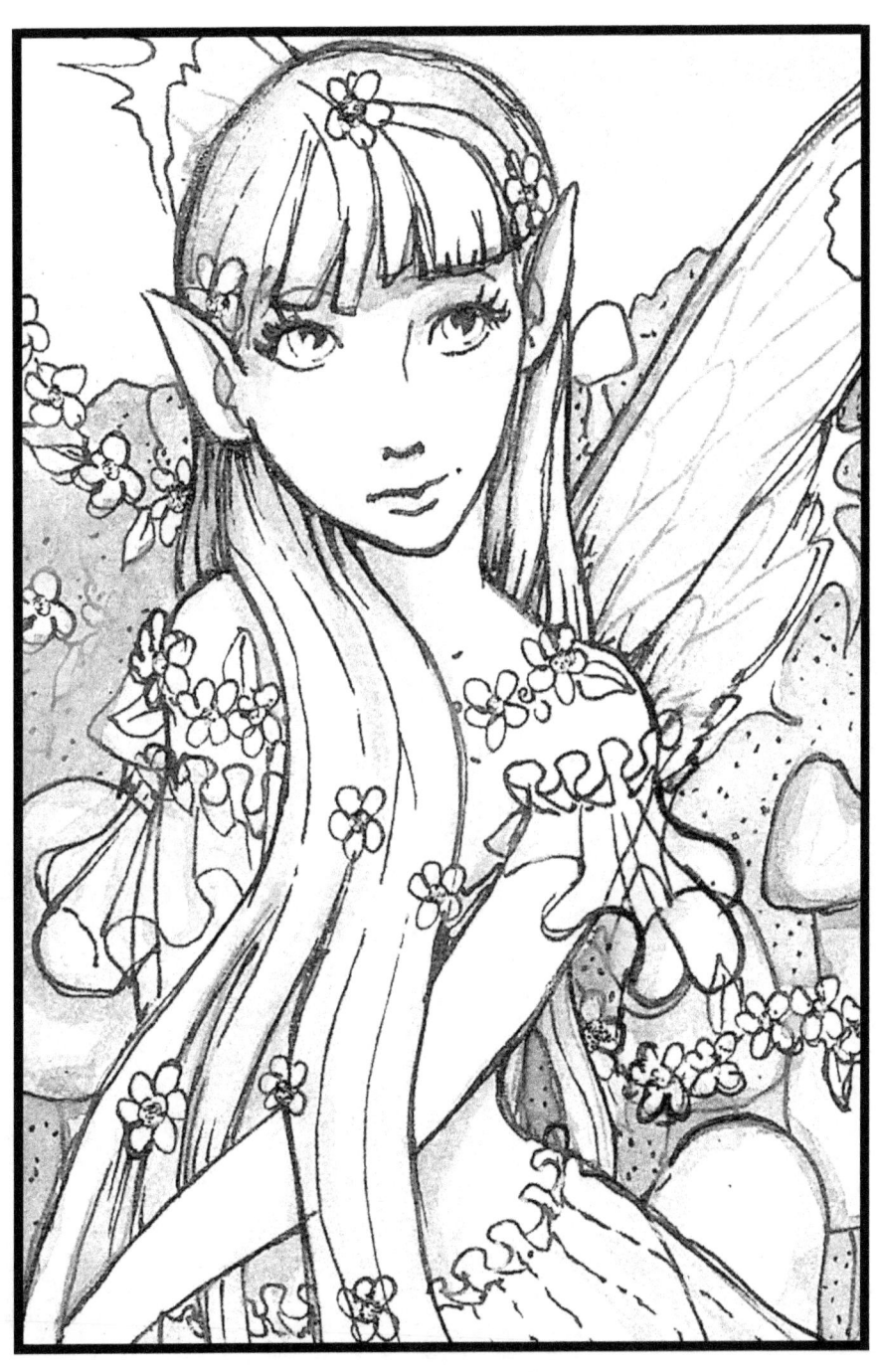

Daisy Chains

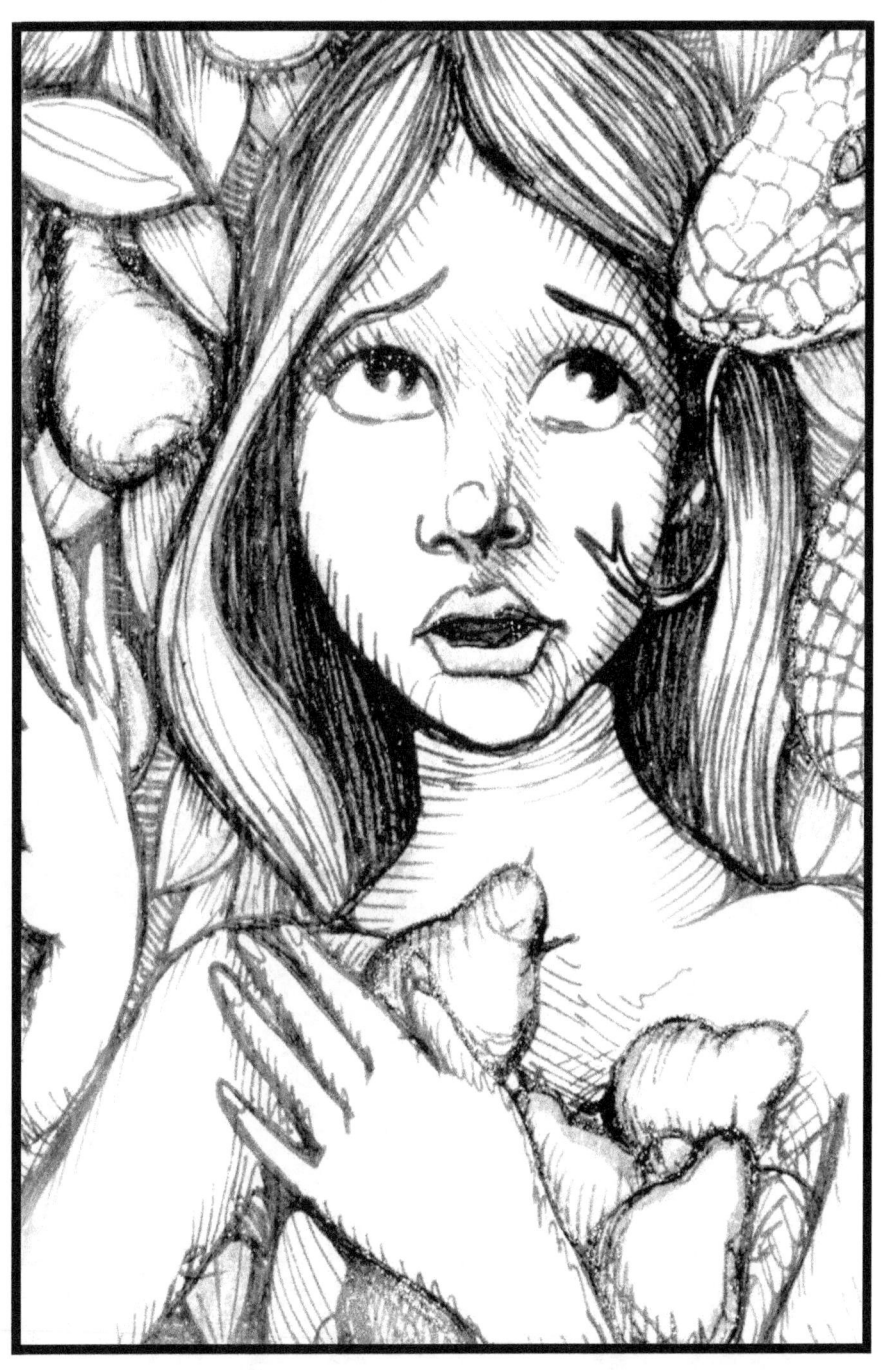

Serpent Whisperer

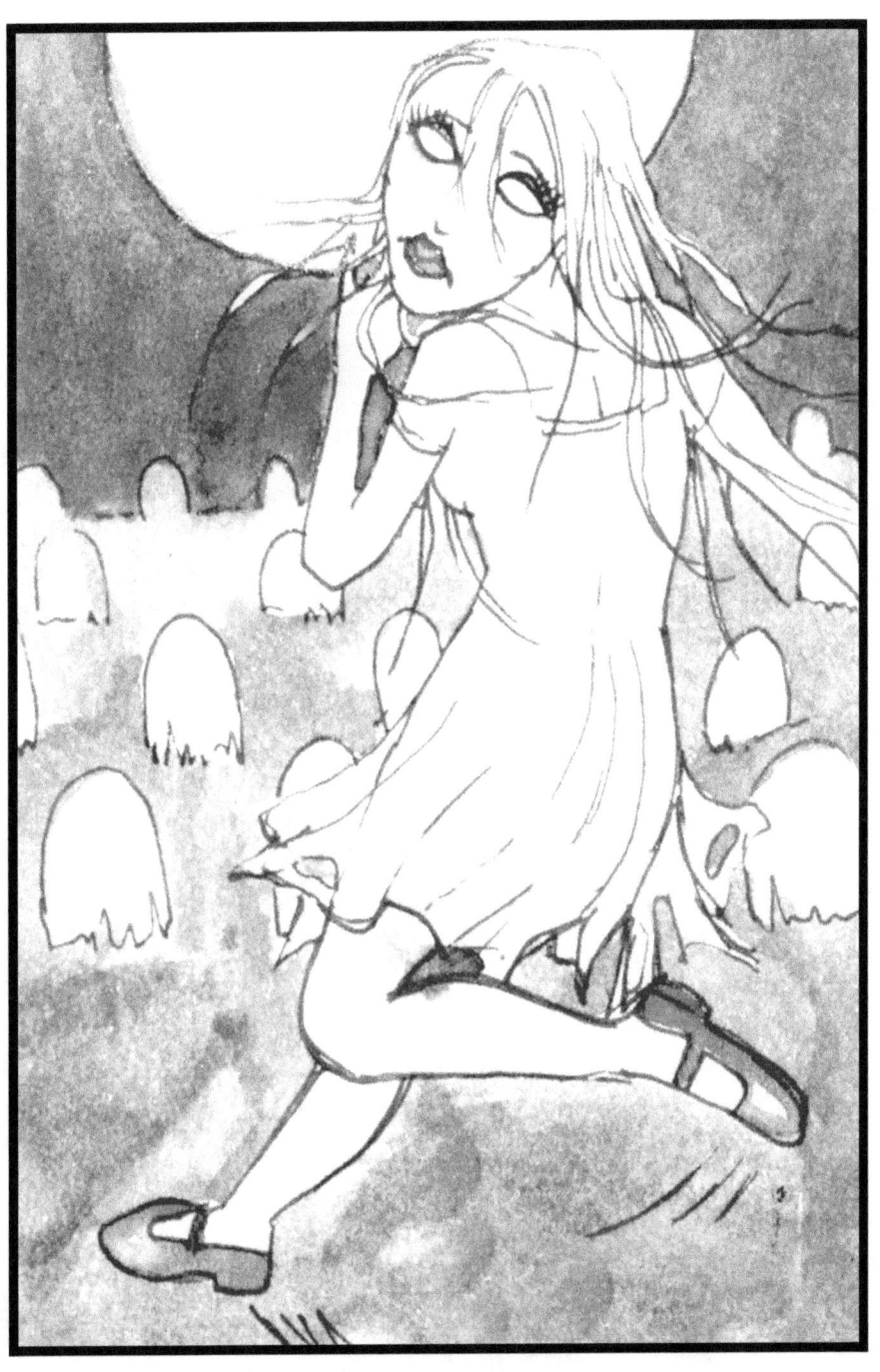

Red Shoes

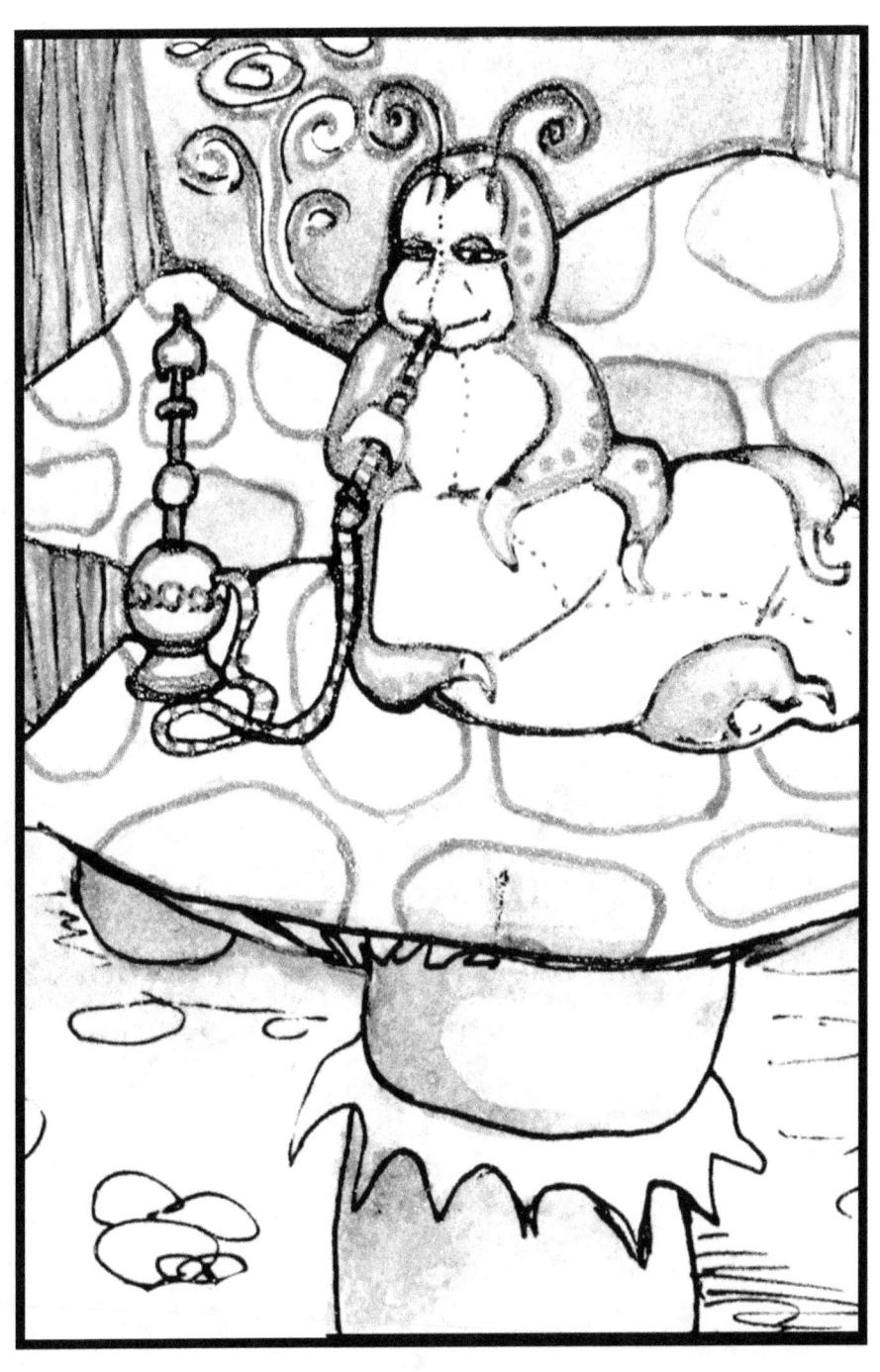

Advice from a Caterpillar

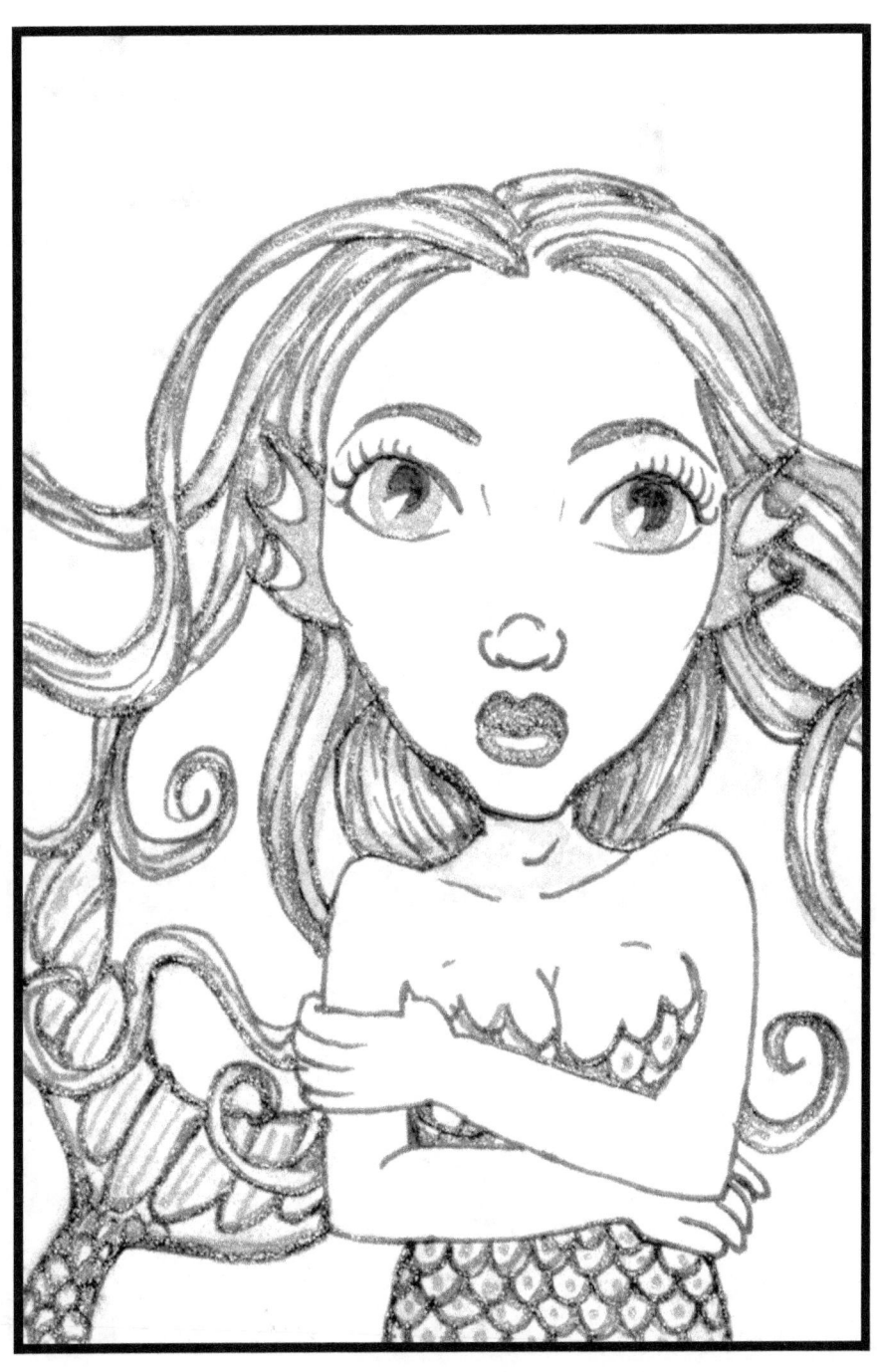

Closed Off

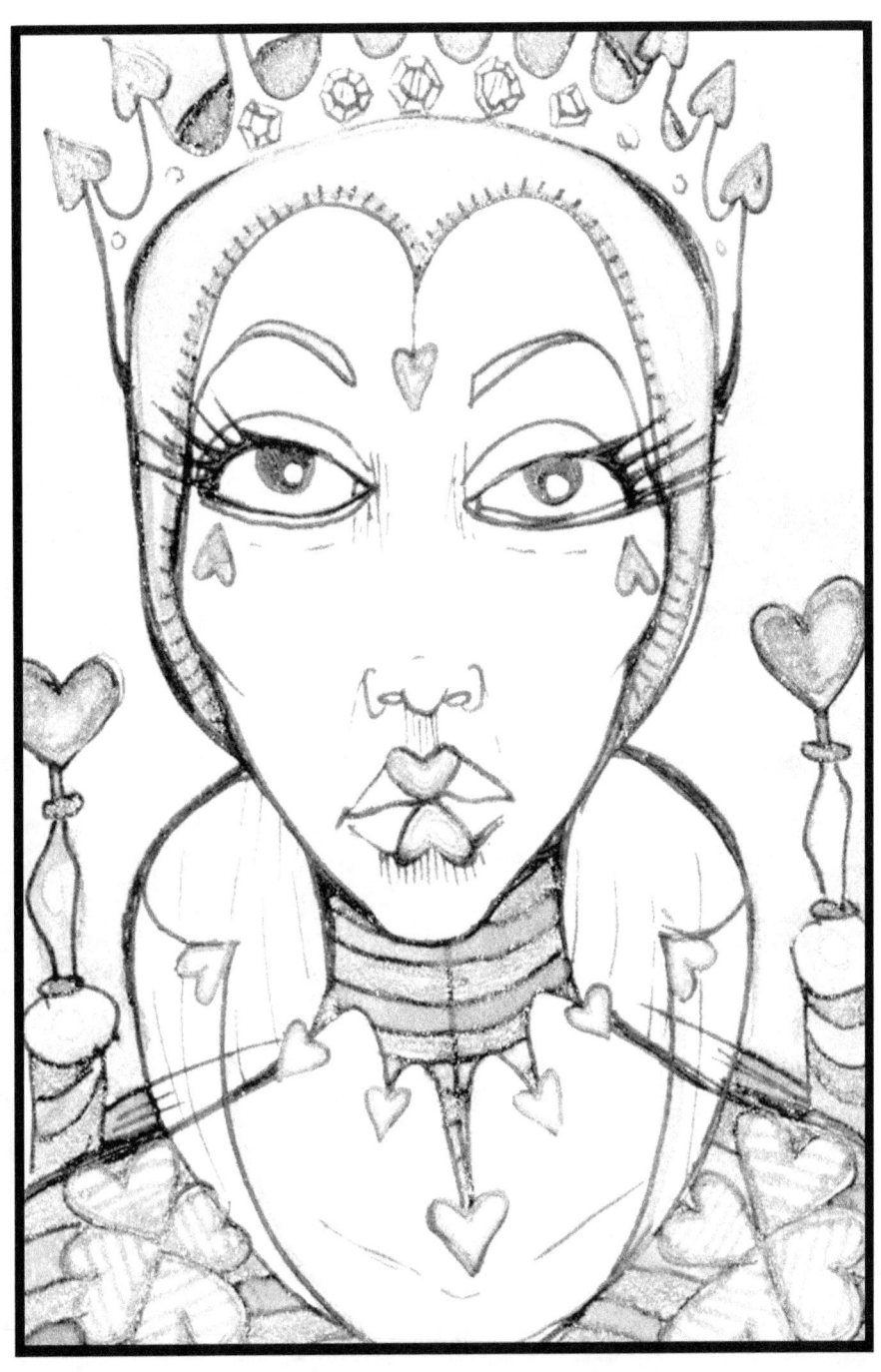

Queen of Hearts

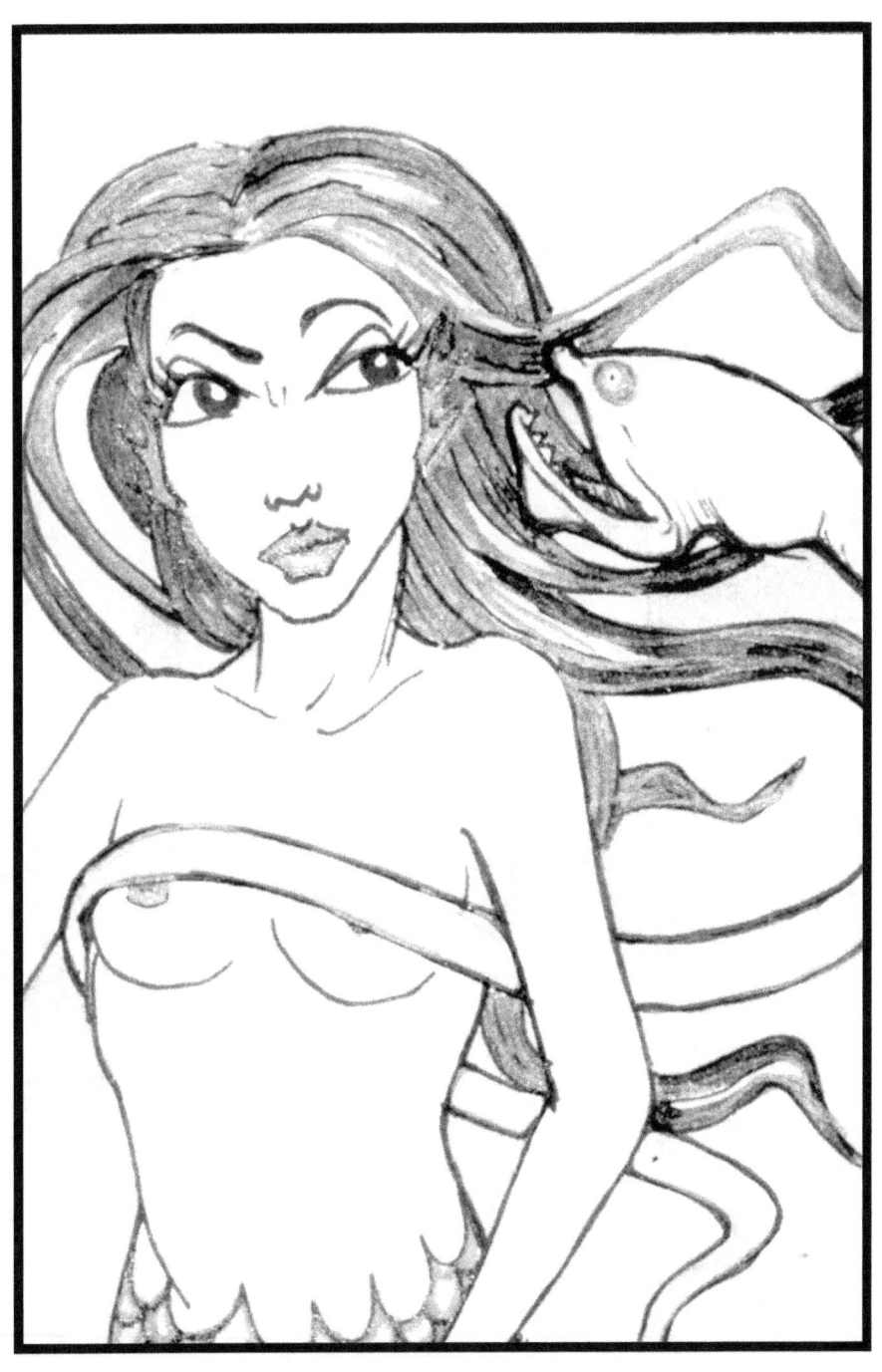

Eel Whisperer

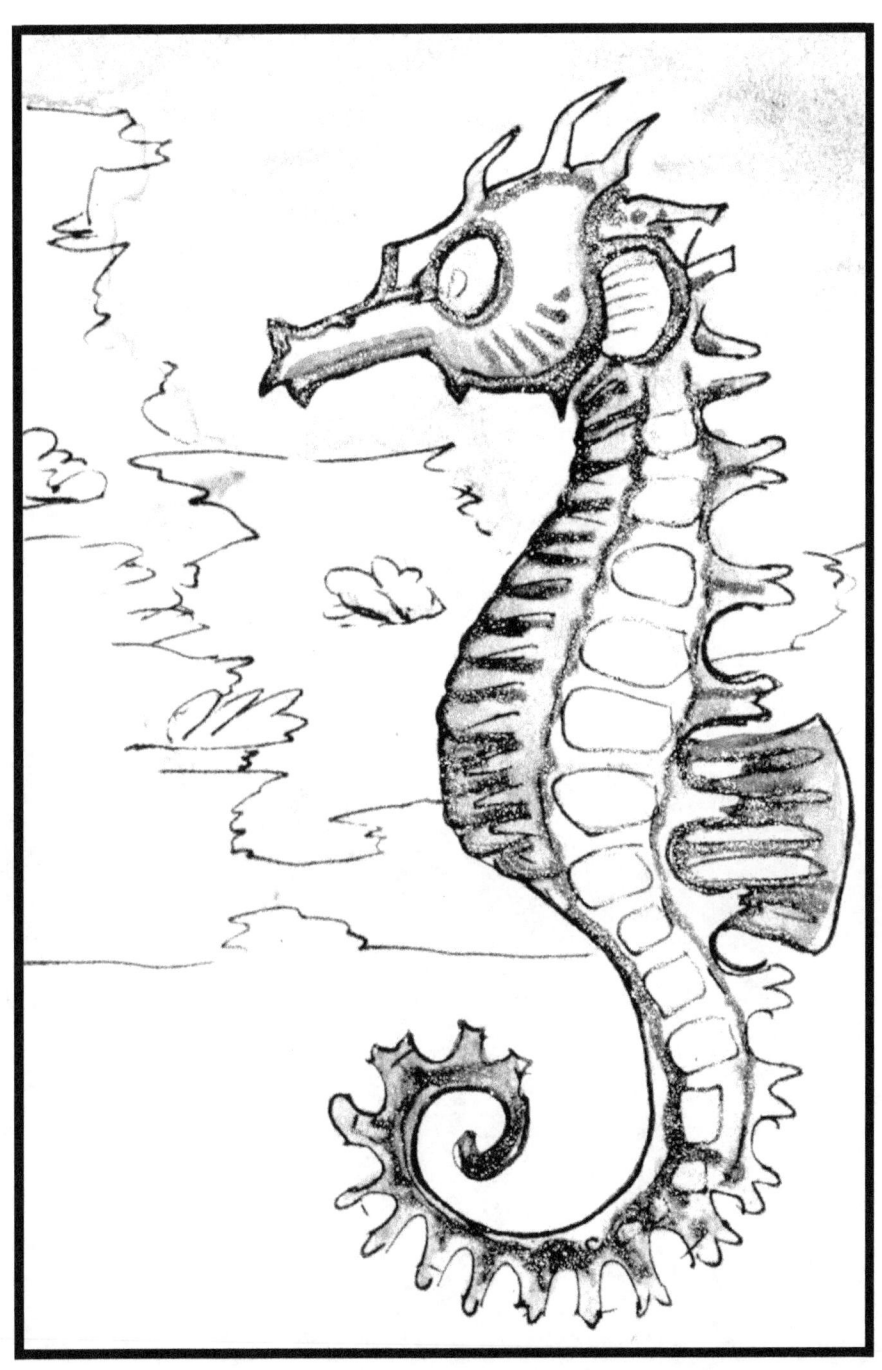

Seahorse

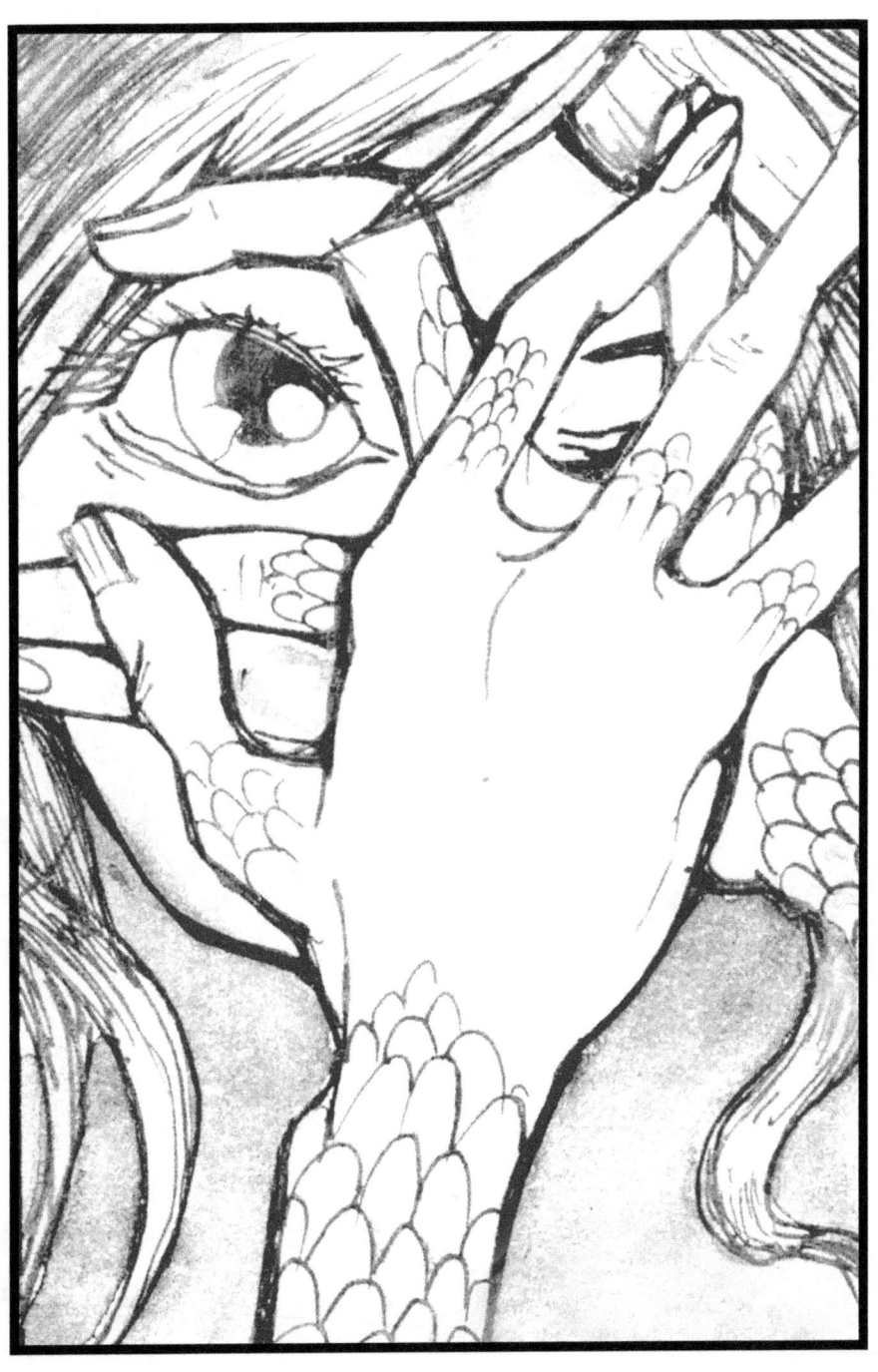

Peeking

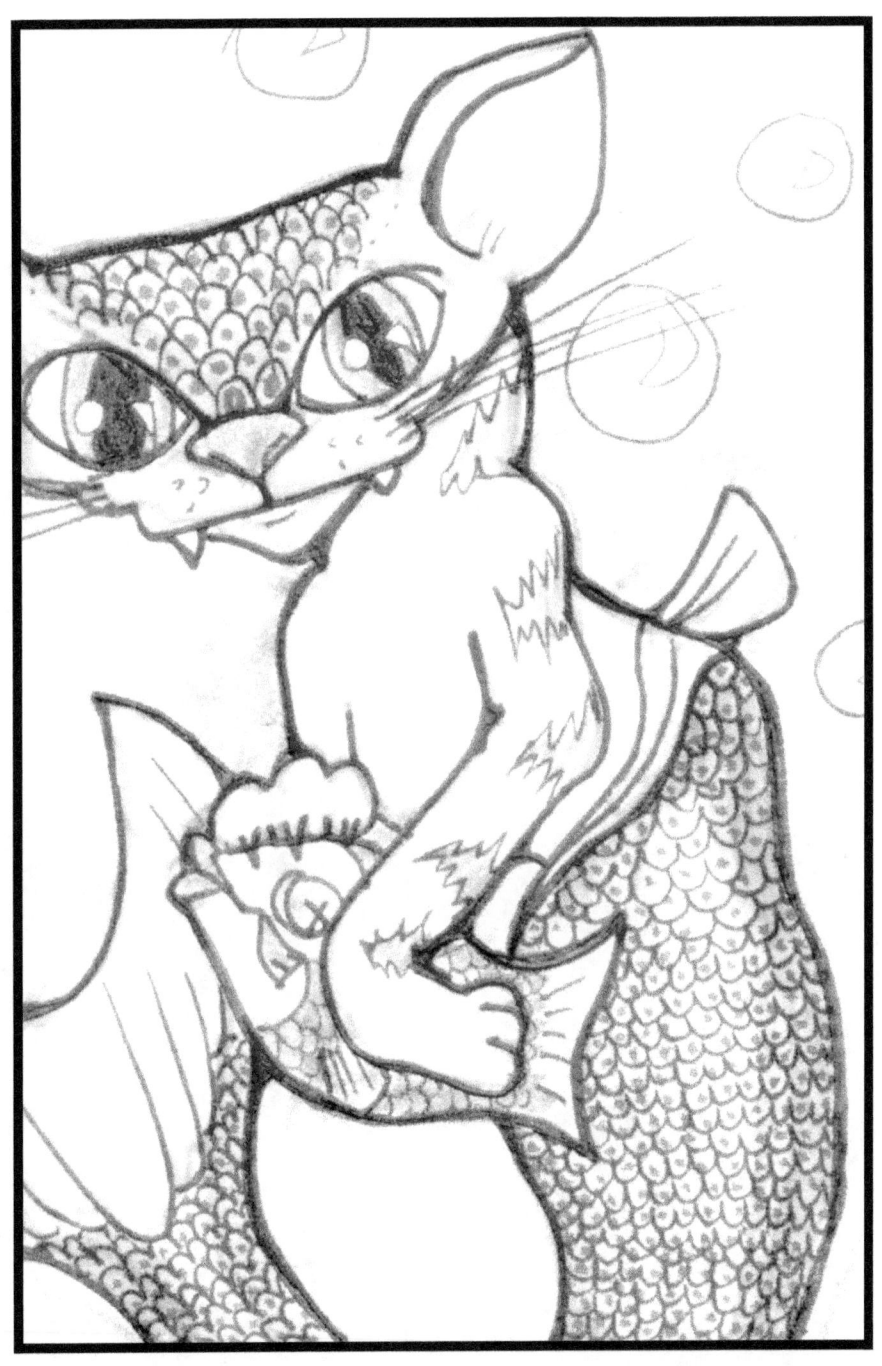

Catfish

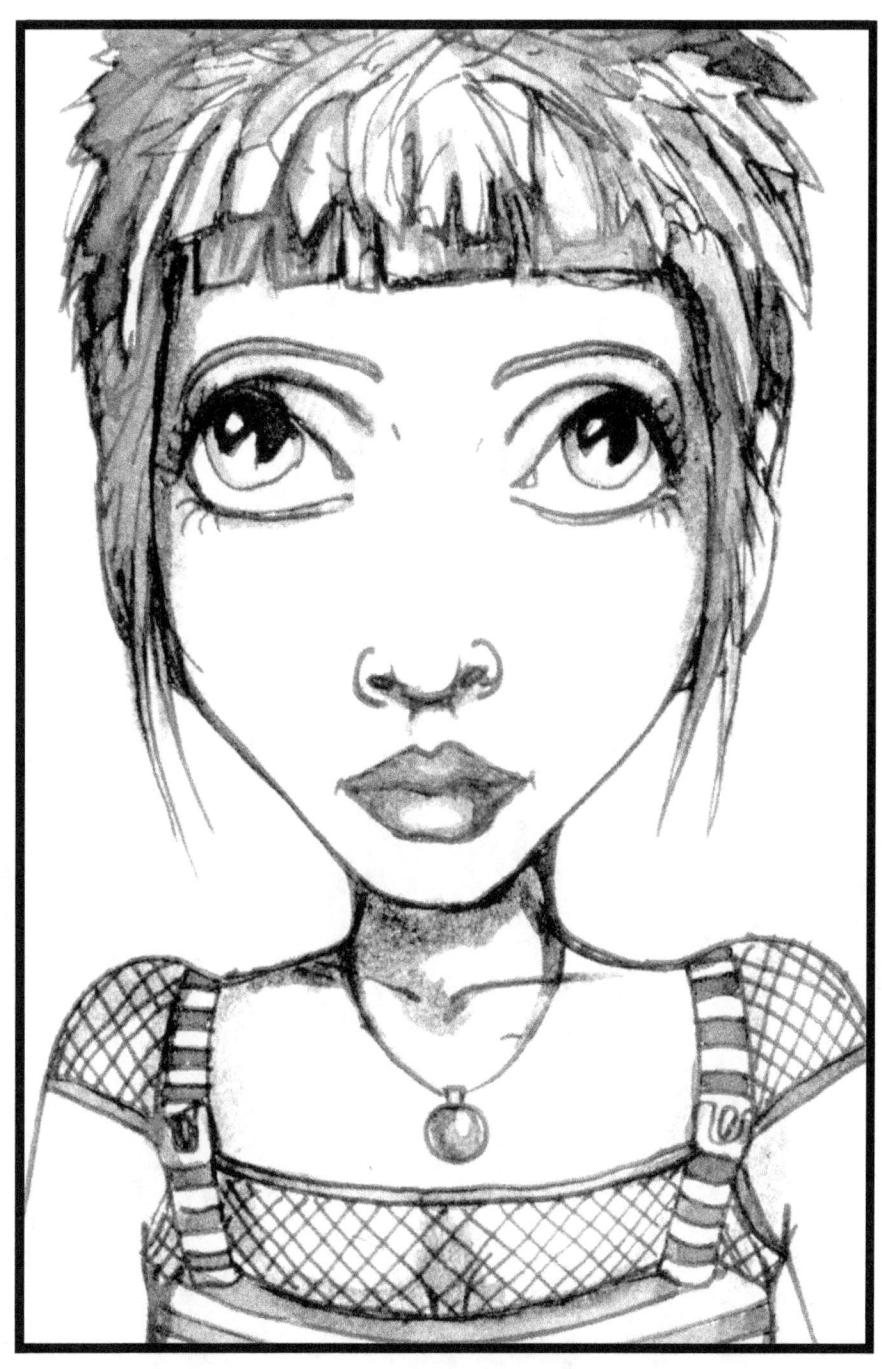

Pixie Cut

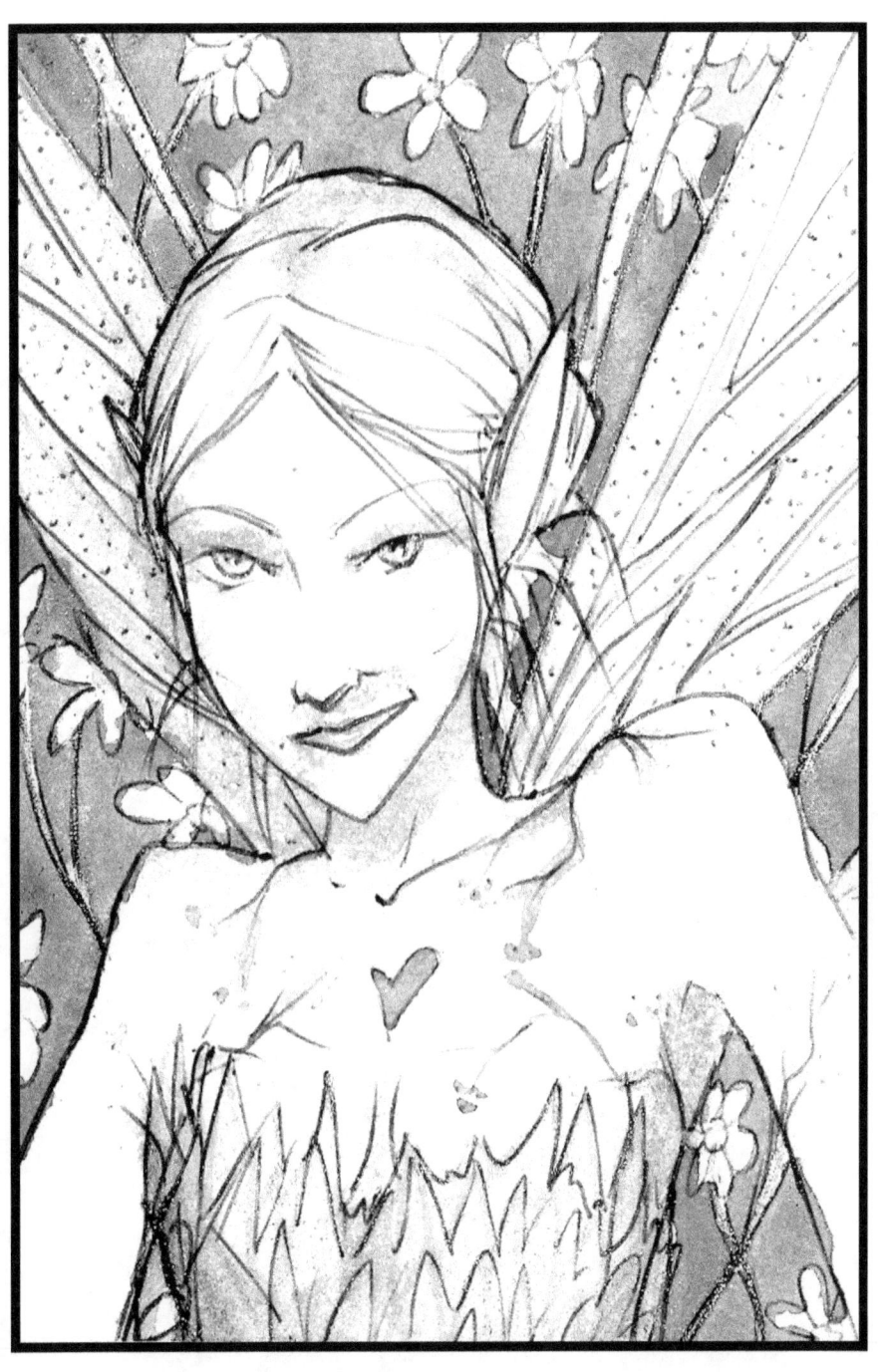

Snarky

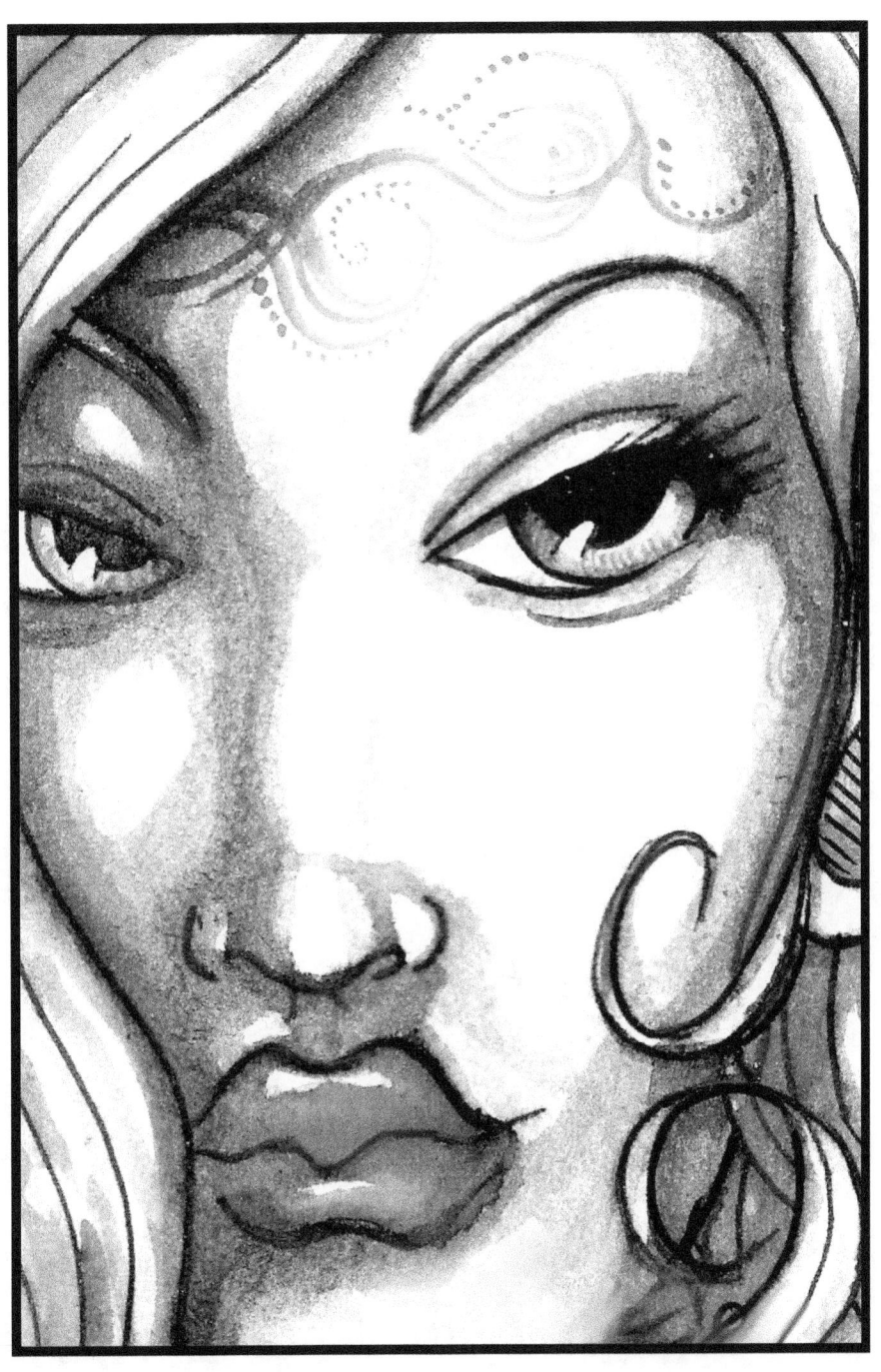

Close-Up

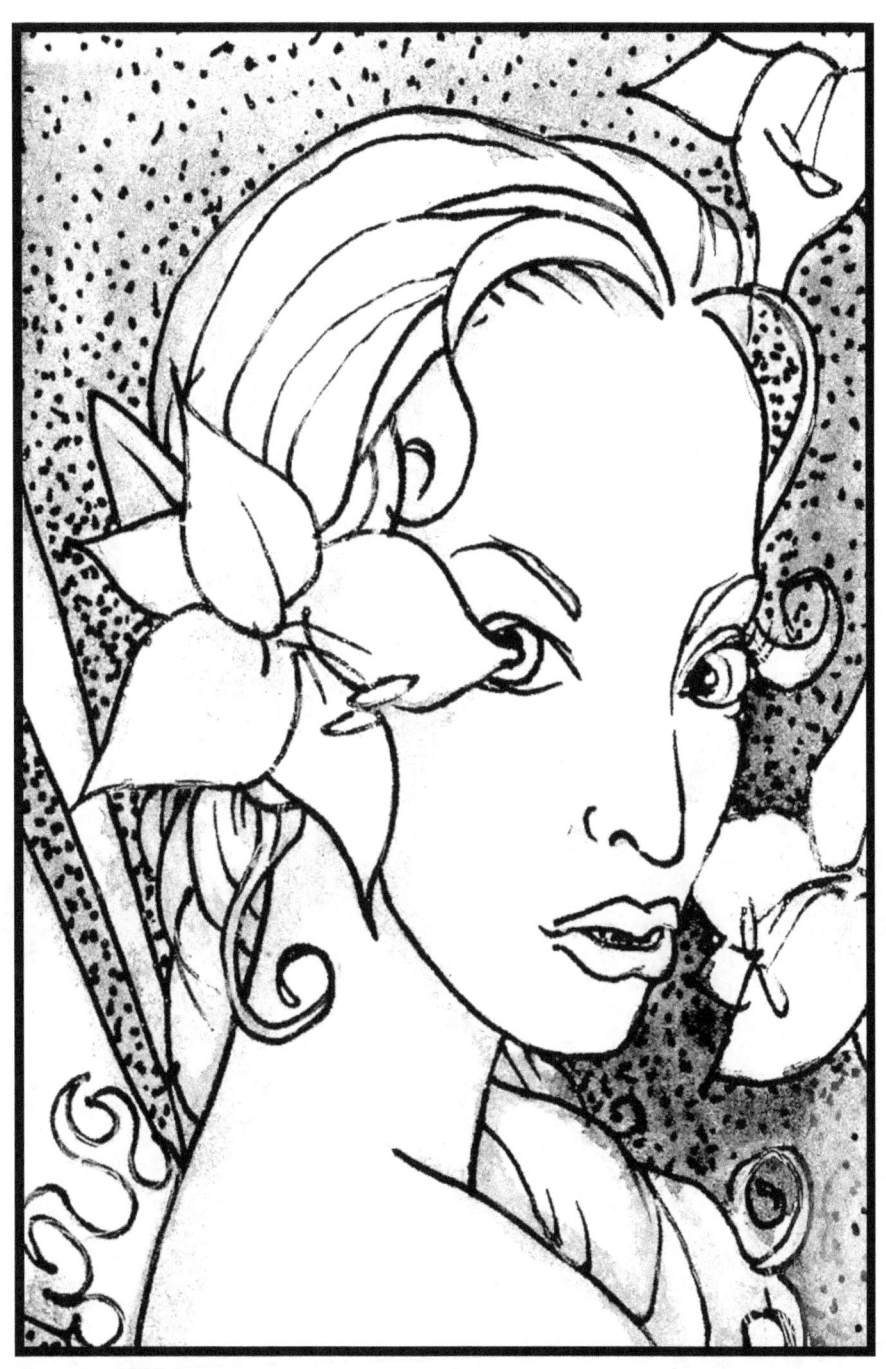

Elusive

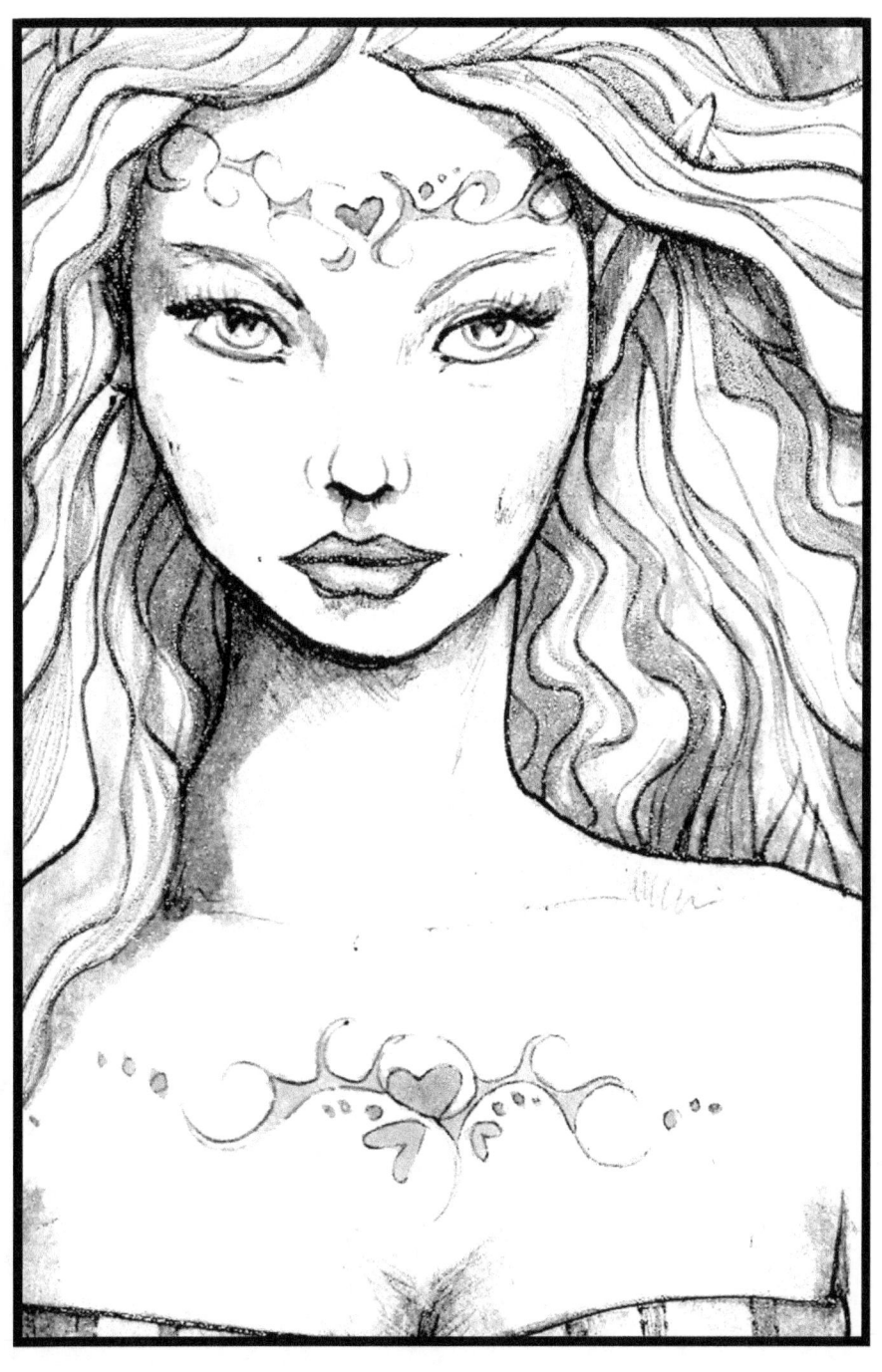

Confident Fae

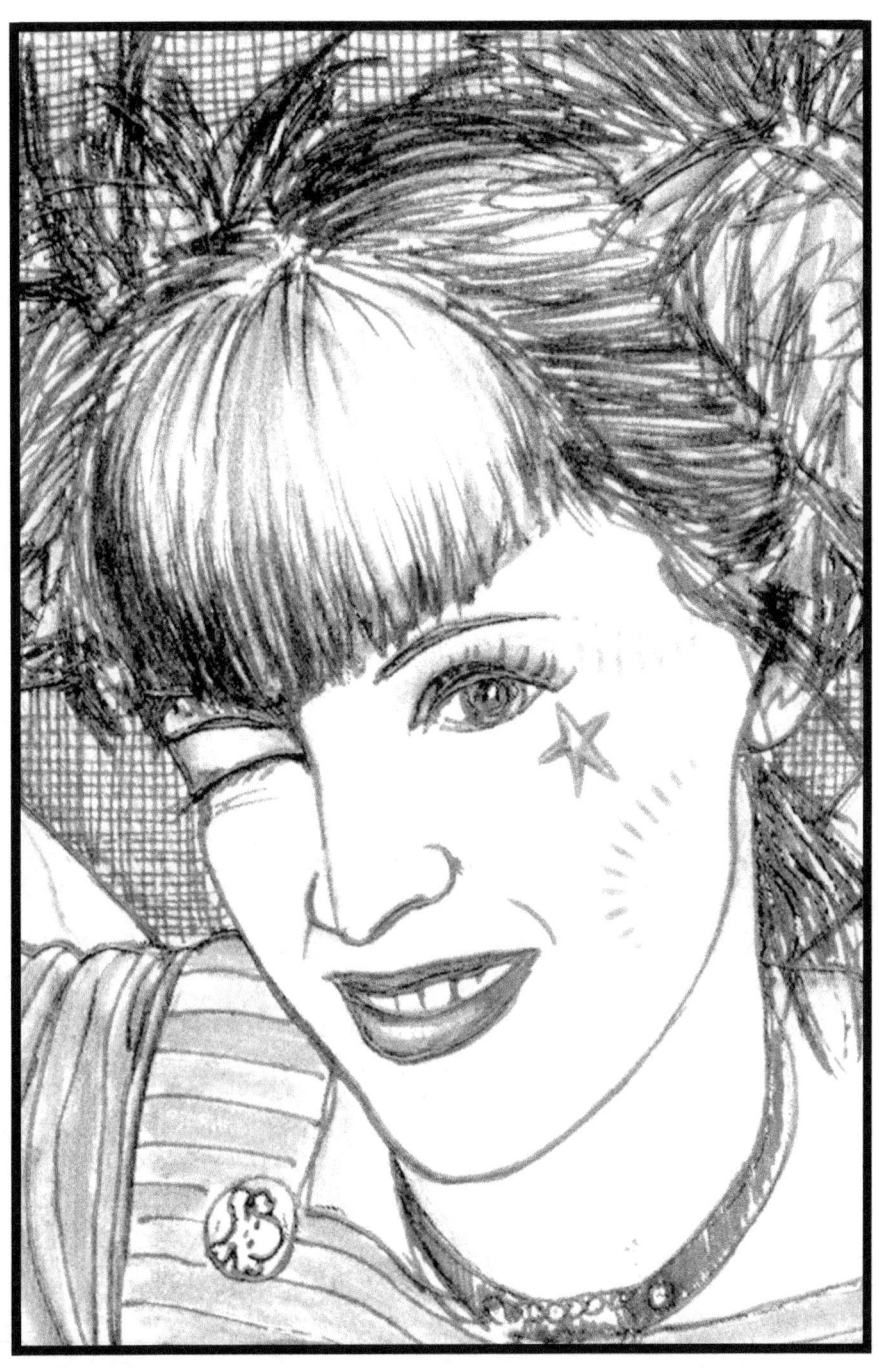

Punky

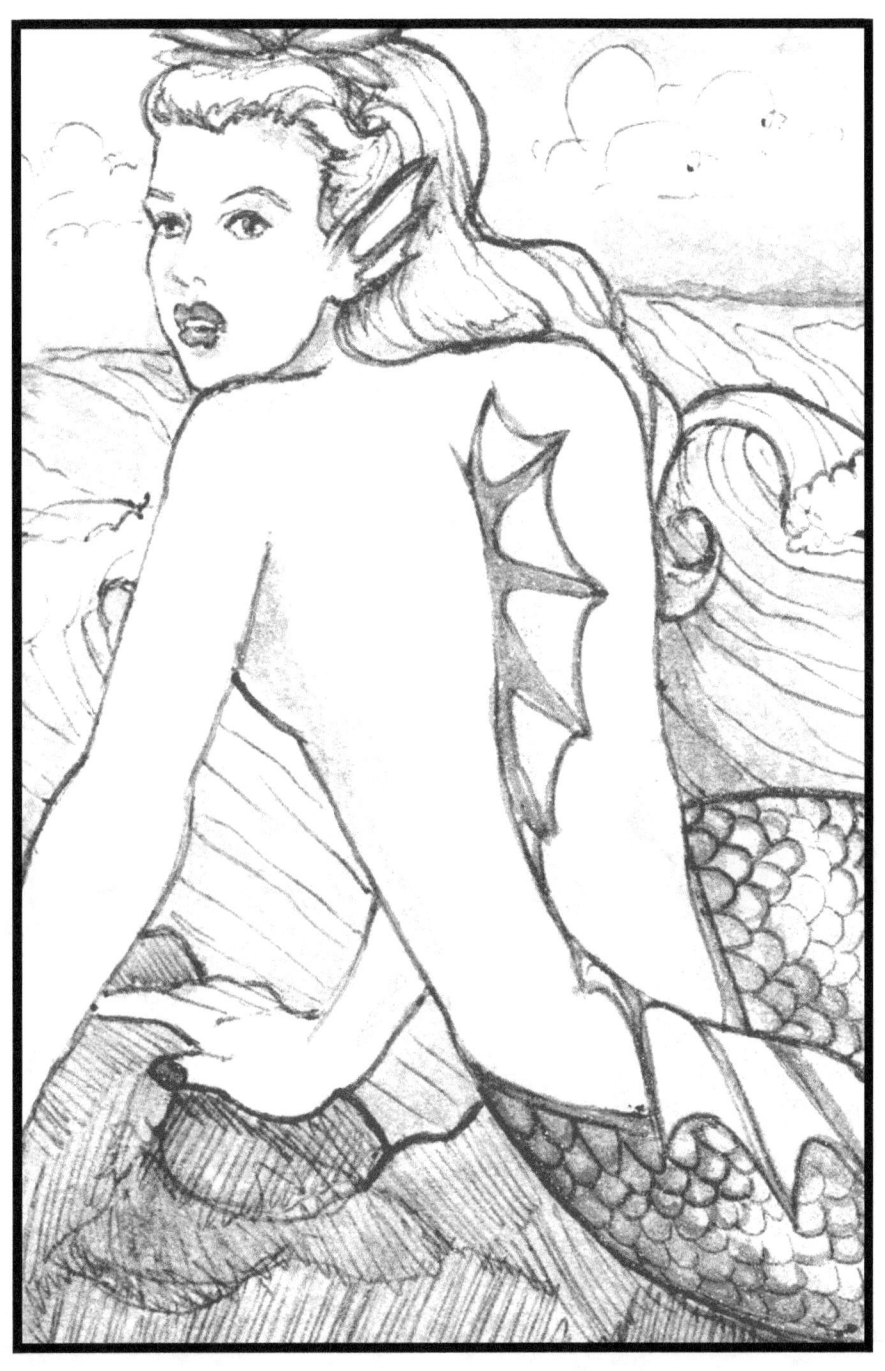

Backfins

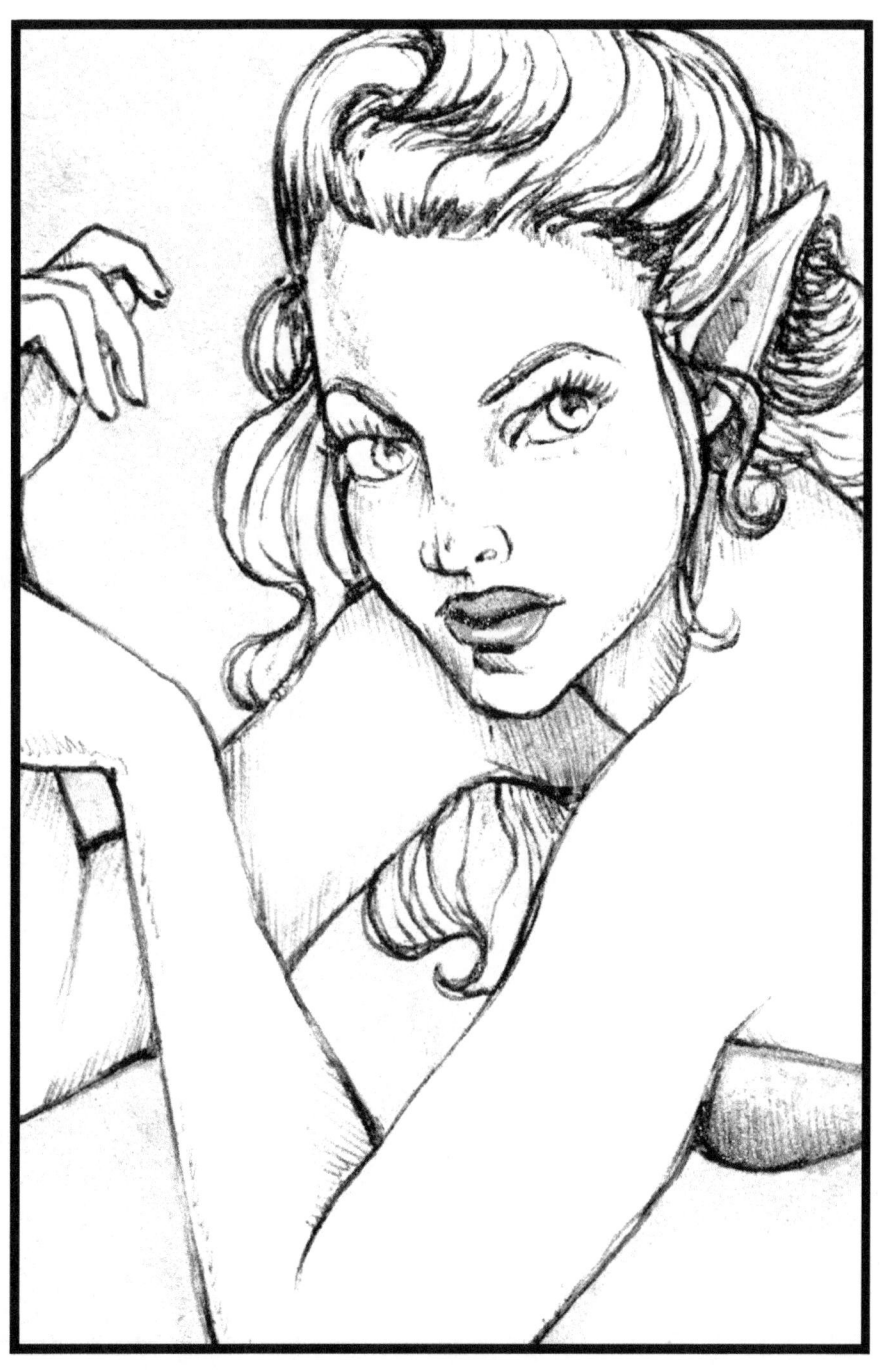

Fae Pin-Up

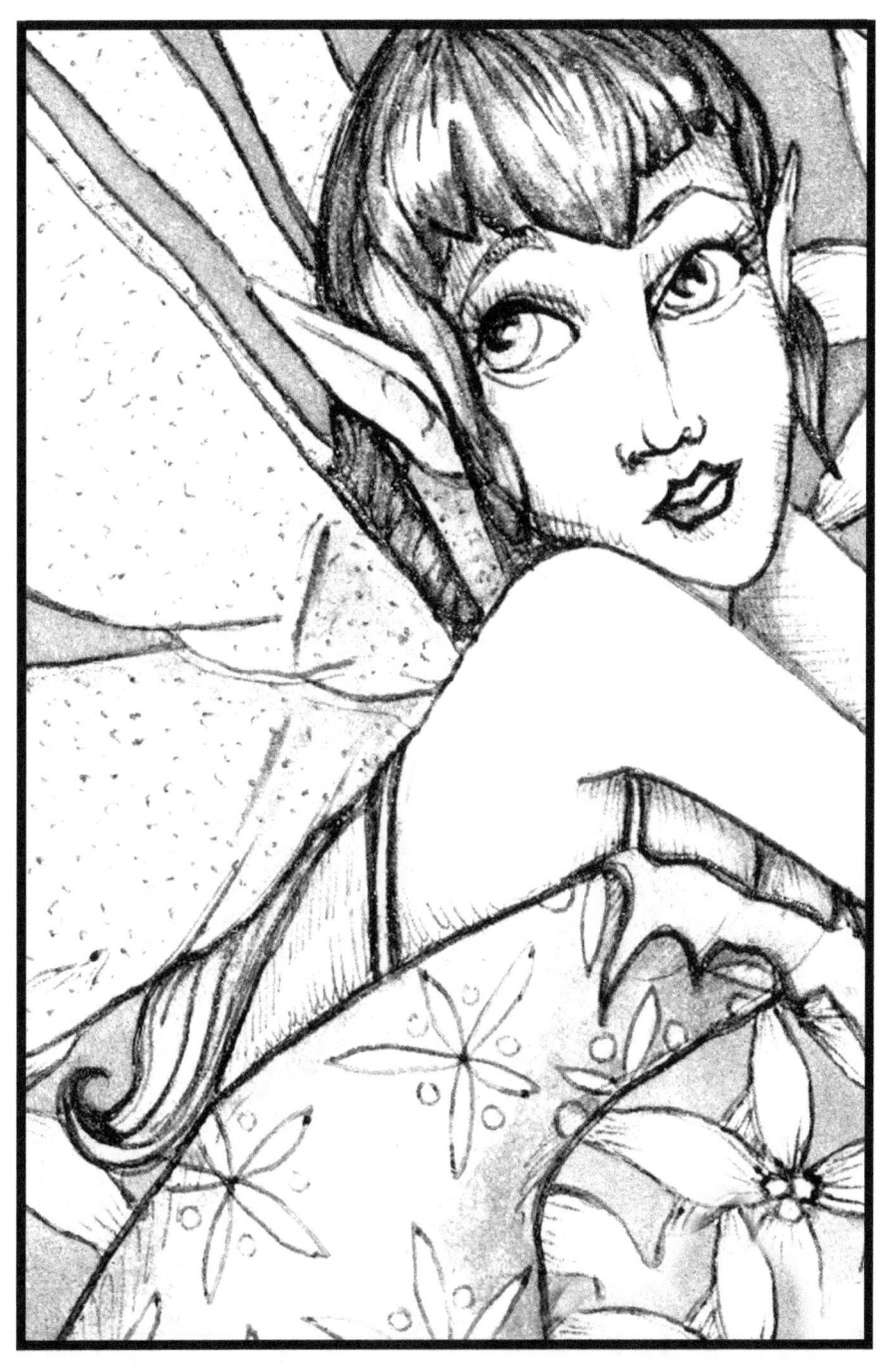

Working & Daydreaming

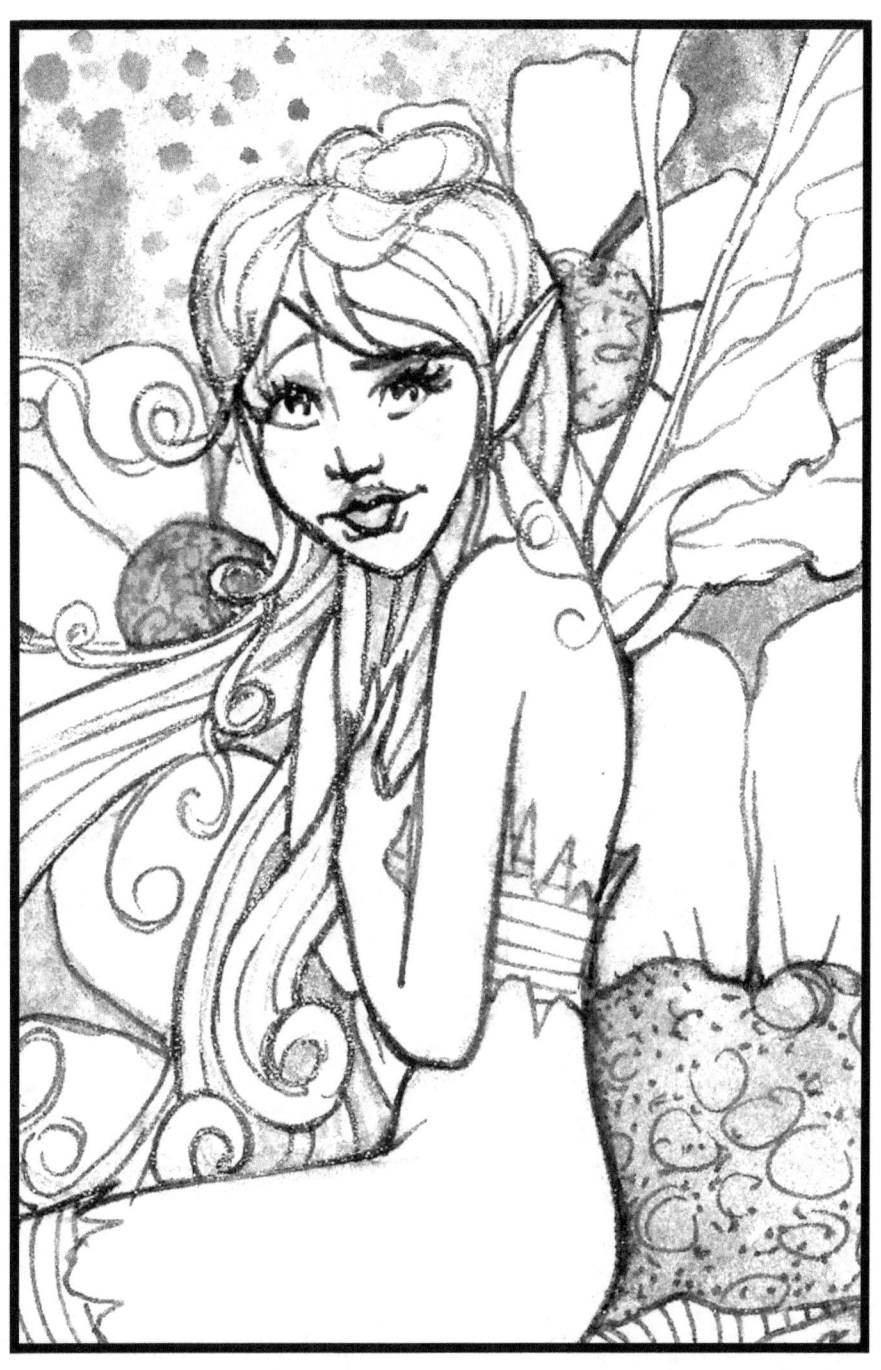

Brushing Hair

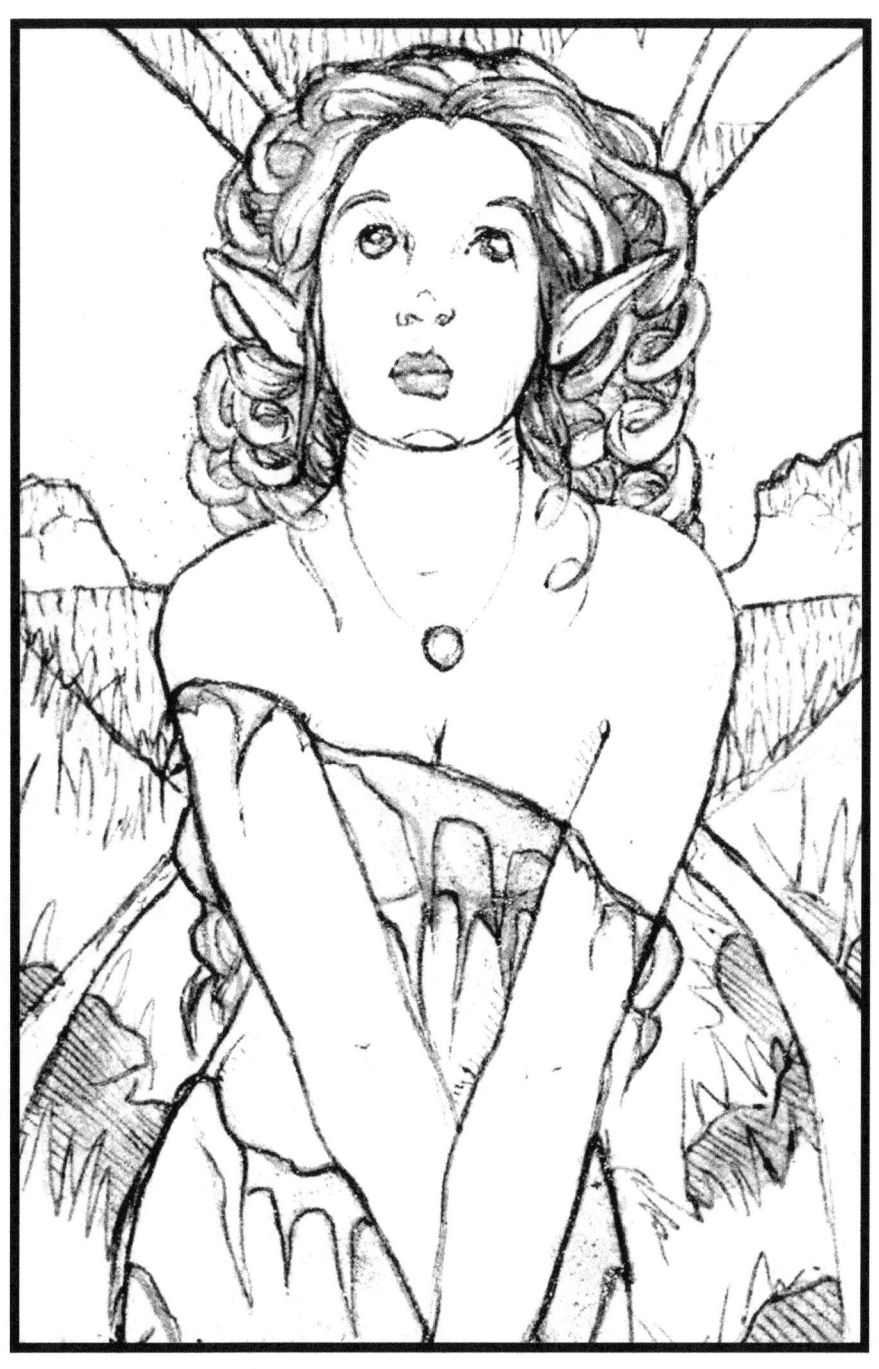

Hopeful

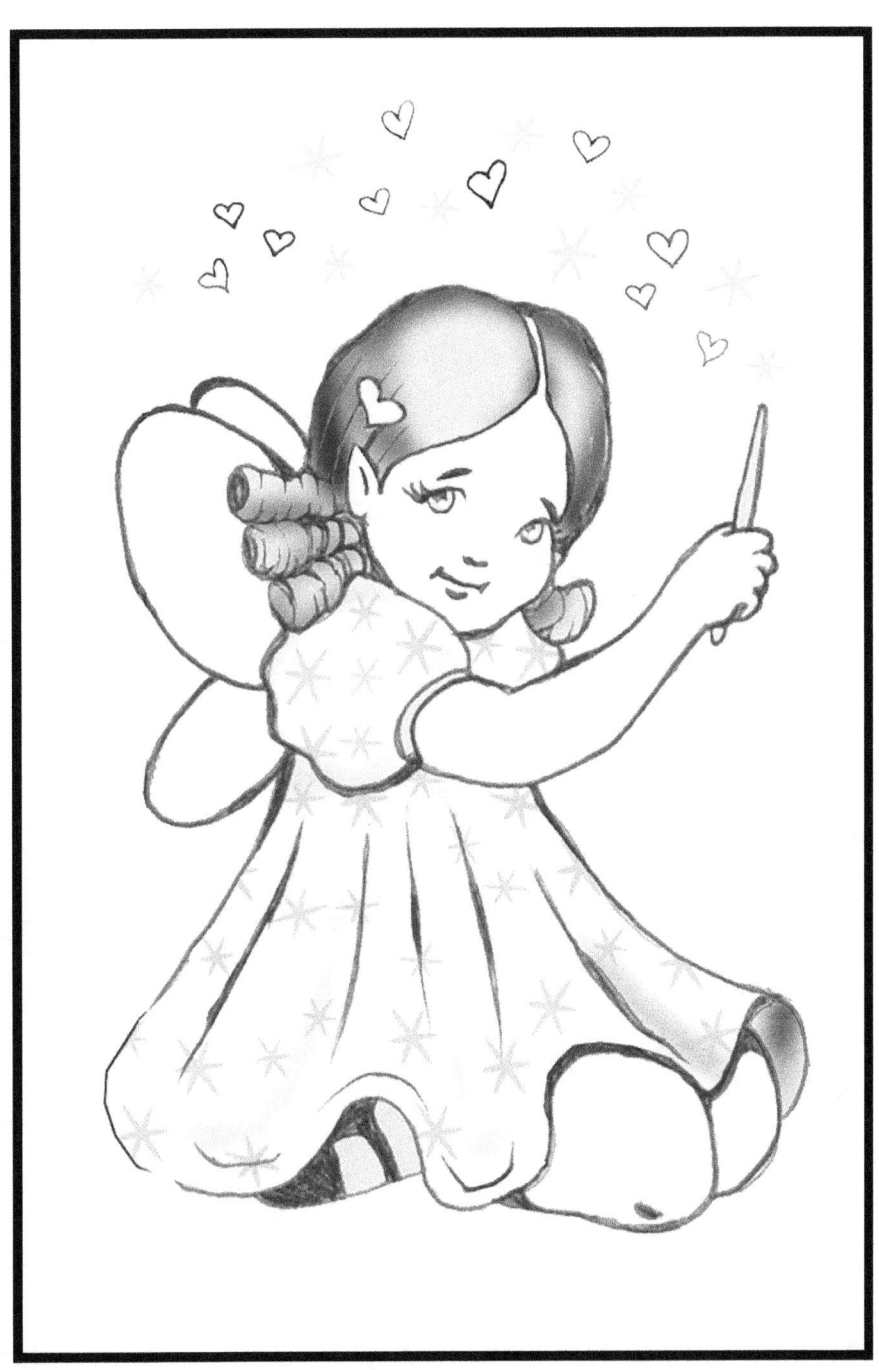

Child's Play

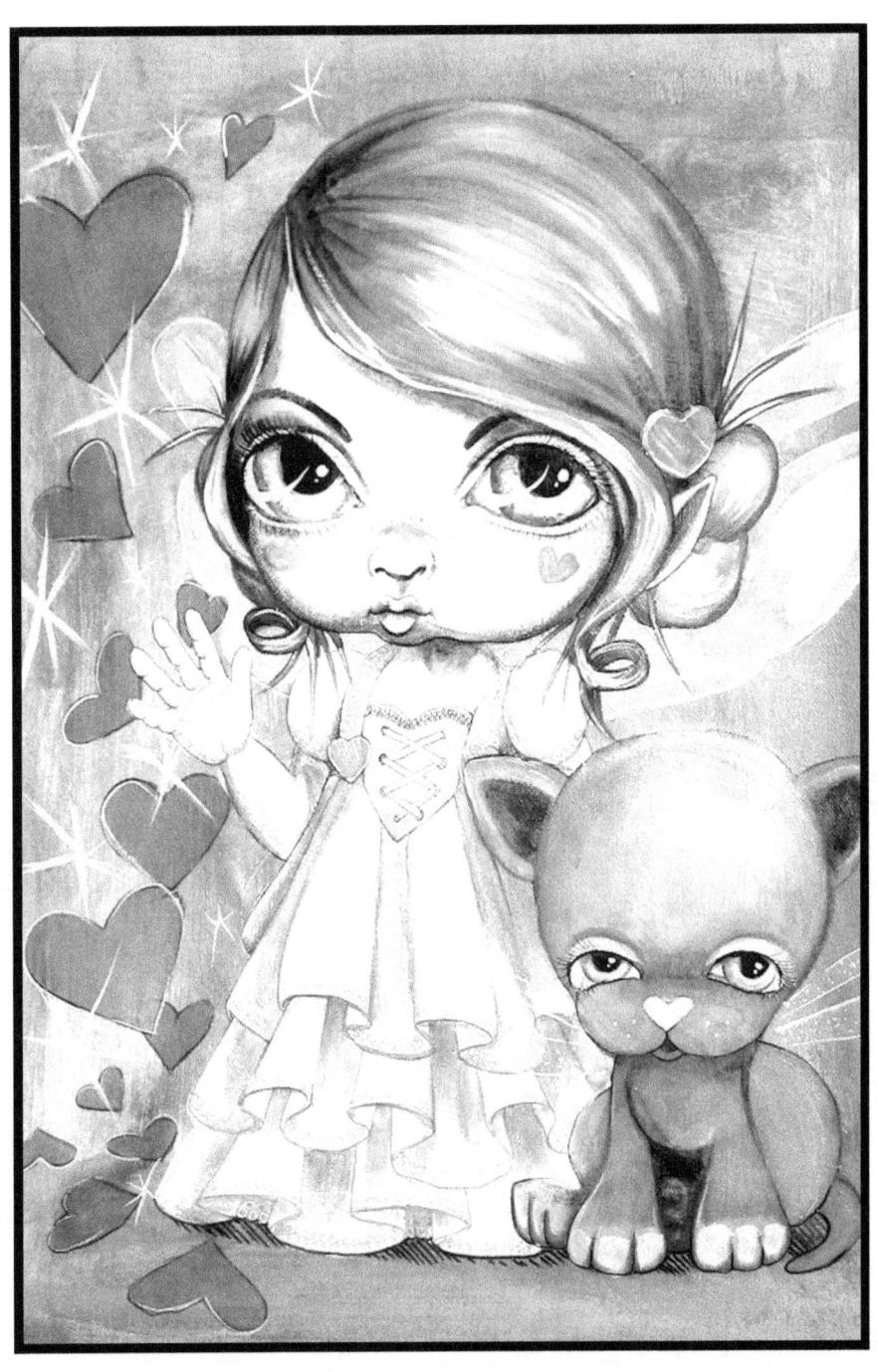

Hearts of Plenty

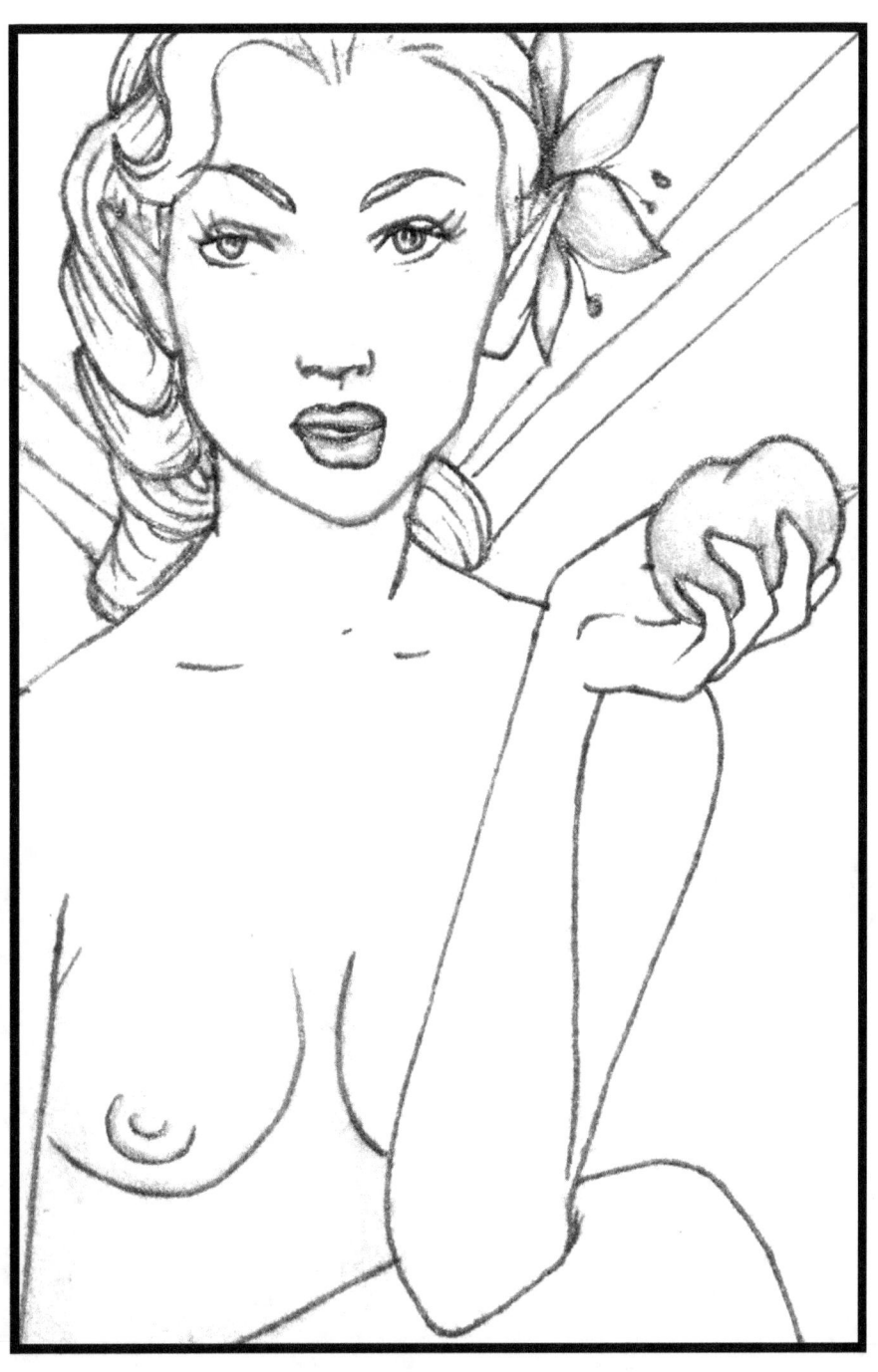

Apple a Day

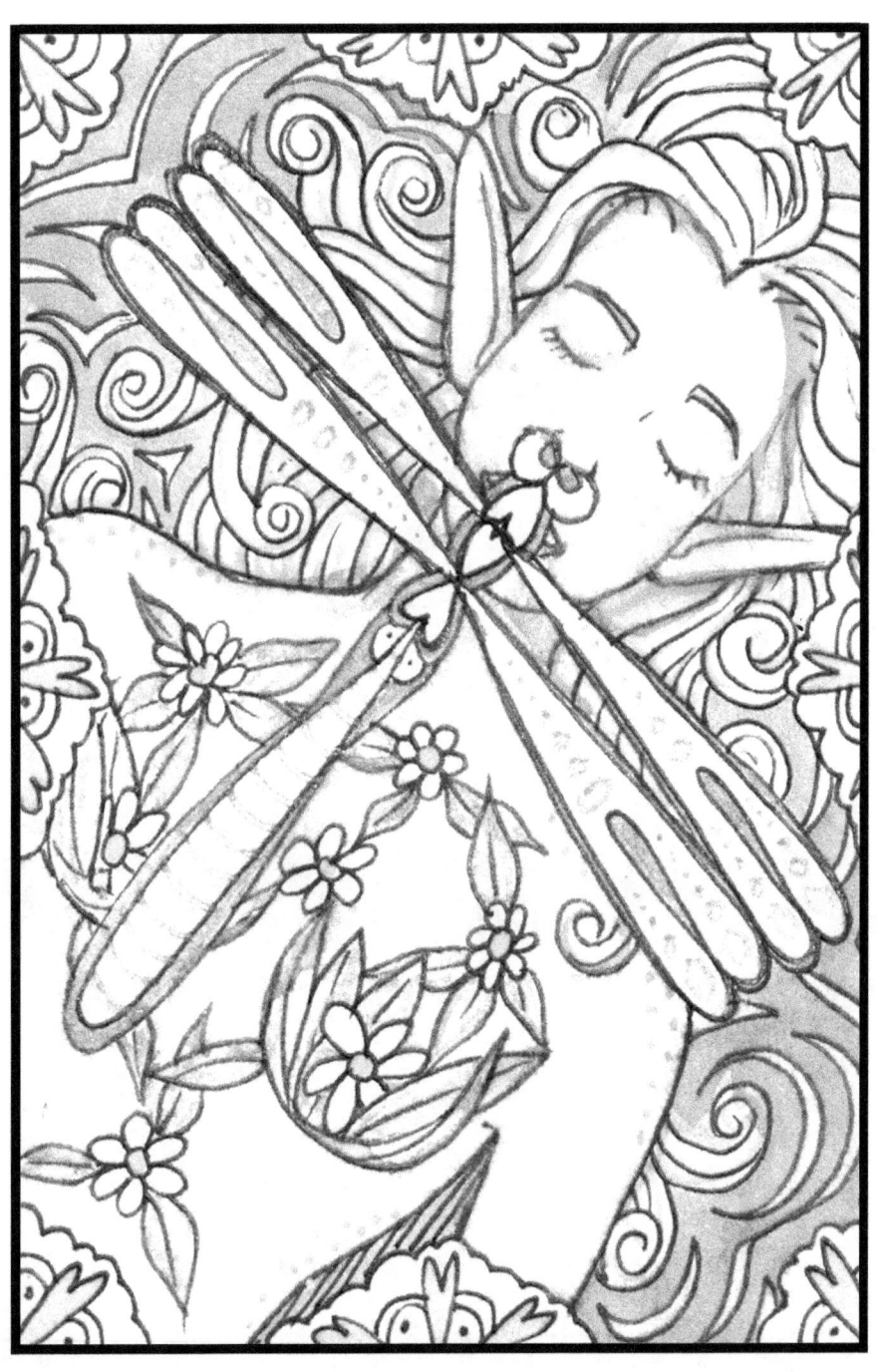

Dragonfly Kiss

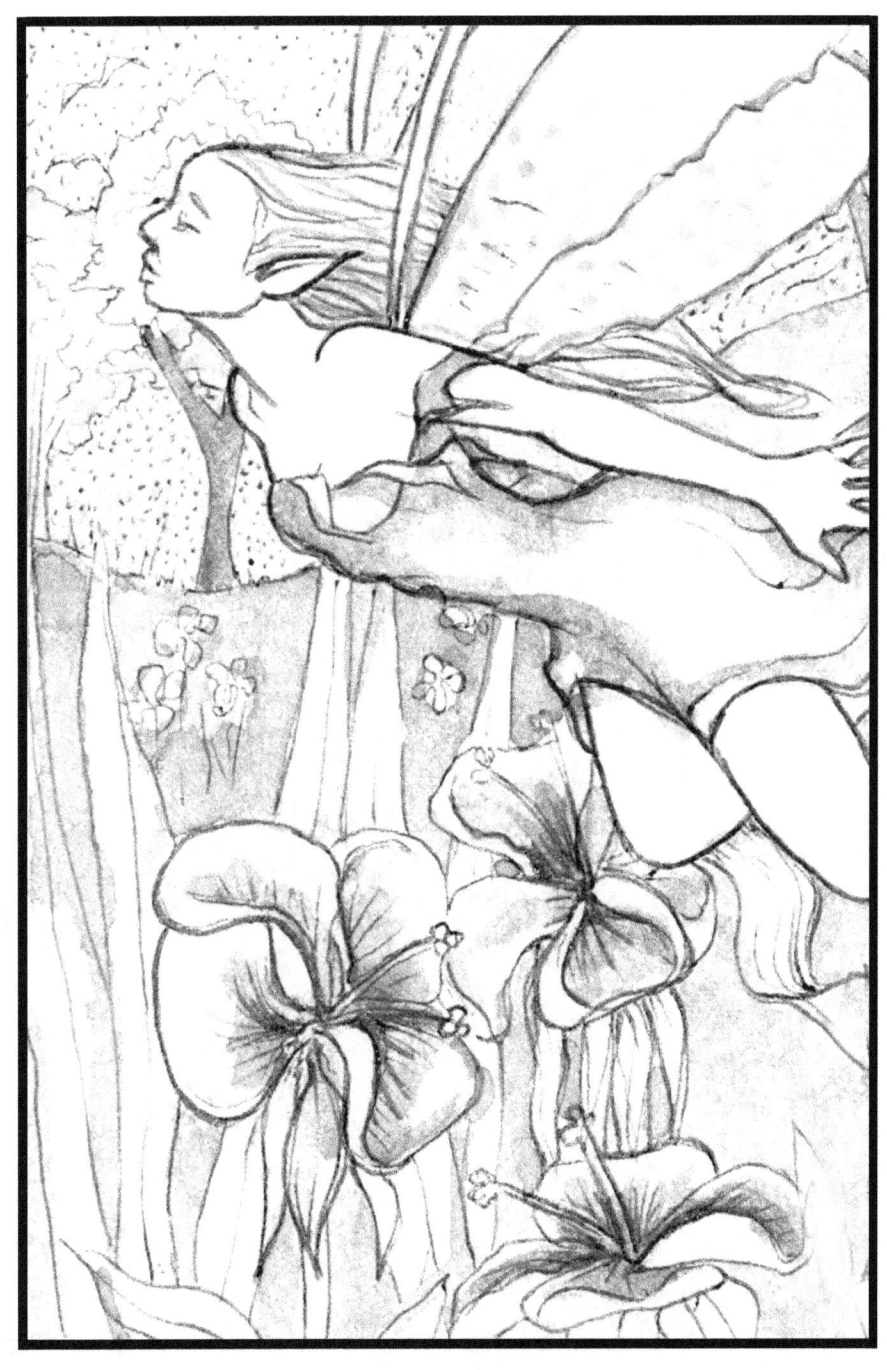

In Flight

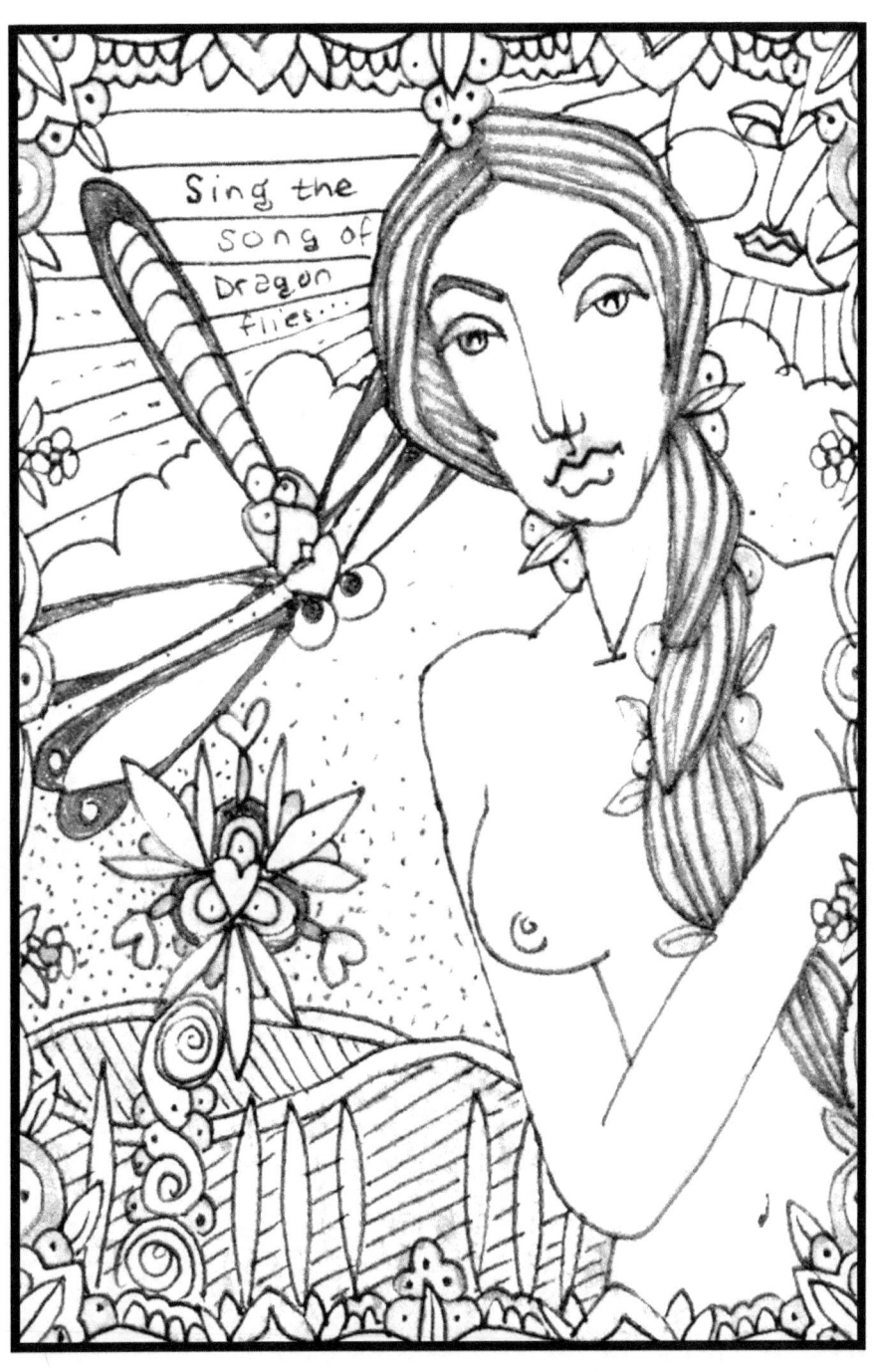

Song of Dragonflies

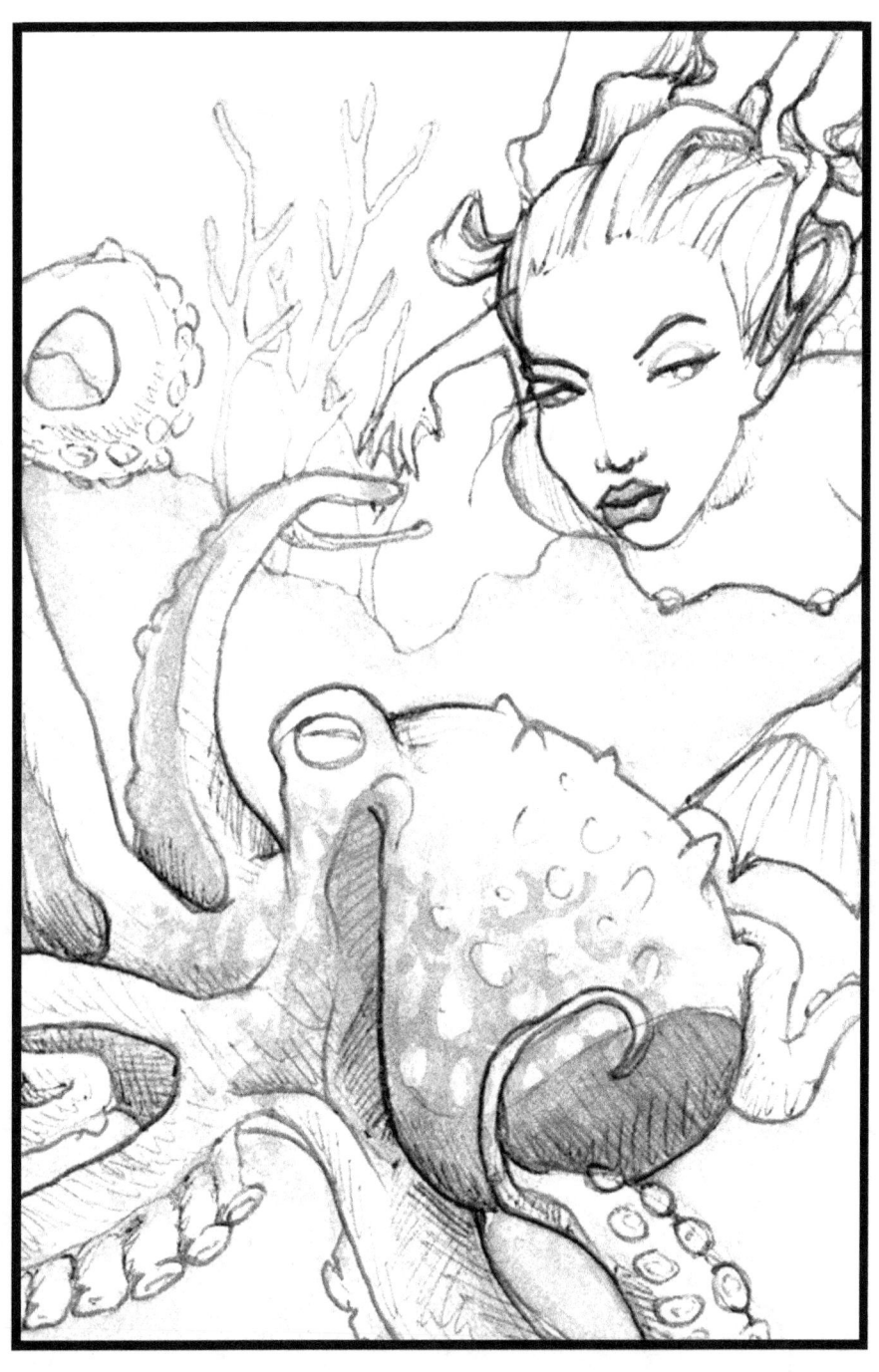

Swimming With an Octopus

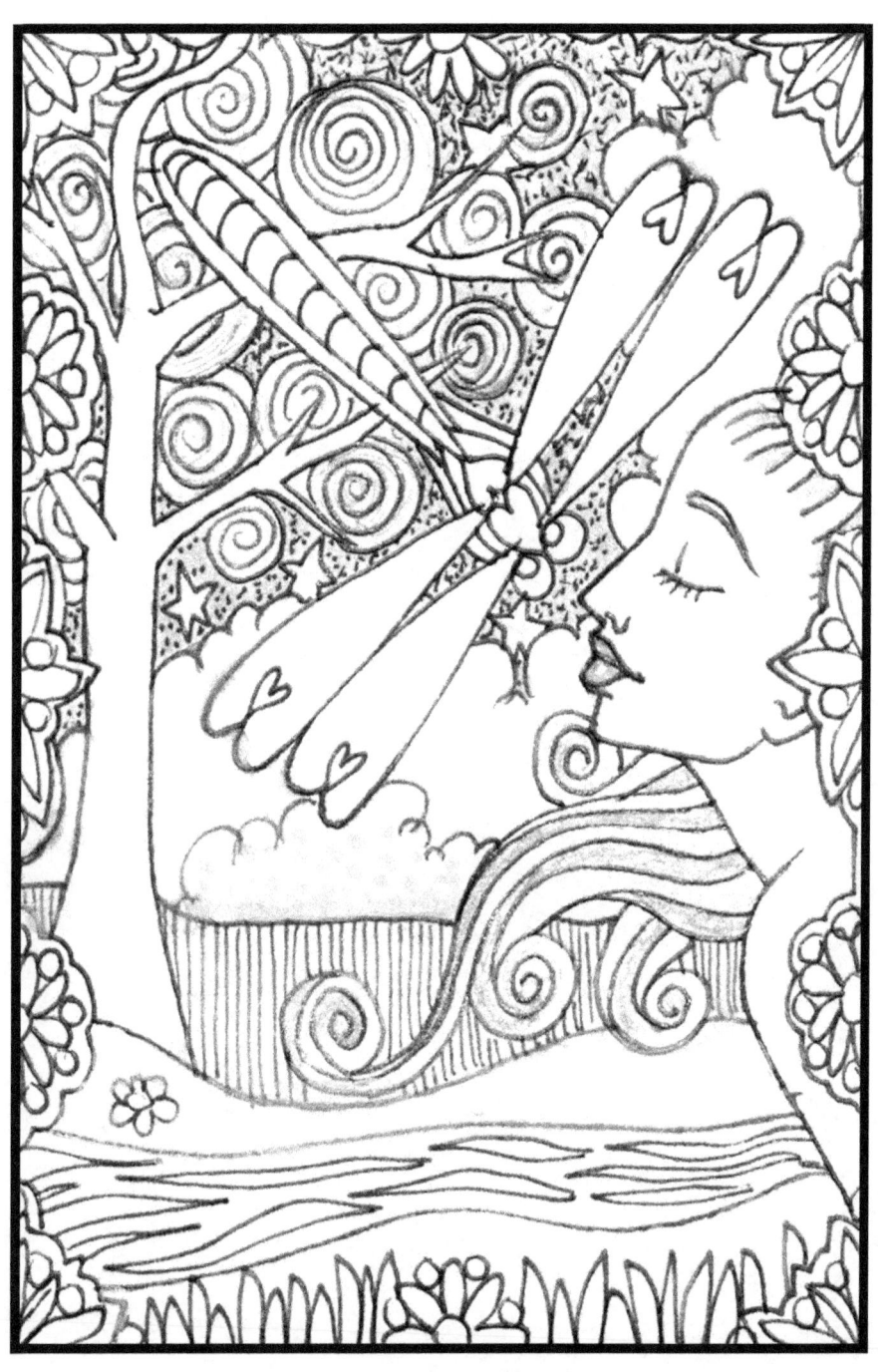

Dragonfly Whisperer

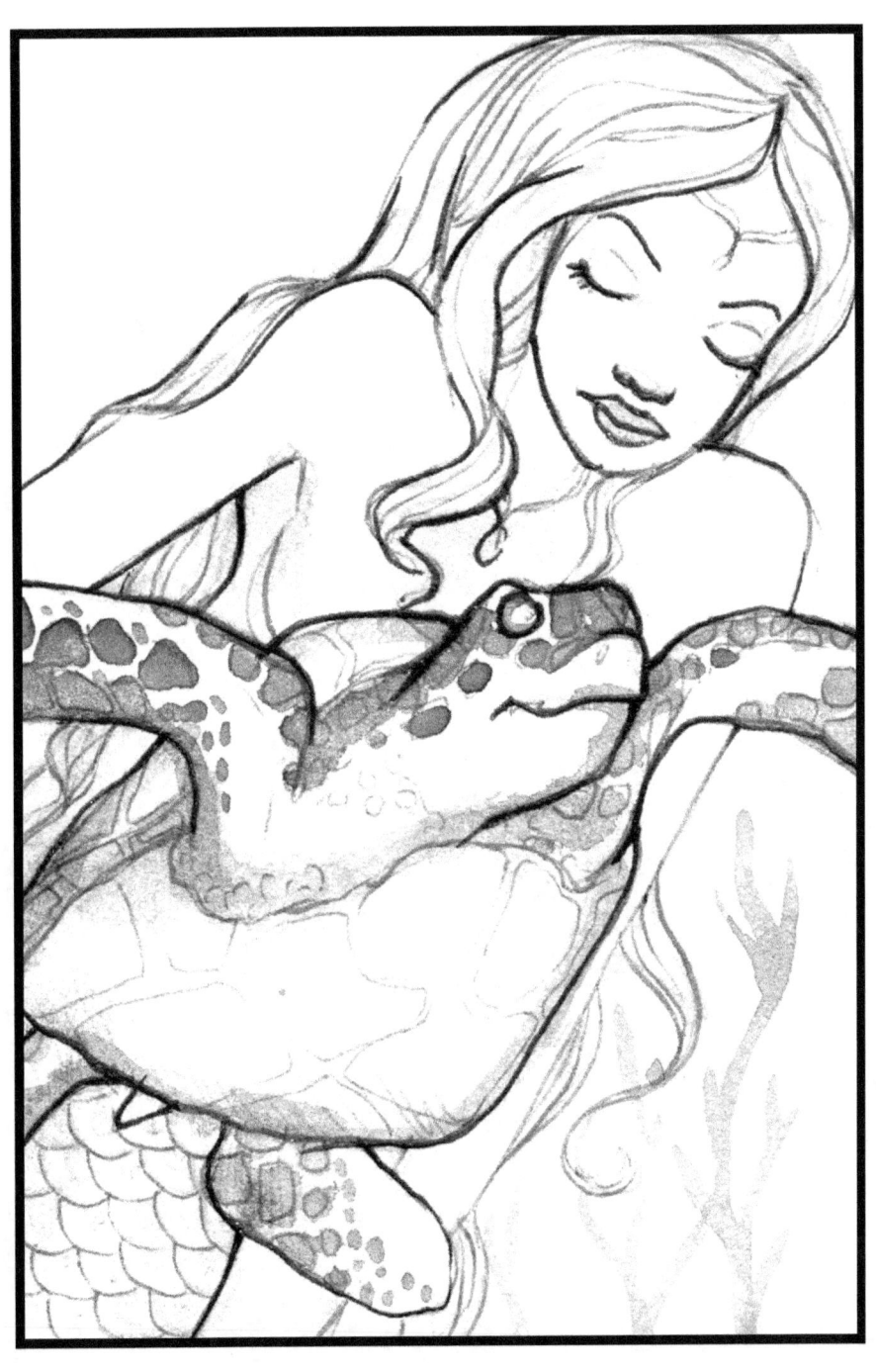

Swim With a Sea Turtle

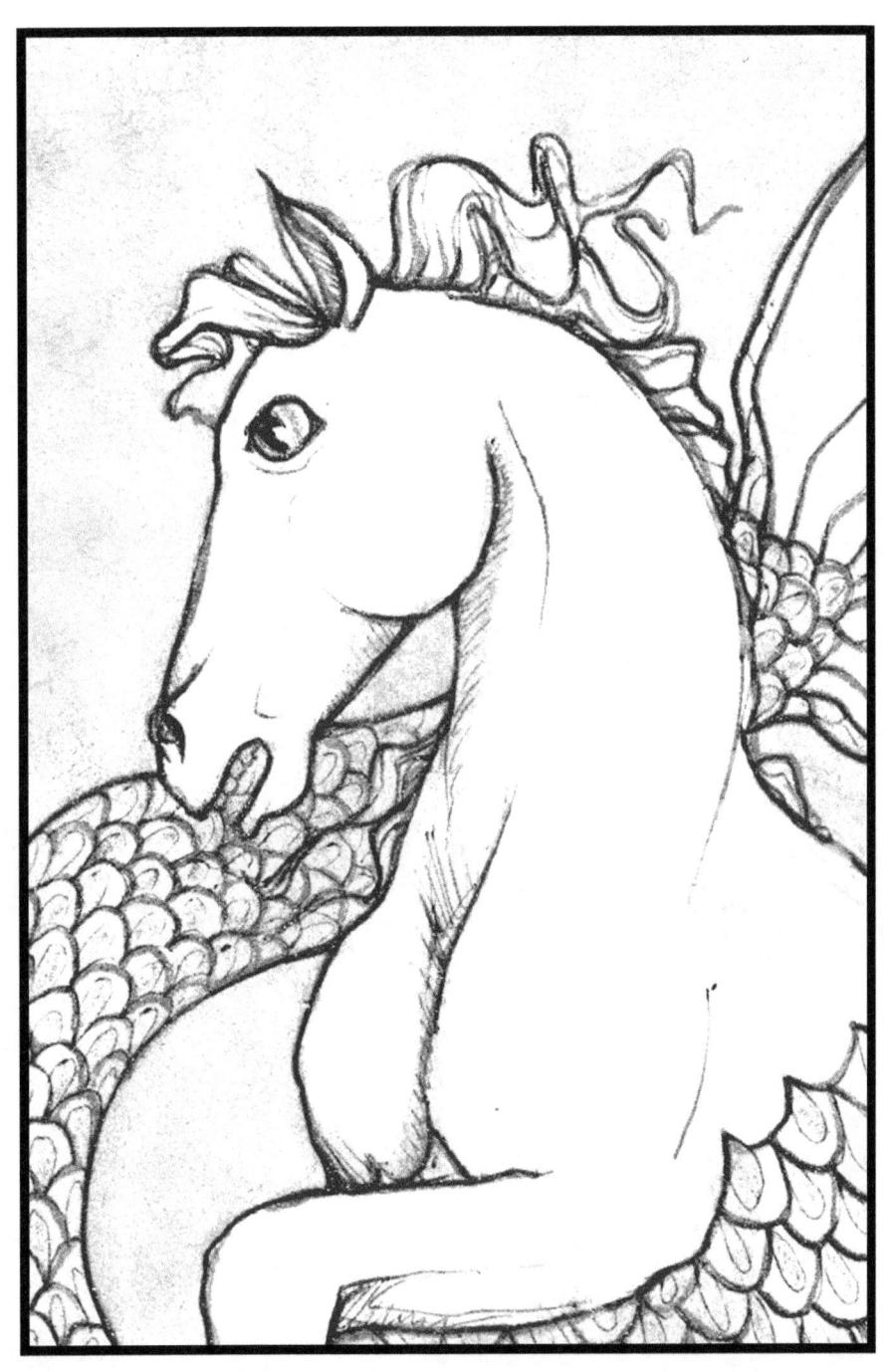

Water Horse

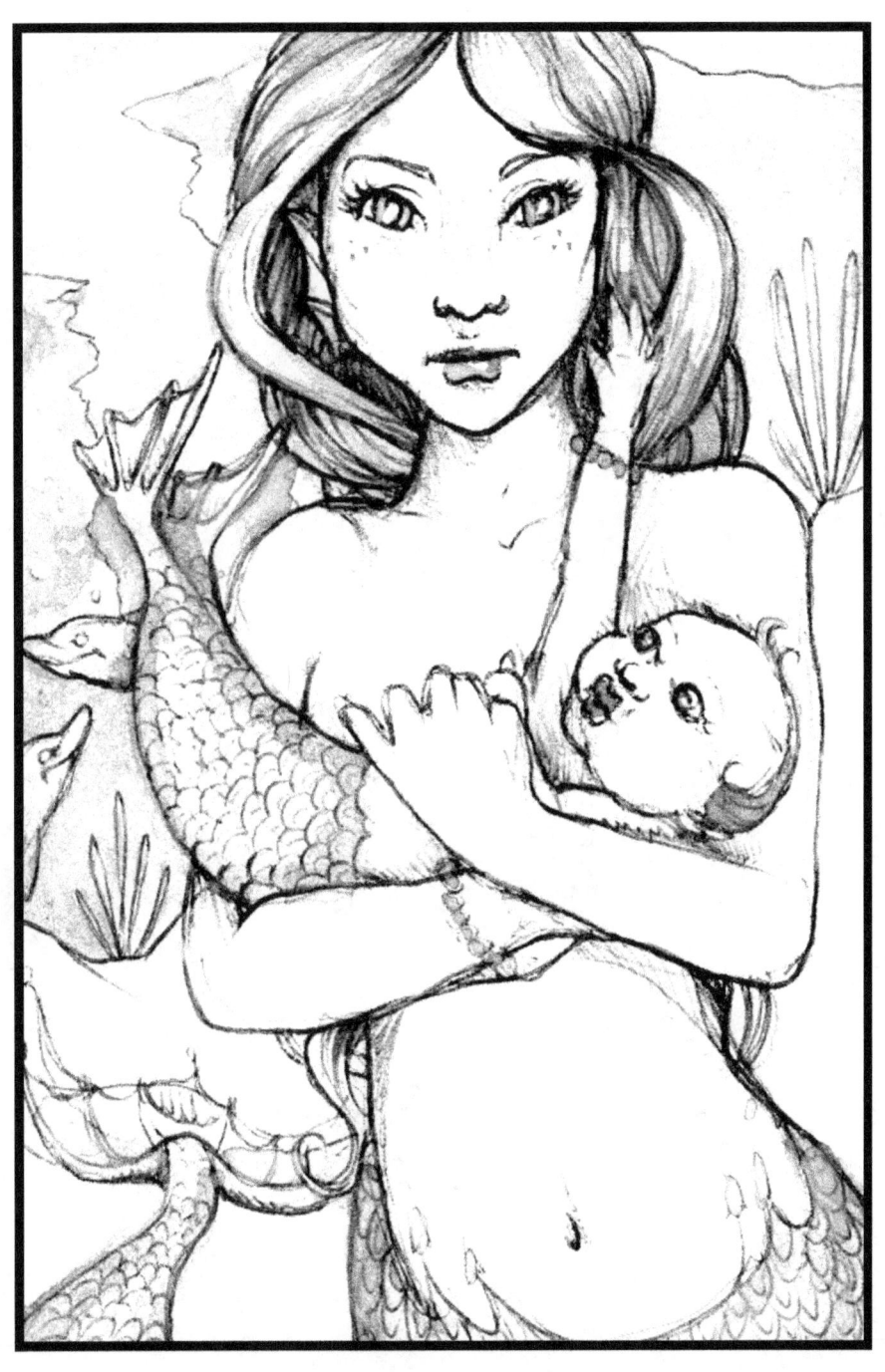

Baby's Awake!

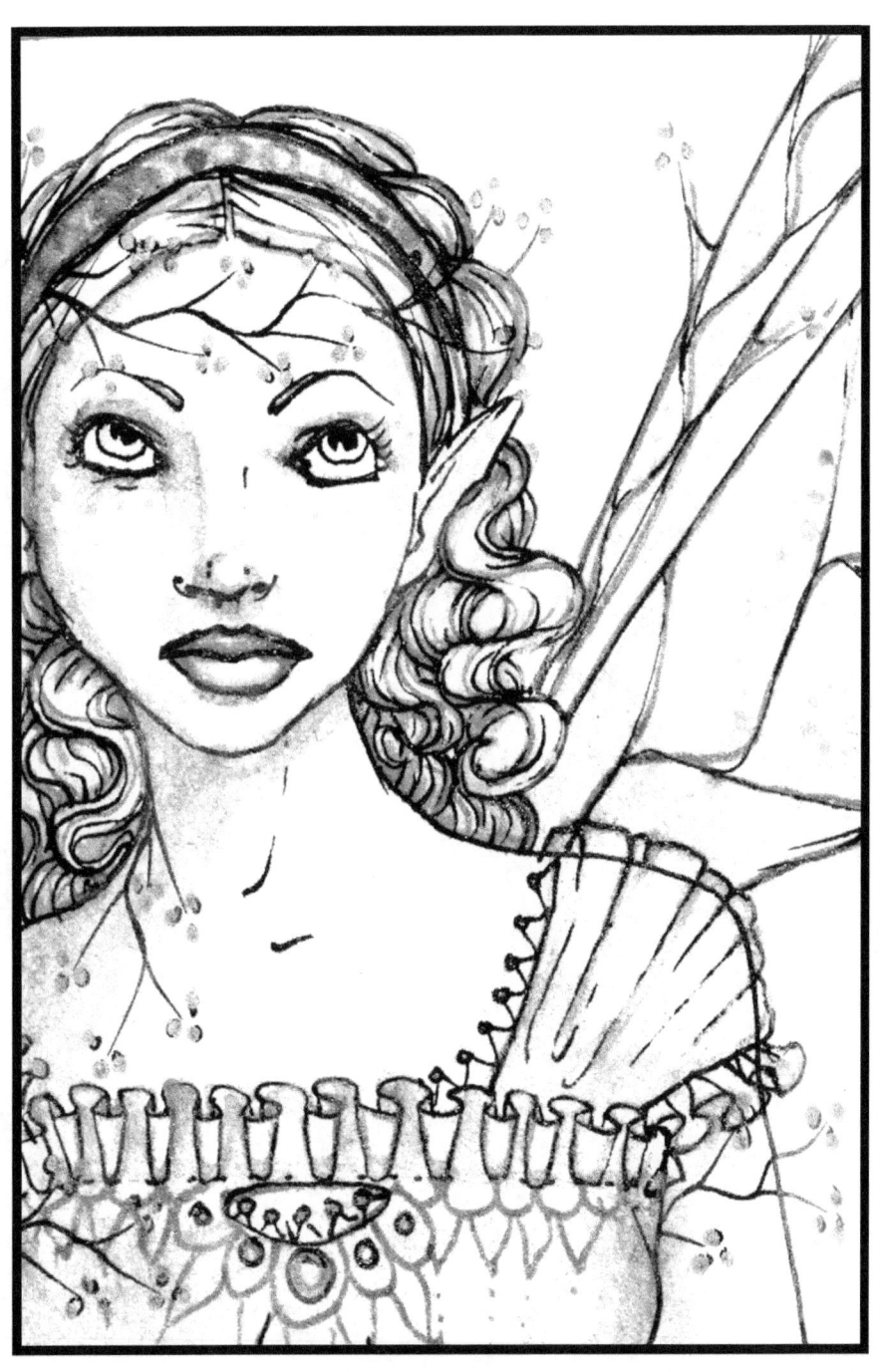

Resolute

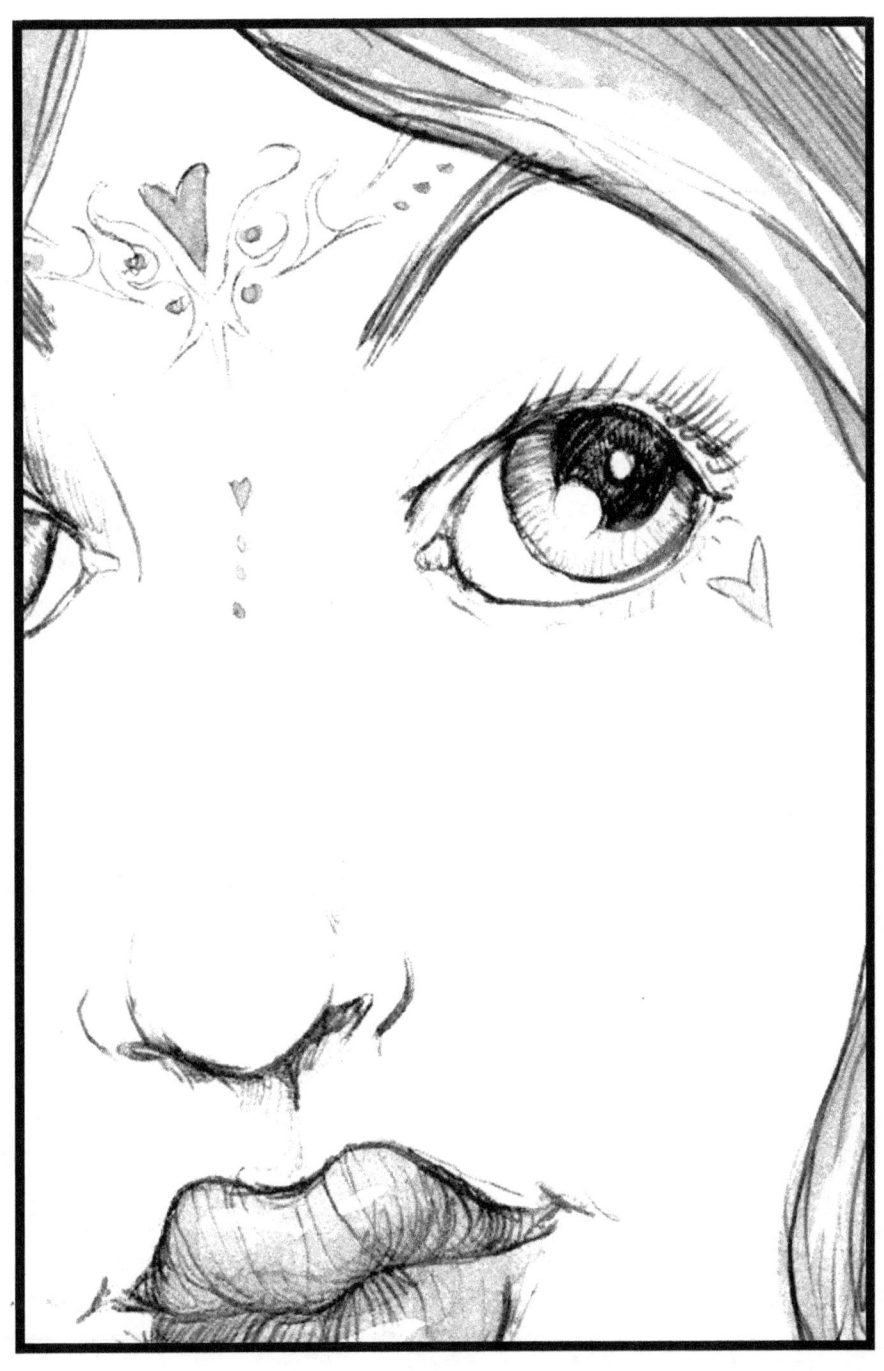

Close Encounter

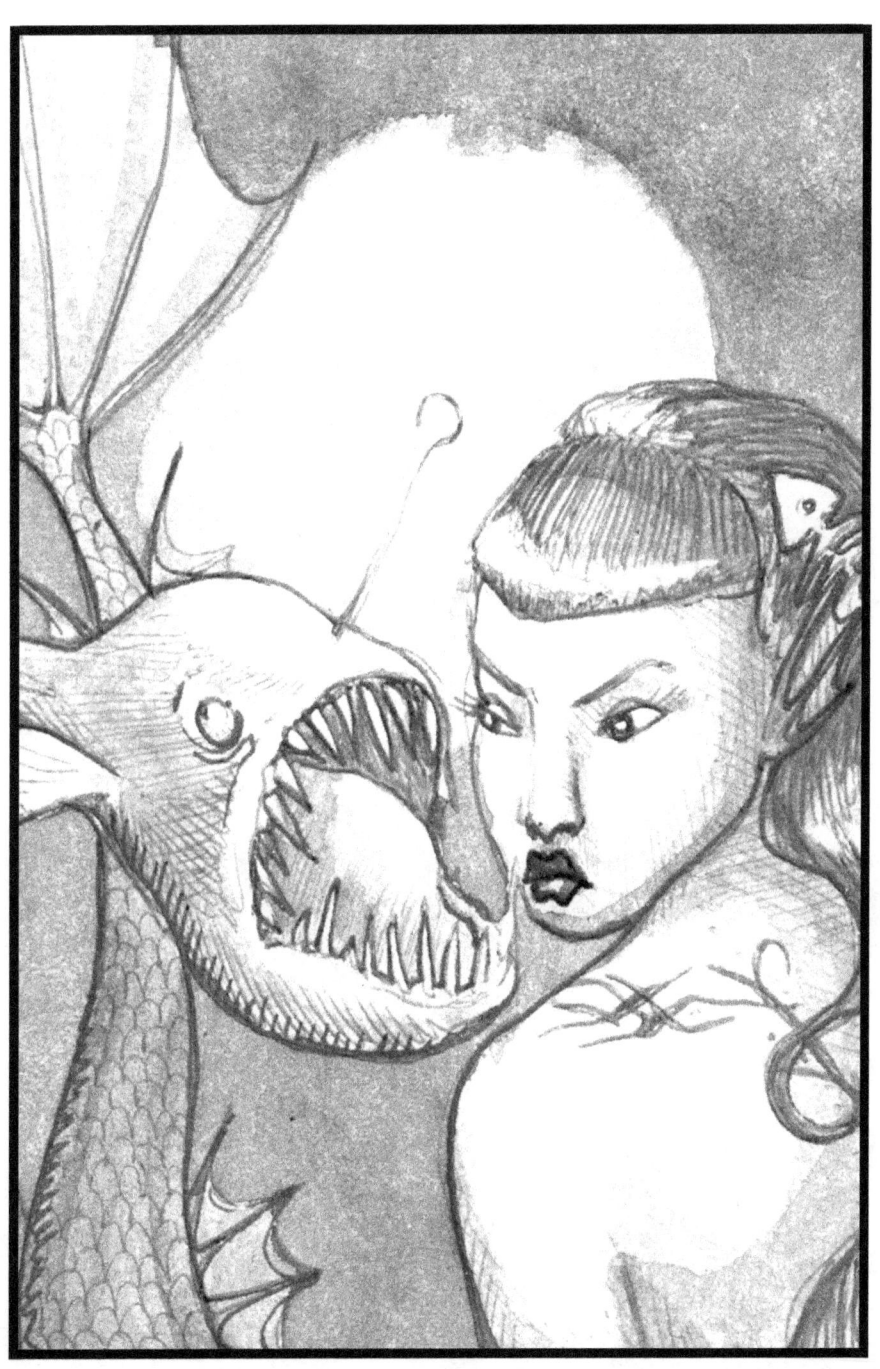

Angler Fish Argument

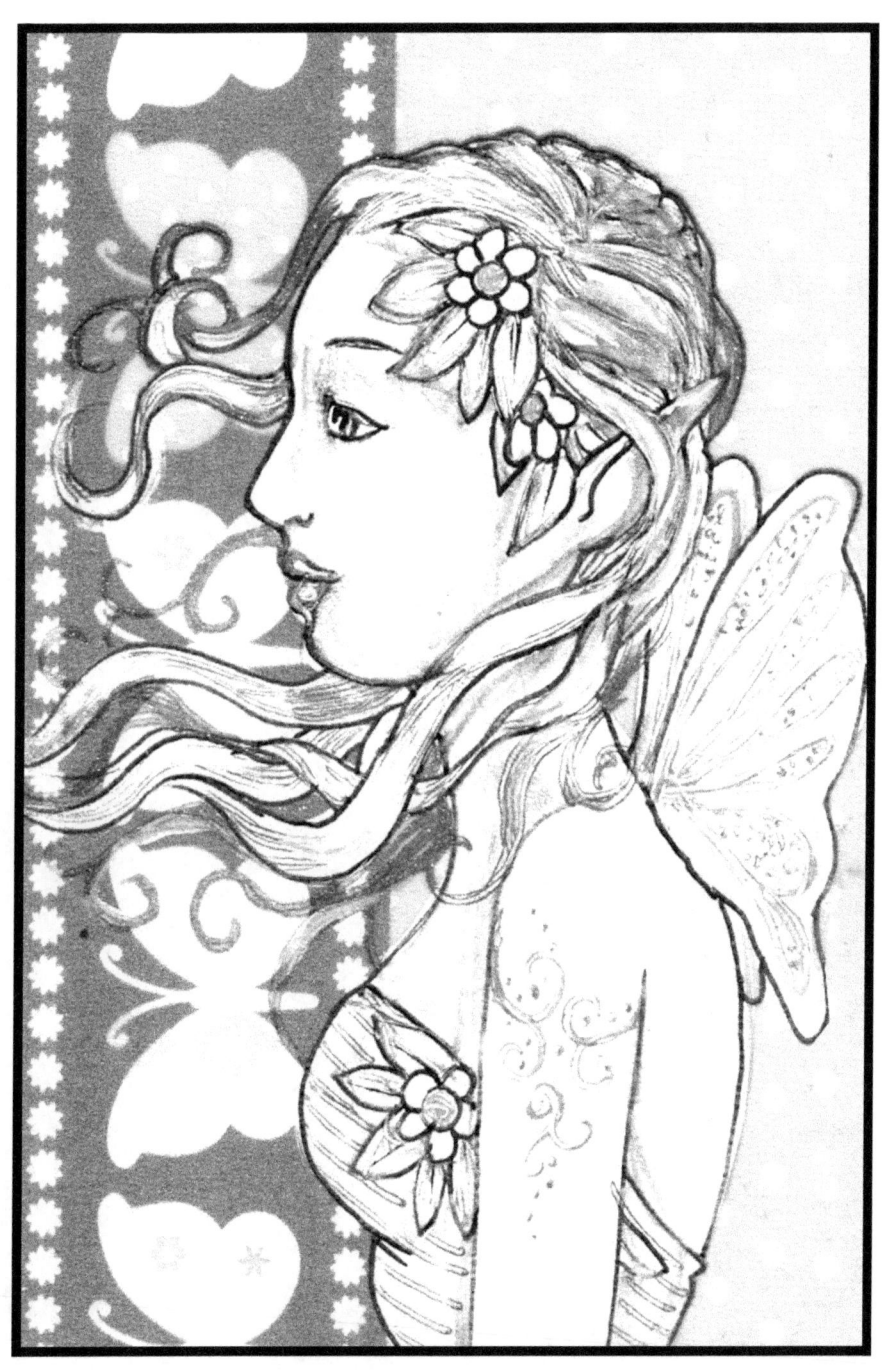

Miss Butterfly

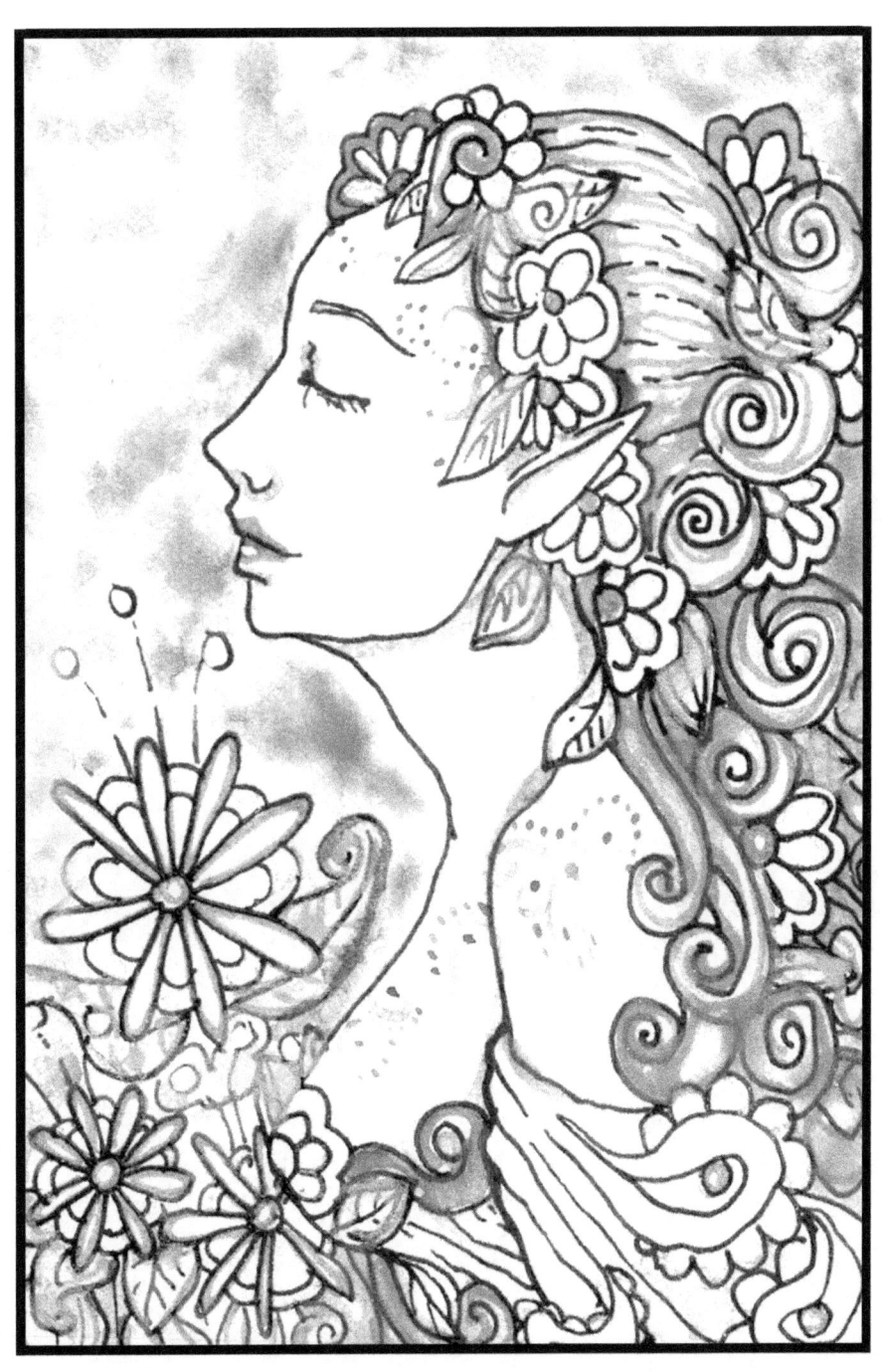

Botanical Bride

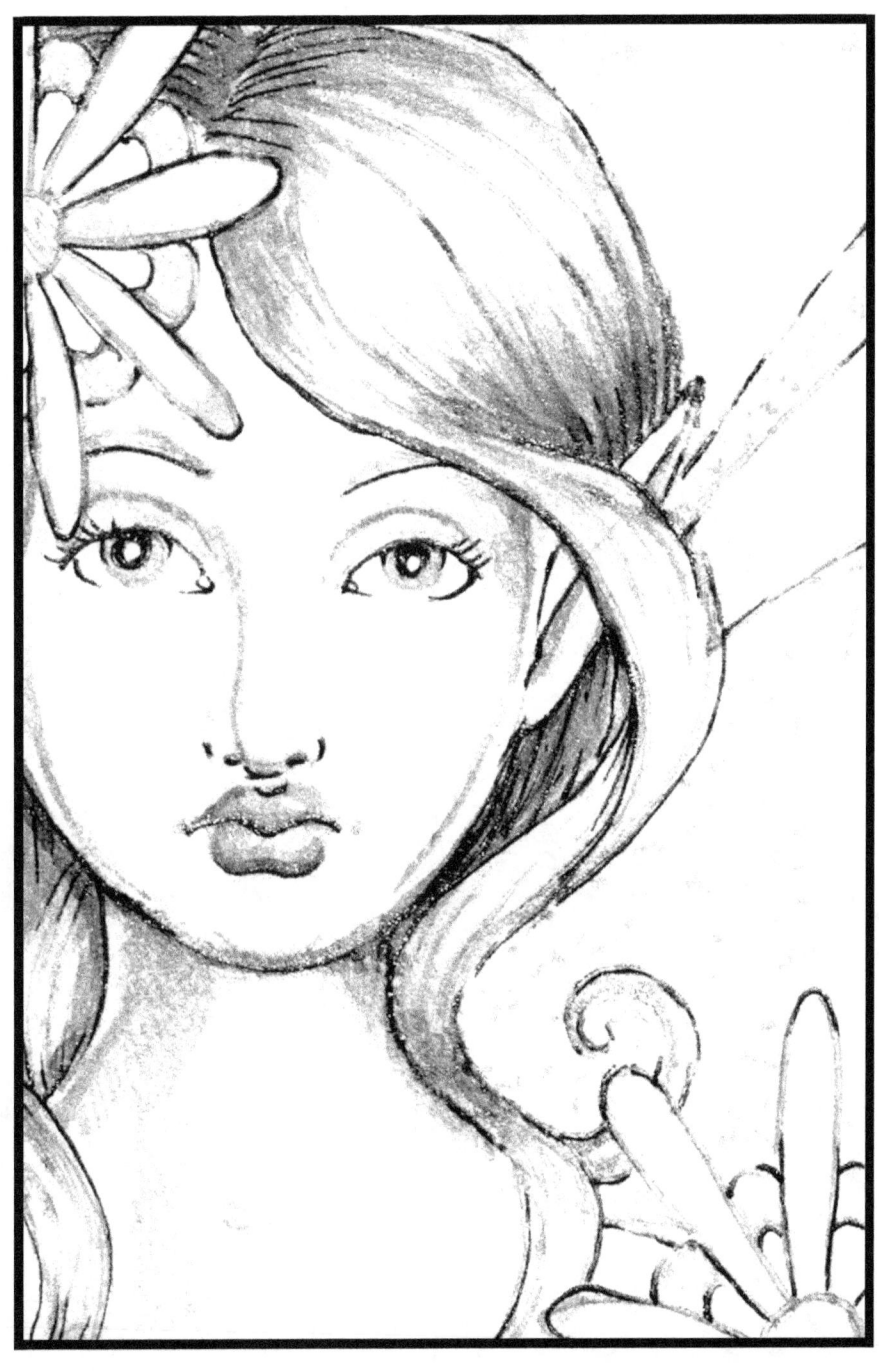

Refined

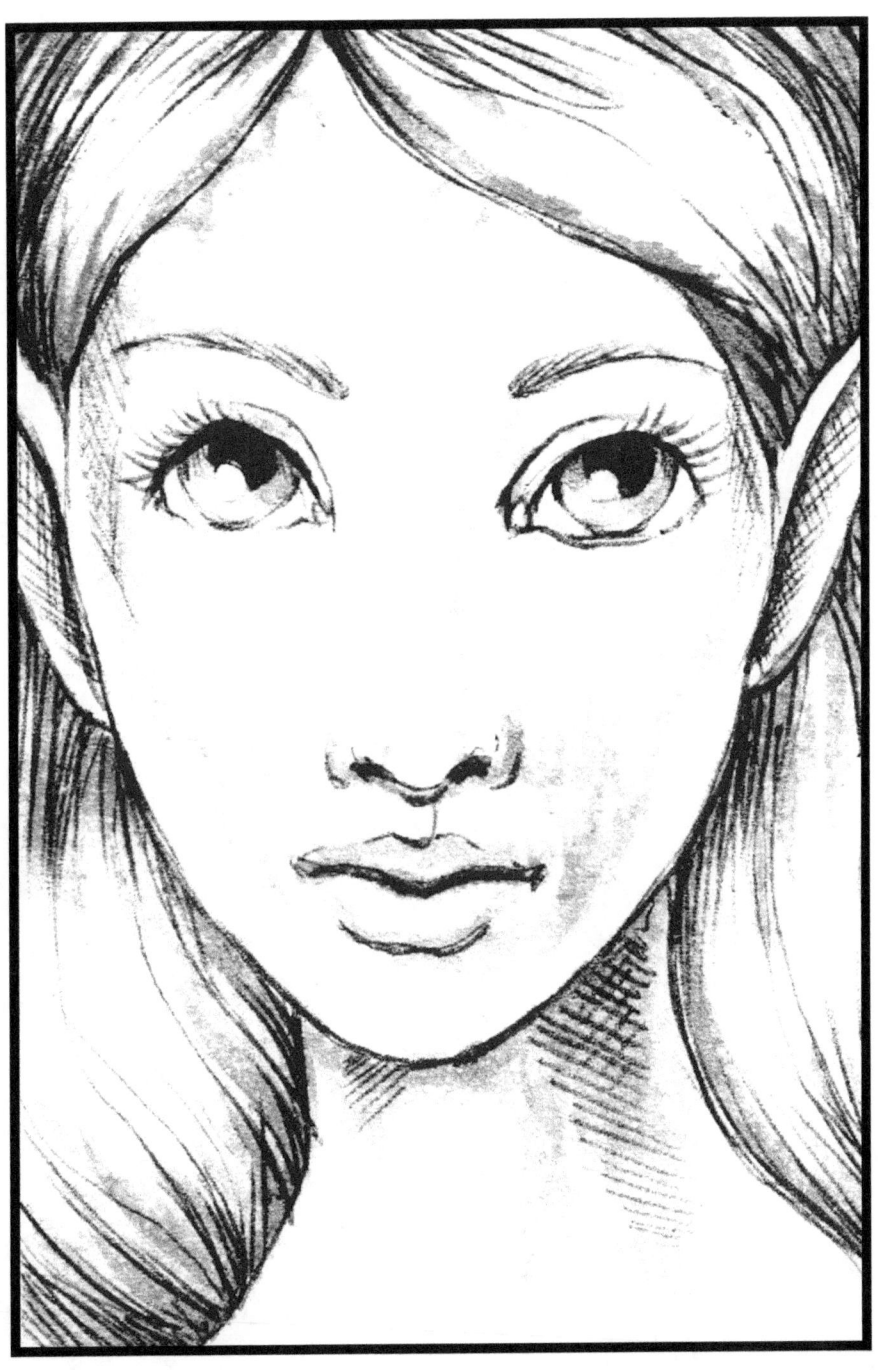

Innocent

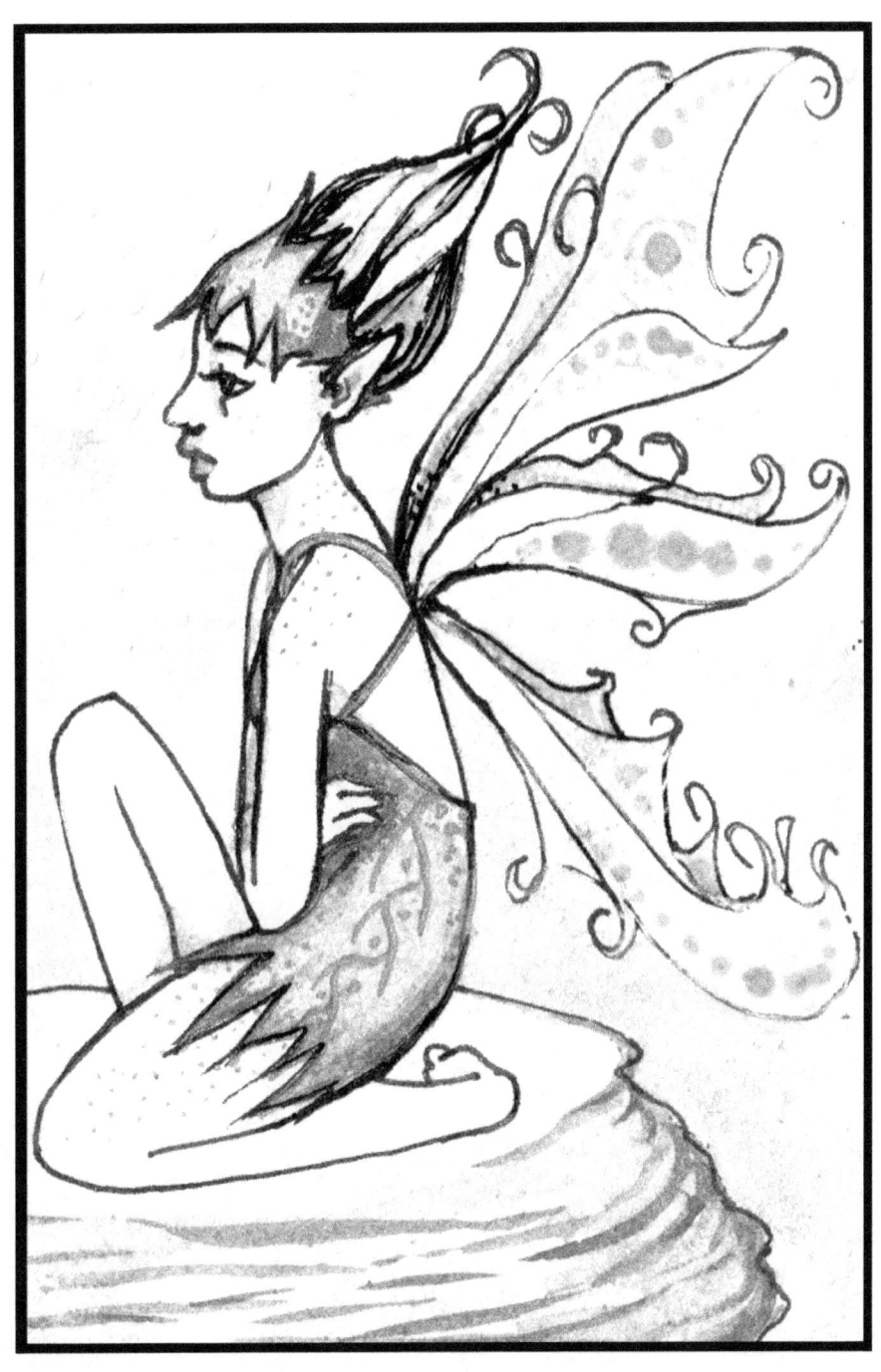

Thoughts on a Rock

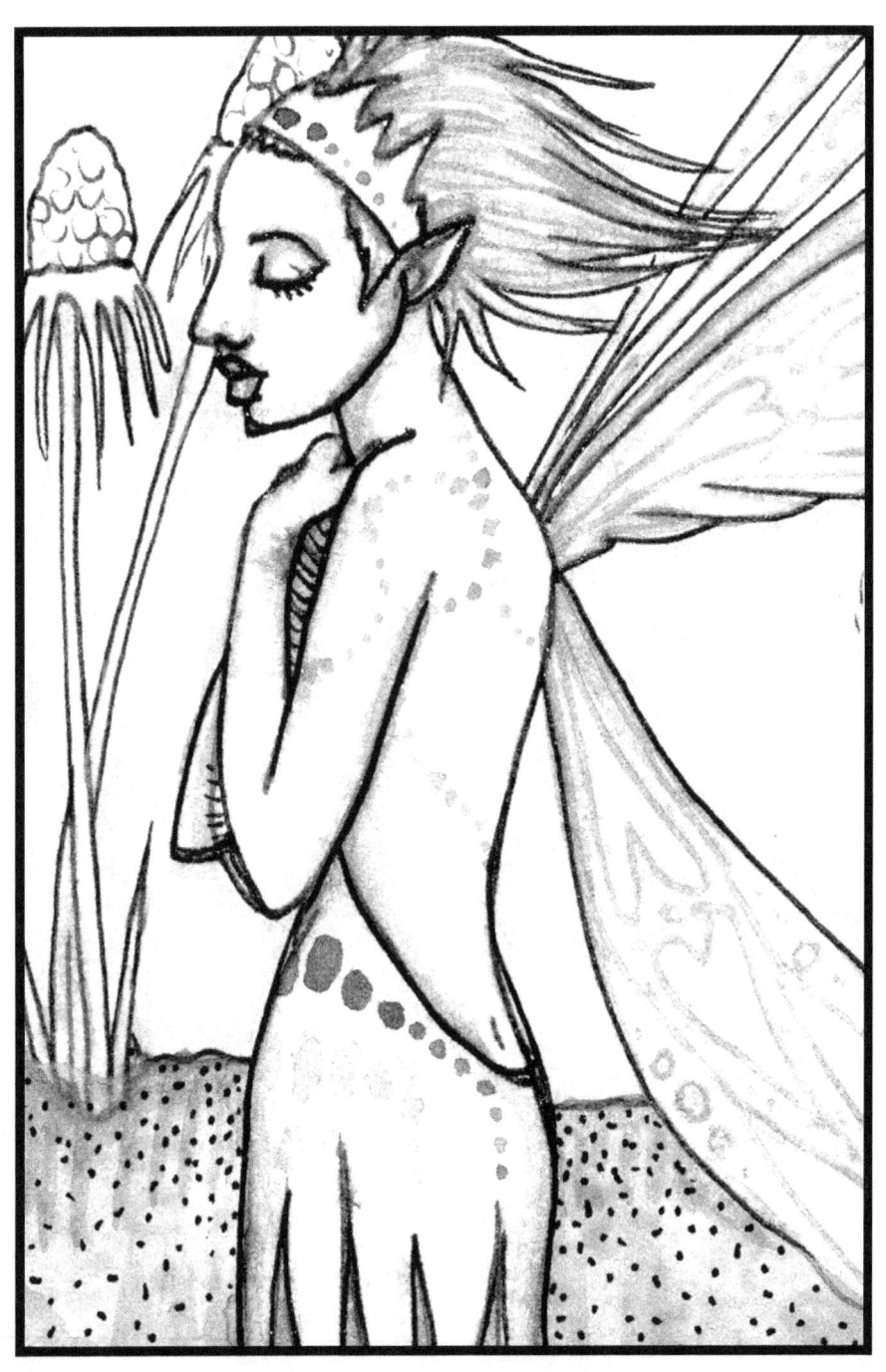

Backless Dress

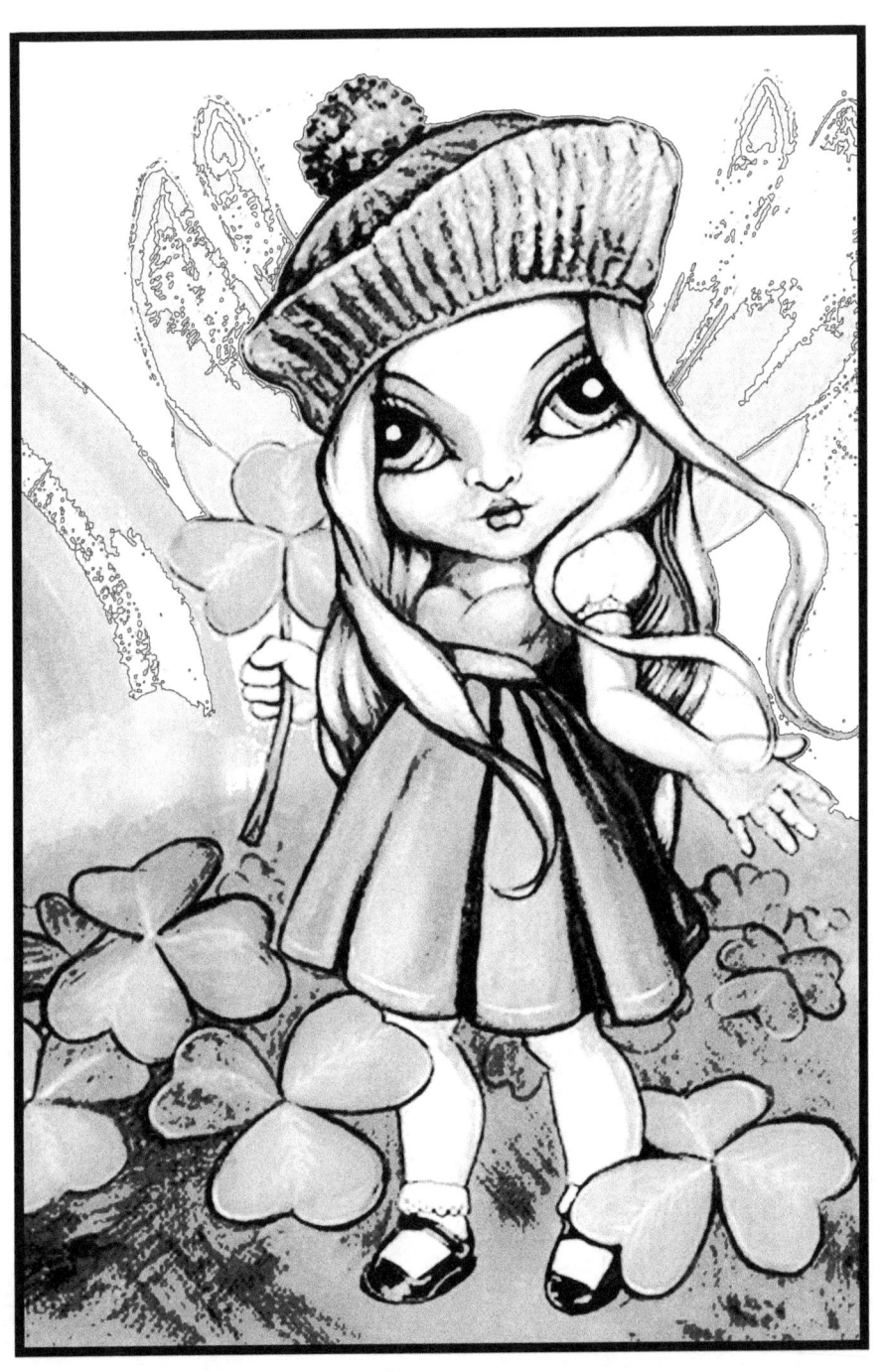

Lucky Lady

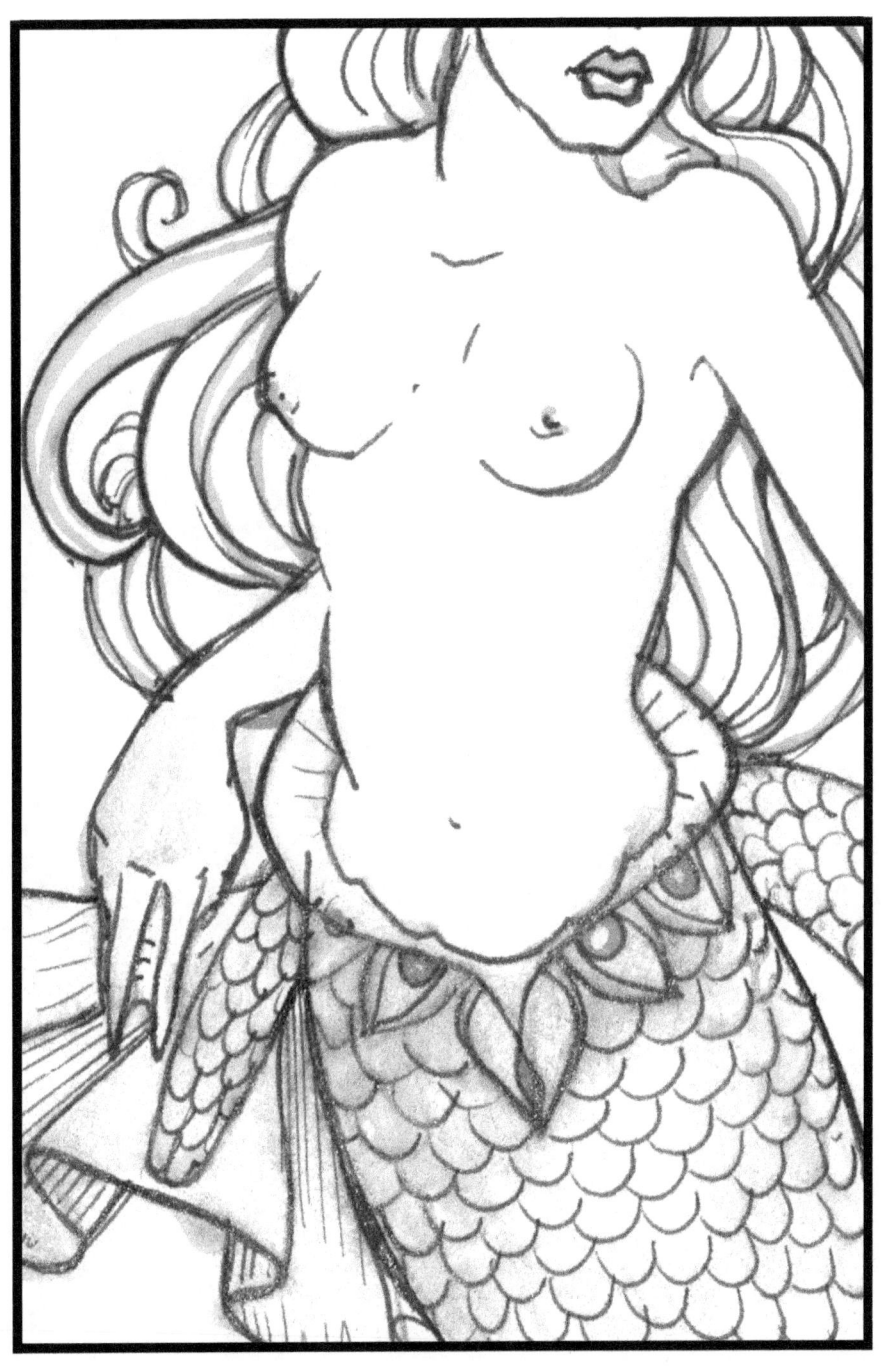

Bust

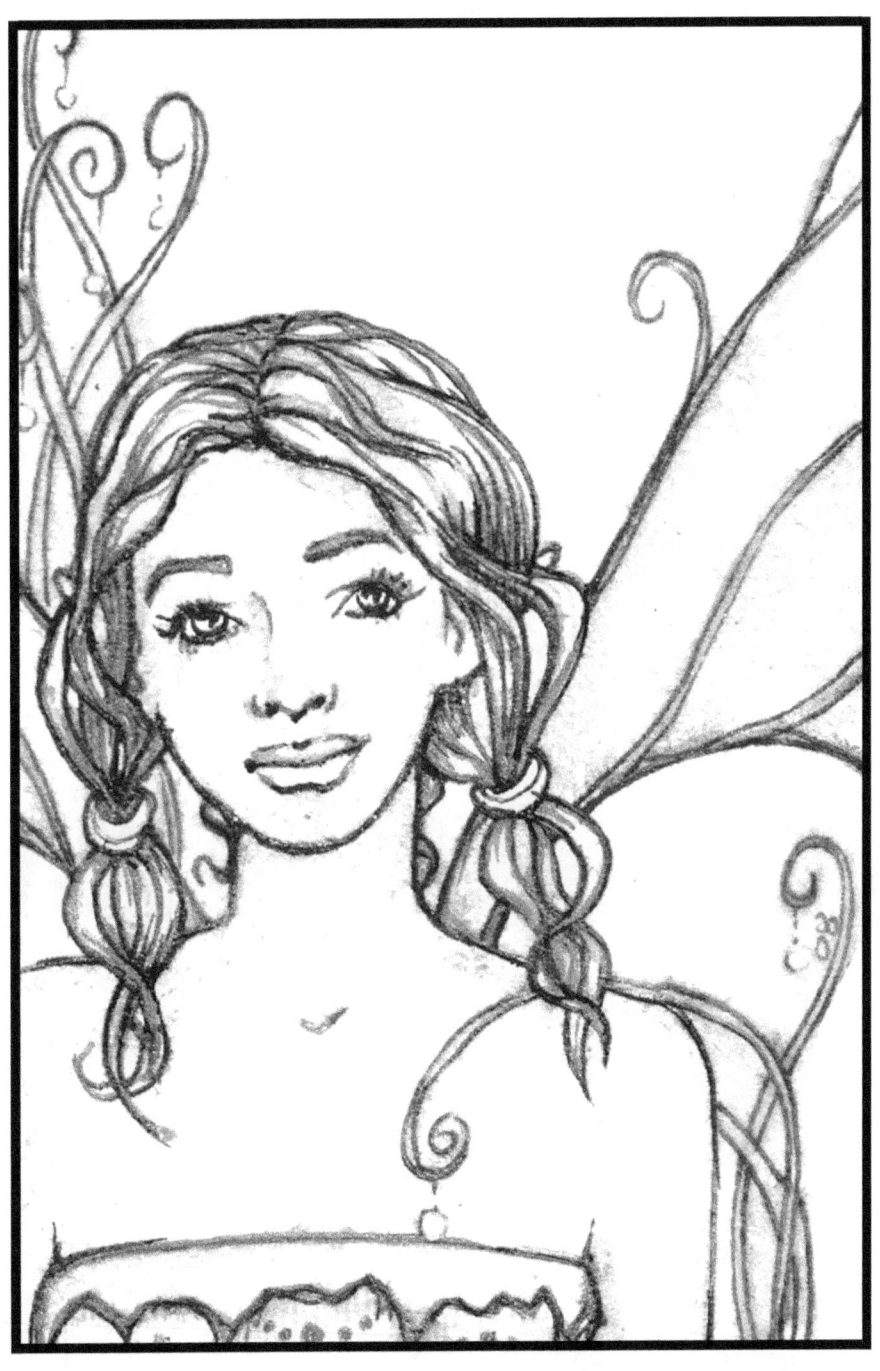

Hair Ties

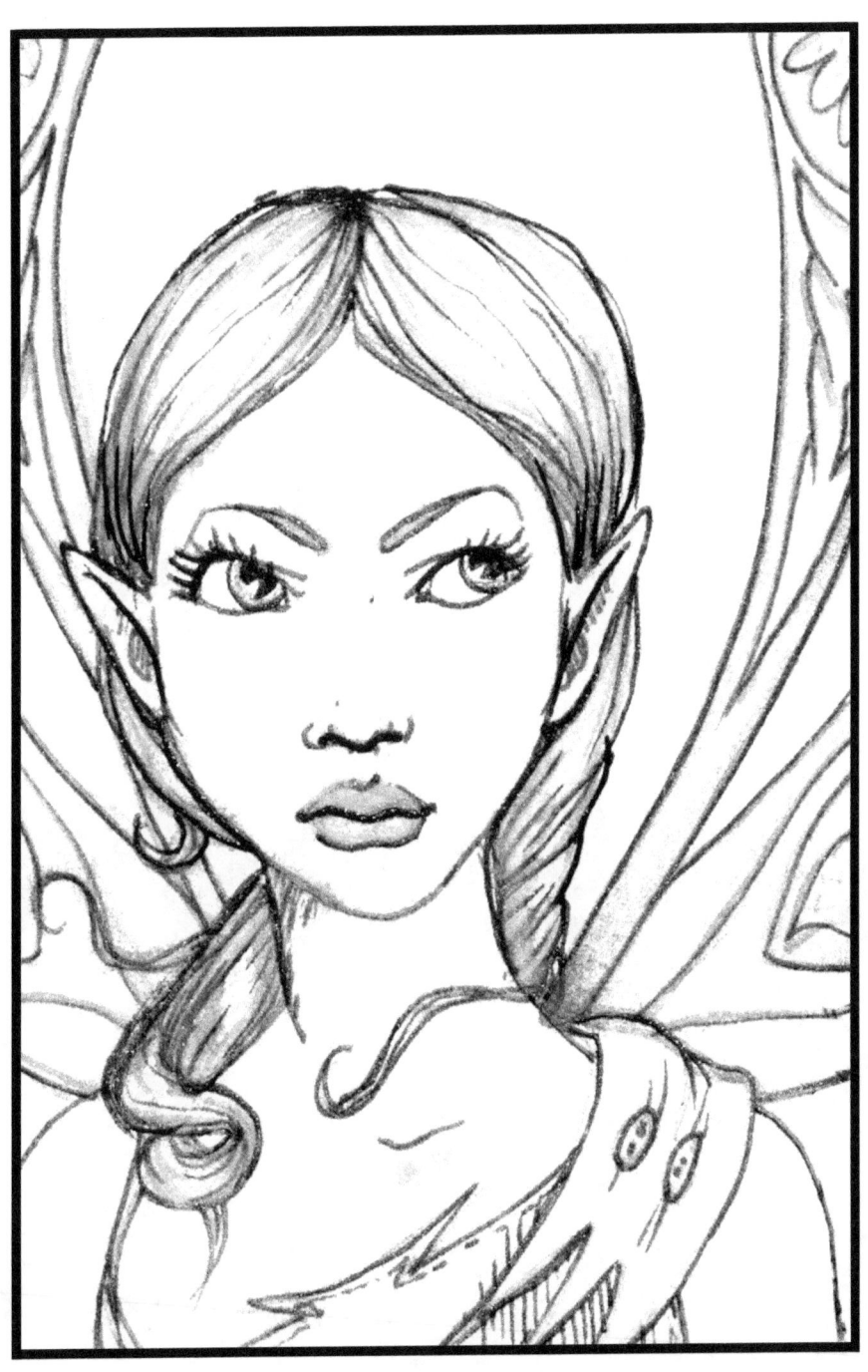

Seriously

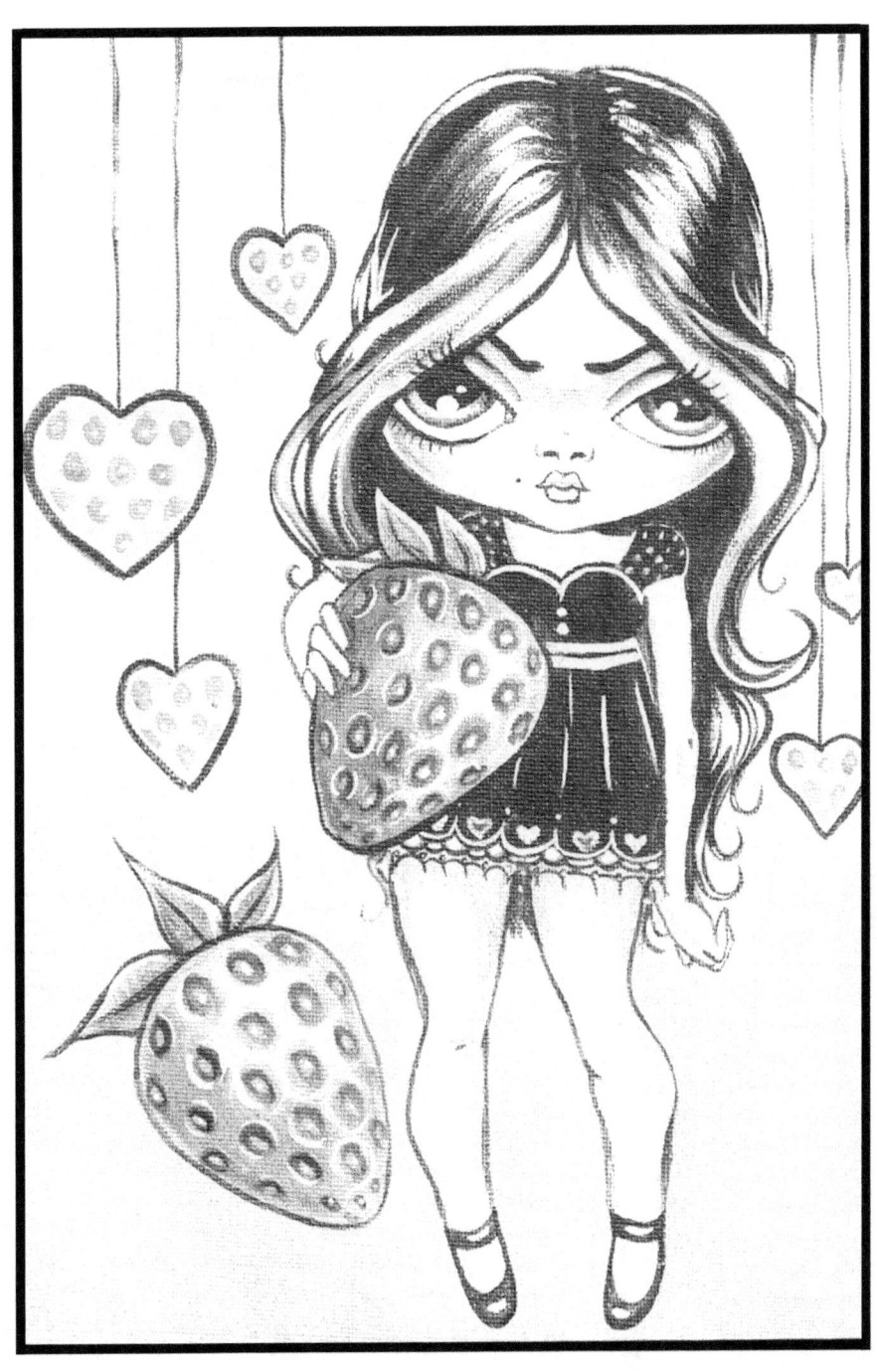

Strawberry Lolita

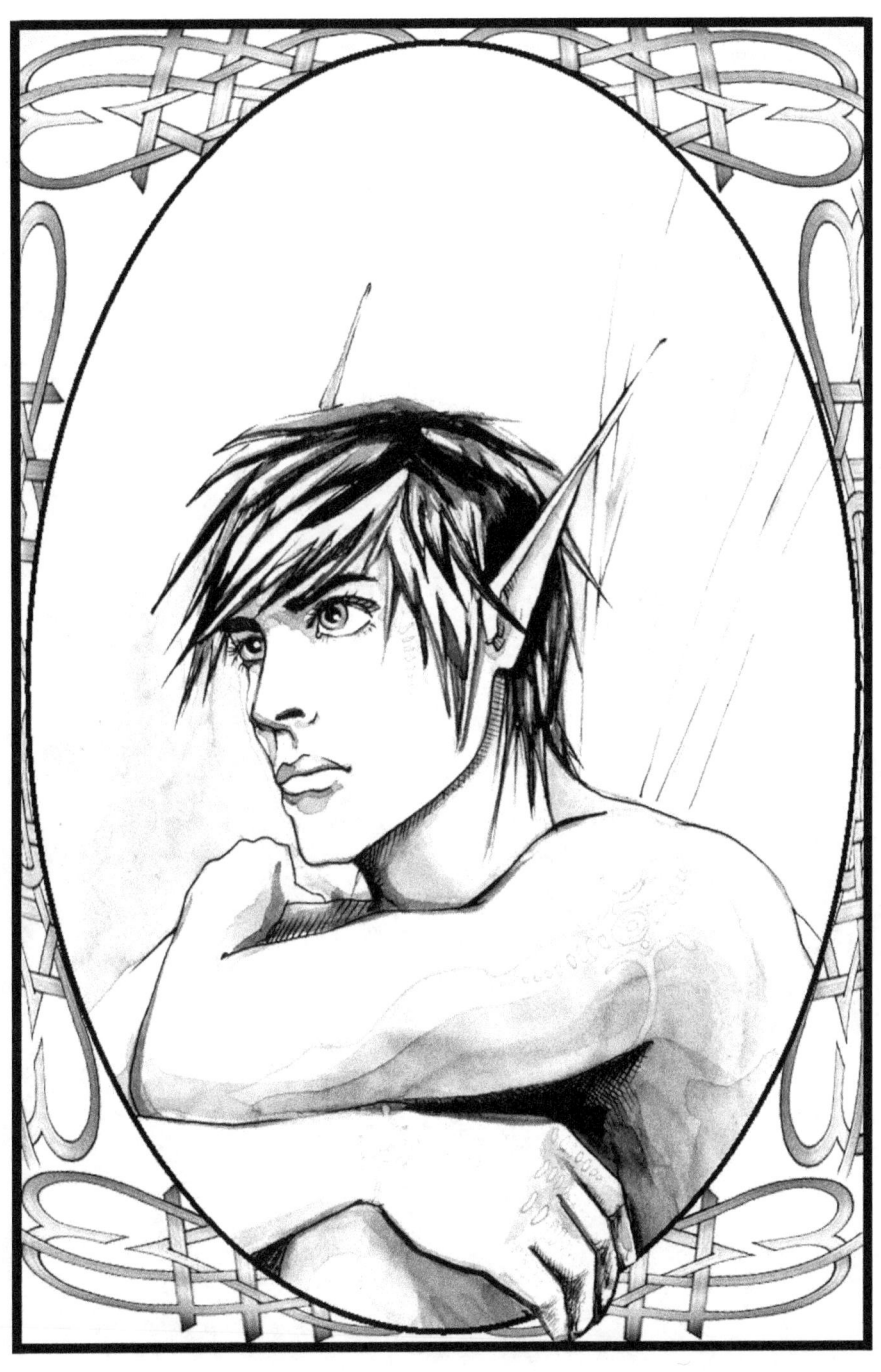

Kalen

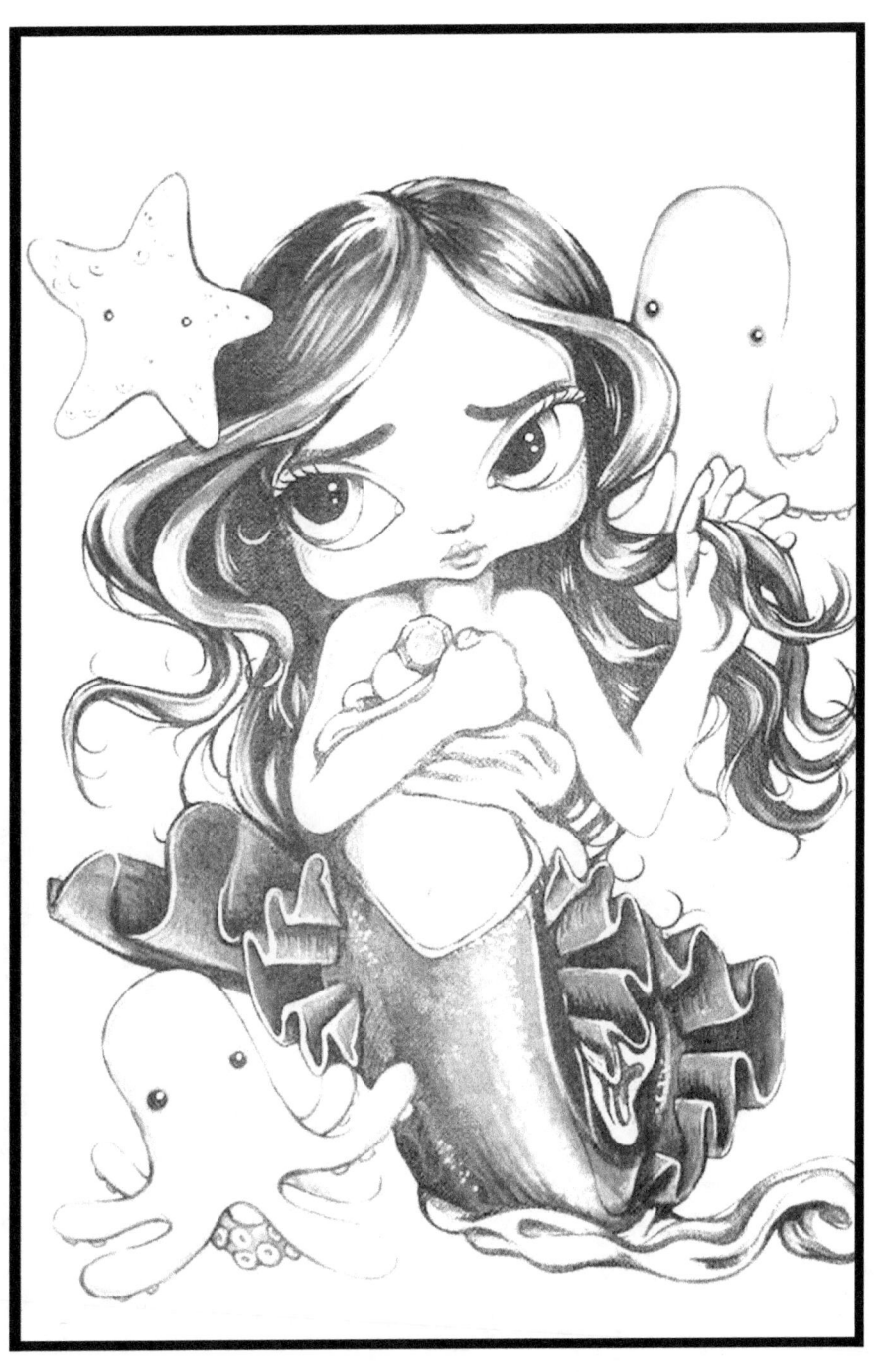

Davey Jones Treasure

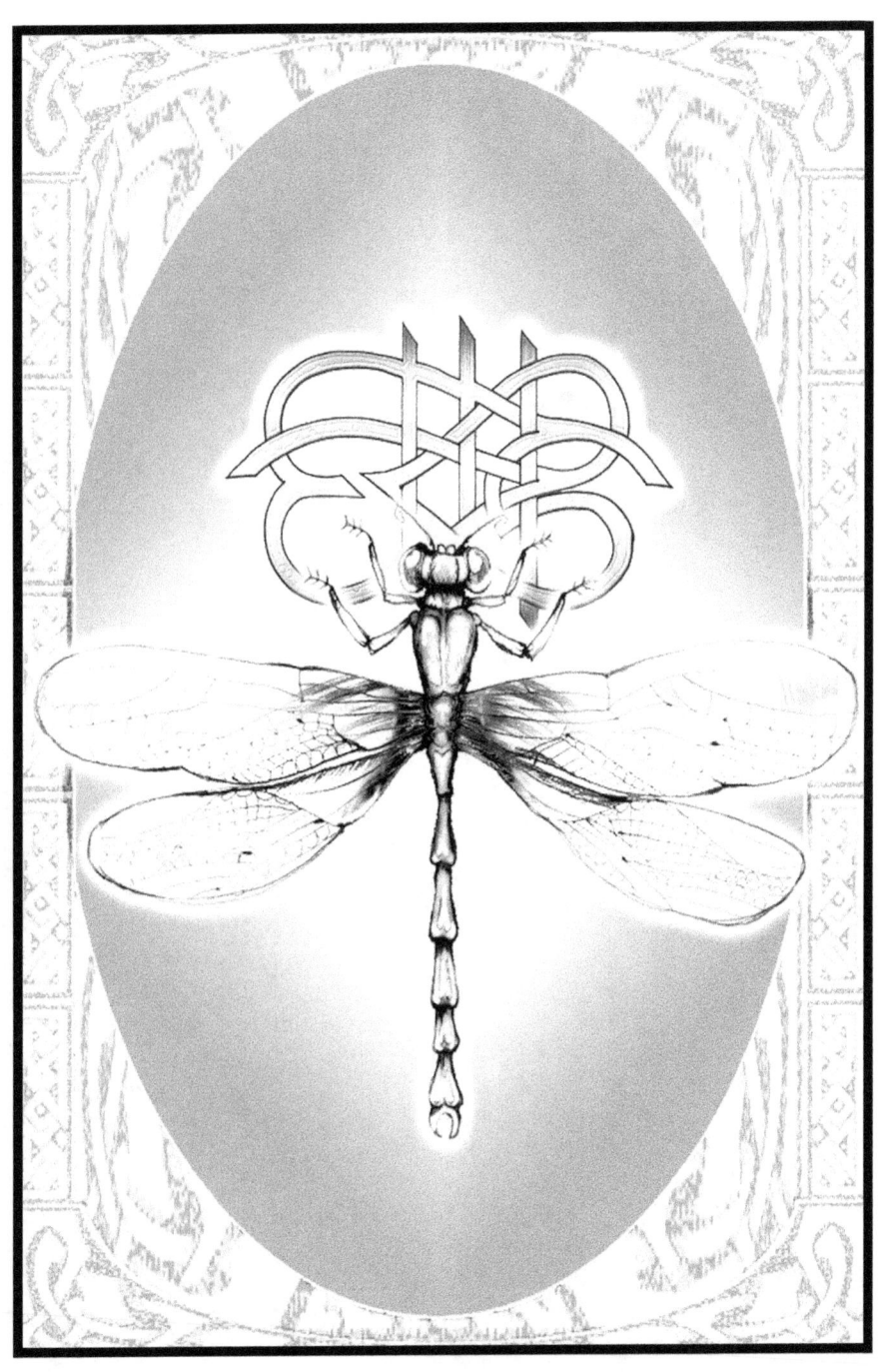

Dragonfly

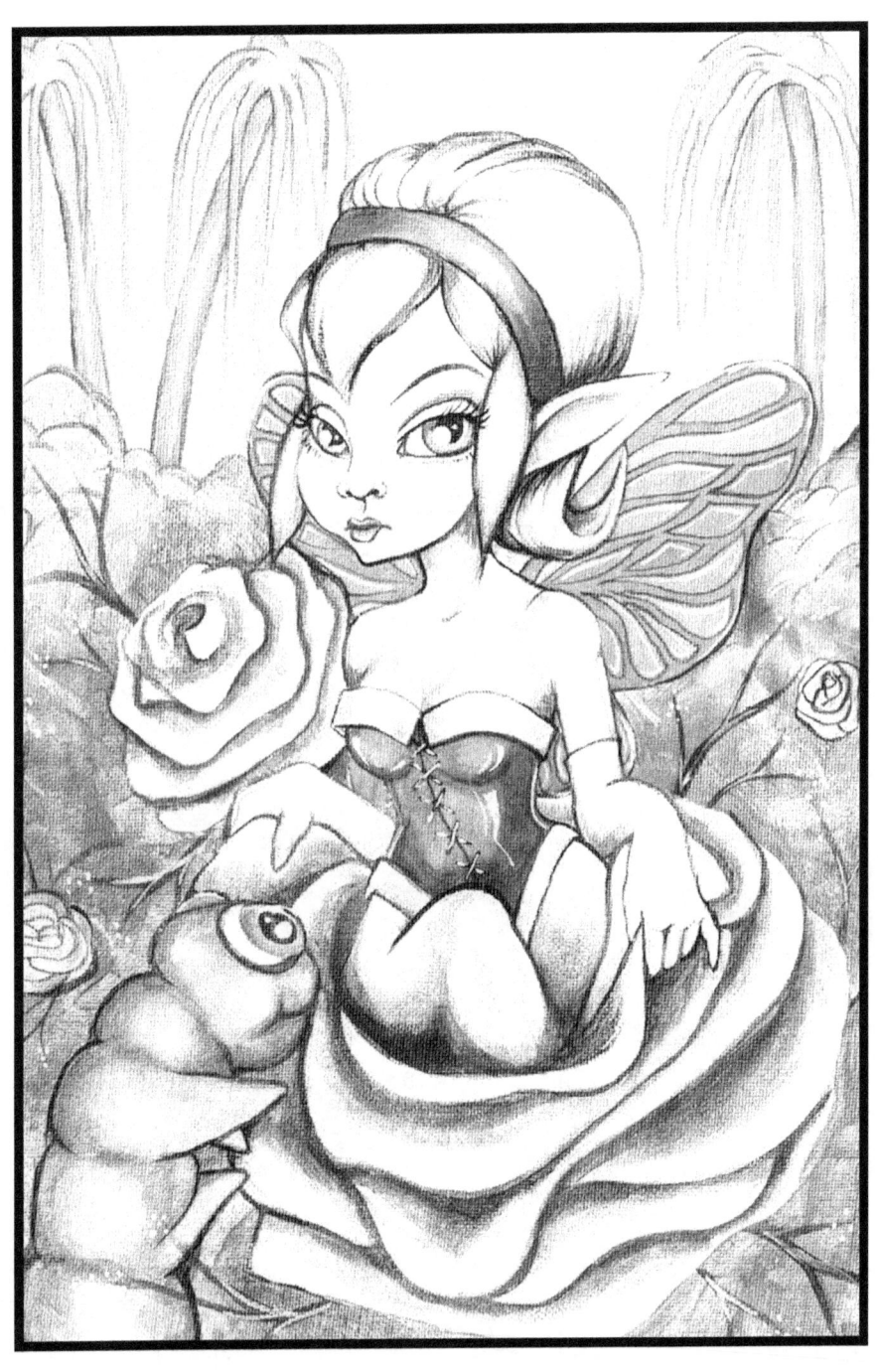

Pin-Up Faerie

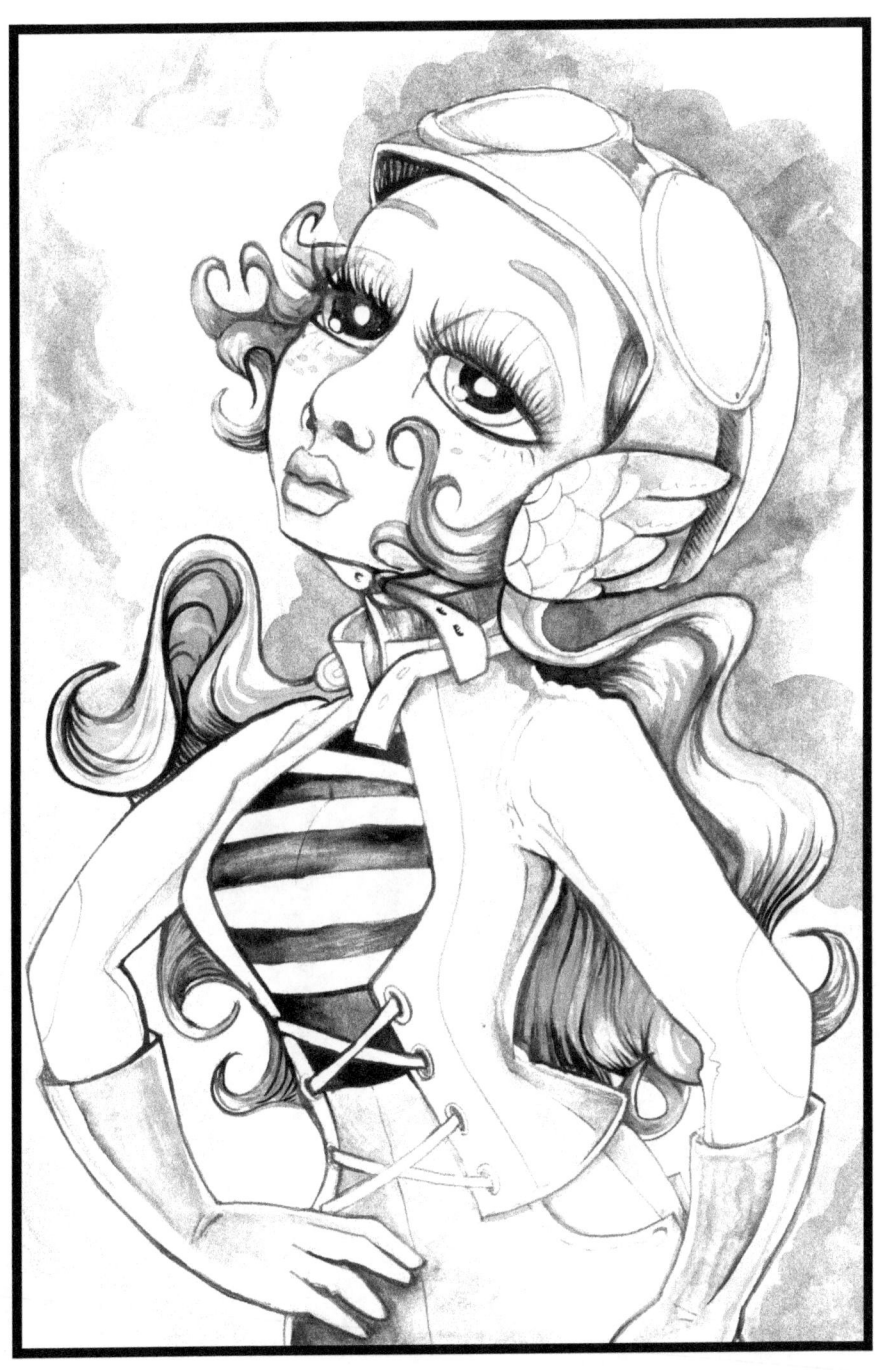

Pilot

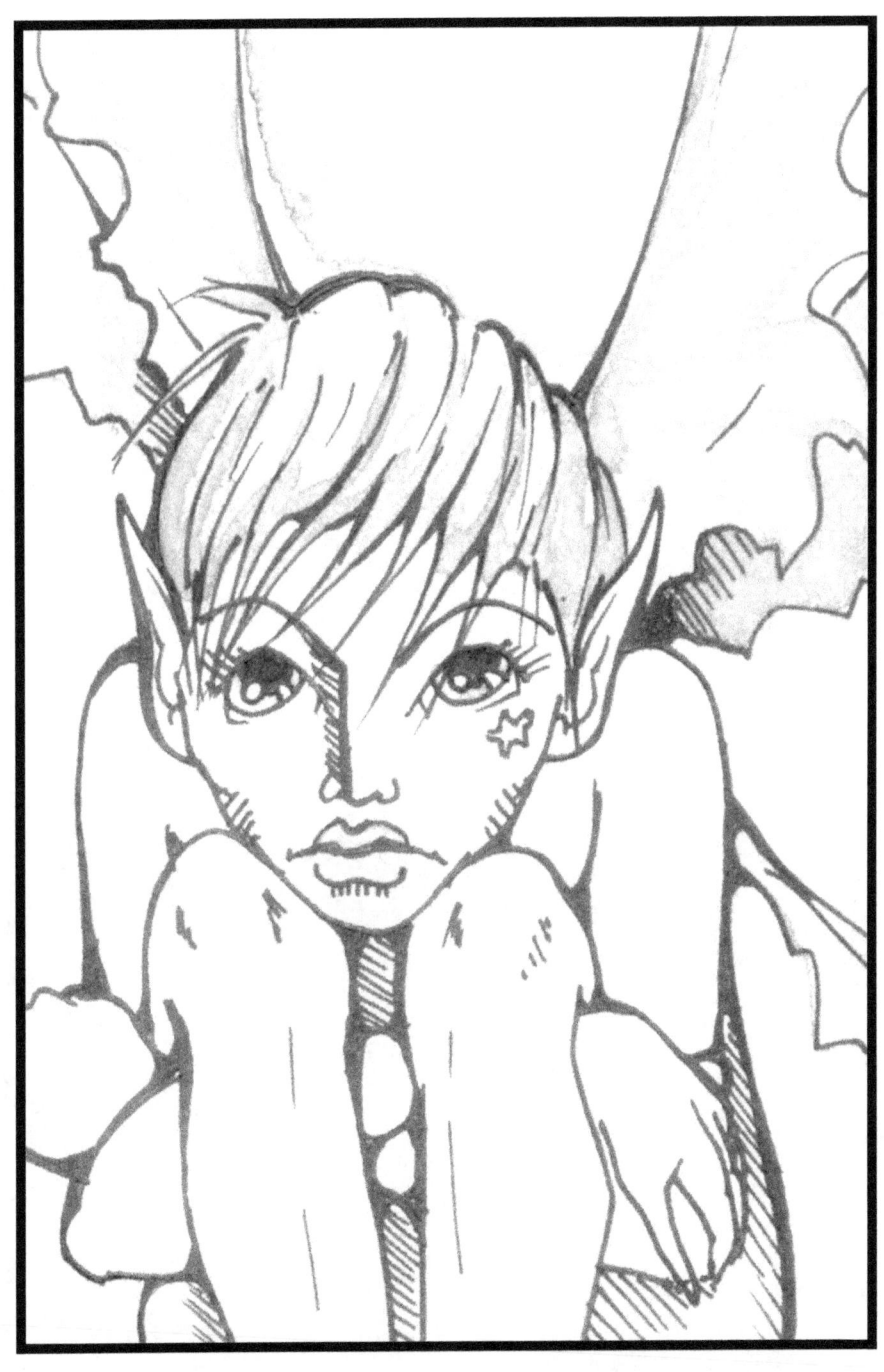

Thinking `bout Stuff

Other books and art by this artist/author can be found on Amazon.com under the following pen names:

G. Desiree Fultz
Desiree Finkbeiner
Vivian Hax

More info at:

www.psychic-insights-astrology.com

www.ingramcontent.com/pod-product-compliance
Lightning Source LLC
Chambersburg PA
CBHW050205230526
45470CB00001B/245